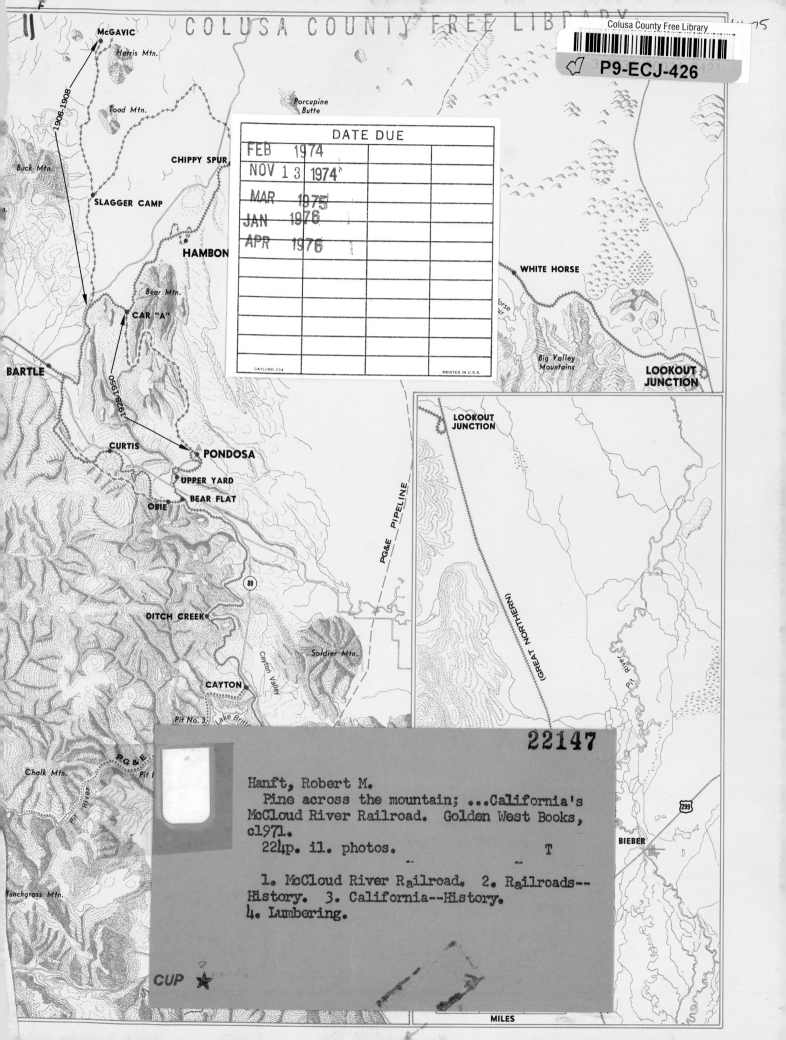

PINE ACROSS THE MOUNTAIN

...CALIFORNIA'S McCLOUD RIVER RAILROAD

Robert M. Hanft

Golden West Books

San Marino, California

ACKNOWLEDGEMENTS

One of the pleasures of writing this story was in meeting and listening to a considerable number of helpful people who gave their time freely and cheerfully to advance the writer's knowledge. A few were old friends who rallied to support the project; many more were introduced because of the need to call on them for their expertise.

I am glad to acknowledge my indebtedness to all who helped make the book possible, but am aware that the list of those who gave a helping hand in some fashion is much more extensive than the names that follow here. To all, my sincere thanks.

Identifying the one person who helped the most is easy. Everywhere I turned I was told the man to see was Chino Haines. Charles M. Haines is an historian in his own right. McCloud and its railroad were his home and his love for most of a long and capable lifetime. Not only has he preserved the photographs that illustrate this volume so substantially; his mind holds much of the story that I have tried to put on paper. He read and criticized the manuscript in its entirety and his stamp of approval yielded the first realization that a major goal of the writer had been accomplished. Chino is truly the grand old man of the McCloud River Railroad.

Flake Willis, former president of the McCloud River Railroad, set the signals to proceed with the book in the first place. His words: "Here are the records. Help yourself to whatever information you need," opened the door to company files. The open books and his willingness to answer every question I asked evidenced a trust I sincerely hope he will regard as merited.

Any story requires a publisher to become a book. Donald Duke, publisher of Golden West Books, has done a good deal more than set type, form layouts and bind paper. Along with the usual needle reserved for writers he has provided encouragement and his own considerable knowledge of the subject.

I would like to list the following names of those who have been most helpful with information and illustrations: Ora Anders, Gerald M. Best, Al Carter, Guido Cottini, John Frizelle, Milton C. Gerlicher, Ed and Dolly Glover, Don Hansen, Jack M. Holst, Tom Irion, John Kirkland, Karl Koenig, John Krause, John T. Labbe, Richard Lohse, Morris Maxwell, Ruel Methvin, Sidney E. Muma, Ray A. Piltz, W. A. Radcliffe, Dan Ranger, Jr., D. S. Richter, James Robinson, Al Rose, Kent Stephens, George Tolosano, Gerald Wetzel, Reginald Wetzel, W. C. Whittaker and Ted Wurm. Also to the librarians and curators of the following collections: The Bancroft Library, Chico State College Library, The Library of Donald Duke, The Huntington Library, Siskiyou County Court House, Siskiyou County Historical Society, Siskiyou County Library, The State Library of California, and The University of California (Berkeley) Library.

The locomotive roster is the work of Gerald M. Best, Donald Duke, John Kirkland, D. S. Richter and Kent Stephens. To these locomotive historians I am most appreciative for their contribution.

Manuscript typing is a necessary and extensive chore. A number of charming ladies assisted with this one. They are: Mrs. Dorothy Charroin, Aileen Cordell, Mrs. Annabelle Hanft, Karen Kuzara, Mrs. Erma Orendorff, Mrs. Grace Riemens, and Mrs. Kathy Rice.

TITLE PAGE ILLUSTRATION

The era of steam nears its end as No. 24 gets a roll on an eastbound consist from McCloud. The fireman on engine No. 21 crowds in the fuel, sharing the effort to move tonnage. The empty log flats on the front end of the train will be dropped off and spotted at log loaders; box cars east indicate fresh lumber from the McCloud Mill to the Great Northern connection or empties to be spotted at on-line mills. —JOHN KRAUSE

Golden West Books

A Division of Pacific Railroad Publications, Inc.

P.O. BOX 8136 • SAN MARINO, CALIFORNIA • 91108

To Charles M. "Chino" Haines
A dedicated and talented railroader, with a keen
sense of history and a willingness to share his
memorabilia with us

Profile — McCloud River Railroad

FOREWORD

MANY years ago, in the summer of 1924 to be exact, my wife and I spent two weeks' vacation at the Mt. Shasta Springs Hotel, a few miles north of Dunsmuir, California, in the upper reaches of Sacramento River Canyon. Perched high above the Sacramento and still popular in those days as a resort, Shasta Springs was also famous for its spring water, which was shipped in tank cars to the cities and bottled there as the most popular mixer of the day. Patrons of the hotel were taken to and from the Southern Pacific trains by means of a cable railway. It was not long before I tired of the amusements the hotel offered and began riding up and down in the cable cars to meet each train. After studying the timetable, I found I could board a northbound train after lunch, get off at Sisson, have time there to walk around and get a really good look at Mt. Shasta, then return to the hotel on a late afternoon train.

At Sisson, a small locomotive and combination coach of the McCloud River Railroad was standing in the station. I had seen this train on previous trips to Portland from San Francisco, but knew nothing about the railroad. The train's brakeman volunteered that it went 18 miles or so to the town of McCloud, and that I could go over there and back before my southbound main line train arrived. No sooner said than done, and I was on my way through deep woods, then cleared areas where the great white mountain to the north appeared to be just over the next ridge. I was surprised to see a switchback with change of direction; this type of railroading was not new to me but it had been a long time since I had been over one. We arrived all too quickly in a valley which smelled of seasoning lumber, sawdust and pine trees, ending our run close to a great mill which teemed with activity. I had no time to explore as the train began its return journey in a few minutes, but the ride made an indelible impression on me. Though I never rode that shuttle train again, I visited McCloud by automobile in later years, and became familiar with its motive power.

Knowing very little about the railroad's early history, I was delighted to hear that Robert M. Hanft had undertaken the long task of researching and writing this book. Bob is especially well qualified, since he spent over 30 years photographing steam locomotives all over the North American continent, travelling untold thousands of miles by motorcycle, car, train and plane in that period. This experience combined with his PhD in transportation has enabled him to do an exceptionally fine job of writing a text which is entertaining to the exacting railfan and the layman alike. Where else could you find the combination of college professor and expert railroad photographer than in Robert M. Hanft?

Unlike the histories of most shortlines, the McCloud River Railroad story covers the larger part of a century yet has not become a relic of a bygone age. It is a high class railroad, with the most modern equipment and top grade management. Dr. Hanft has given some of the reasons for this fortunate situation in the last chapter, which covers the future prospects of the McCloud River Railroad as well as all other shortlines. The remarkable collection of pictures presented in this book represents a condition which authors dream about but seldom realize. For those who buy railroad books for the pictures and don't read the text, and there are many who do just that, they should be highly pleased at the contents of this one. It was a privilege to read the manuscript of this book and to relive the days of pioneer logging and lumber railroading in northern California.

GERALD M. BEST.

Beverly Hills, California

TABLE OF CONTENTS

1

PIONEERS
BEFORE THE RAILROAD

THE volcanic upheaval that created Mt. Shasta, the most majestic peak on California's long spine, helped to establish one of the richest forests of the West, sweeping in a deep crescent for some 80 miles southeast of the mountain. Sugar pine and ponderosa shared sunlight, soil and water with cedar and fir. The twisted terrain of the Cascade Mountains provided a barrier against early exploitation by man; the cities of a century ago were built with timber from more accessible areas.

It was inevitable that the development of the West would bring the day when lumbering would invade the naturally protected forests and when a railroad would penetrate the barrier and push into the wilderness opening the region to men and their activities.

This is the story of that area and particularly of that railroad.

The first explorer of record was Peter Skene Ogden, who ventured through the area and sighted the lofty cone on a cold February day in 1827. Just two years later Alexander Roderick McLeod set out for California from Fort Vancouver, employed by the Hudson's Bay Company to explore the Buena Ventura River and seek sources of fur. By April his party was in the valley of the Sacramento, which he may

have surmised to be the stream he sought. He evidently did not continue his exploration to reach the Spanish mission settlements to the south but turned back toward the north and east.

McLeod followed a tributary of the Sacramento to its headwaters, set his traps and was rewarded, but cached the fur and equipment and returned to Fort Vancouver. His records do not make clear just which tributary he followed, or where he left his property, but some writers believe his course was along what today is the McCloud River, and that it bears his name. This clear mountain stream in turn provides the name for the venture whose history is described here. McLeod and McCloud are pronounced alike and early pioneers were not always too careful with their spelling.

Discovery of rusty and crumbling remains of the original McLeod cache have been claimed — he never returned to it — near the upper reaches of the river. Whether or not McLeod actually was the first of his race to move into the McCloud area doesn't really matter. Others would come soon, and their record is more important. Even so, the McCloud remains a rather remote stream for much of its length. Its wild downhill race has been partly tamed by two

11

great man-made lakes in its path, but it still passes no settlements, few dwellings, and is by no means easily accessible for the most part. Countless thousands of fine timber specimens line its usually rocky banks. Many of these trees are second growth now coming into maturity.

Two decades after McLeod's exploration, the discovery at Sutter's mill created echoes that reached here and beyond. The '49ers explored every foot of waterway in the gold bearing hills, and made strikes of the yellow metal within a day's walking distance of the McCloud, but only enough traces to tantalize prospectors have ever been uncovered in the immediate area of our concern. With people swarming into California, settlers began to seek something more permanent than the gold claims and some of them looked at this land.

The government looked too, and one result was the first road, still shown on some maps as the Military Pass highway. Today part of this pioneer road is no more than a rather poorly maintained jeep trail for fire fighting access. It hugs the north and east slope of Shasta, and during the pioneer days of automobiles was part of a route that circled the mountain for some 70 miles. Driving the loop around Shasta was popular for a while, and the time required may have been less a half-century ago than it would be today.

Men were impressed by the forest, but without transportation there was no economic value to it. Other valleys offered more promise for agriculture, and few stayed on near the McCloud. Among those who did were the Bartle brothers who built an inn where stage passengers and others traveling the new highway could spend the night. A tiny settlement followed, which took the family name, Bartle's. The "s" has long since been dropped. Another settler was Ross McCloud, whose descendants claim that he gave his name to the river. A fair controversy once boiled over McLeod vs. McCloud, but both men were obviously venturesome and worthy of recognition.

Although the great forest was no more than a potential for the future, as the century moved toward its close several foolhardy investors found the challenge of free trees, a brisk market for lumber in the cities, and an available road too much for them to ignore. They built

sawmills here and there in the forest, and proceeded to lose their shirts. One of these men who perhaps planned better than most of the others, but still could not survive, was A. F. "Friday" George, who built his mill in Squaw Valley directly to the southeast of the mountain on a tributary of the McCloud.

Friday George linked his hopes for success with two new factors in the transportation picture: a railroad, and his means of access to it.

On May 10, 1869, the golden spike signifying that the continent had been spanned by the iron horse was driven at Promontory, Utah. The Central Pacific, building east from California to meet its westward thrusting counterpart, had accumulated not only men and machines to engage in massive construction under impressive difficulties, but a taste for empire as well. Meeting the Union Pacific on a desolate, wind-swept Utah high prairie was by no means the signal for the hard-driving managers of the Central Pacific (or the UP either) to turn off their ambitions. A compass held in San Francisco could indicate that there were directions other than east alone in which to send rails.

One of the ambitions of the "Big Four" who managed the Central Pacific was, naturally enough, to move northward to tap the Oregon Country and reach the Columbia. Rather than trace out the corporate meanderings involved, suffice it to say that the Central became the Southern Pacific, as it is today. Through one corporate arm or another SP reached northward from the Golden Gate in California and south from the Columbia in Oregon until only a day of stage coach riding separated the halves, then they too were linked, with a great deal less fanfare than the meeting of 1869.

The area of our study touches the last hundred-mile gap in this north-south Southern Pacific line. Northward inching steel that had been following the convolutions of the upper Sacramento River Canyon finally broke from the water course by means of Cantara Loop. A steep climb continued to the leveling off called Strawberry Valley, reaching a terminal point at McCloud, November 13, 1886, where it would linger only briefly before resuming the quest for destiny with the Oregon line.

Despite its name, McCloud, entry point for Strawberry Valley, is not the town of primary

In the 1880's, the Mount Shasta Hotel nestled at the foot of majestic Mount Shasta was a delightful stopover. The settlement in Siskiyou County first known as Strawberry Valley, and from 1886 to 1922 as Sisson, was changed to Mount Shasta in 1922. The post office here was named Berryville, since Strawberry Valley was already a post office name in nearby Yuba County. (BELOW) Scott and Van Arsdale built their railroad through the Nelson Harvey Eddy ranch as they pushed their rails toward McCloud. These unusual woodcuts appeared in the Siskiyou County edition of *Thompson & West.* —HUNTINGTON LIBRARY, SAN MARINO, CALIFORNIA

concern to this story. Today it is hardly more than a passing track for the Southern Pacific, and the meeting of the McCloud River Railroad with the Southern Pacific in Strawberry Valley always has been a bit farther north. Because the short line railroad did begin here in Strawberry Valley, a brief background concerned with its settlement may also be in order.

Strawberry Valley has Mt. Shasta to the immediate northeast as its impressive backdrop and today is the turnoff point for the ski slopes high above. Mountains to the west may seldom be noticed because eyes focus on the lofty spectacle of Shasta instead, but they are far from being puny hills. Part of this range is called the Trinity Alps, and the title is not unworthy. Main access to the valley is north and south, no longer a challenge to automobile or locomotive, but still by no means plains country. Strawberry Valley is a small bowl in the midst of mountains.

When the gold-seekers began to swarm, many passed this way, explored the headwaters of the Sacramento with only mild success, and passed on. A few liked what they saw here and stayed. Crops could do well. There was plenty of water, for the source of the Sacramento, consisting of a great spring that gushed endlessly, was here. Best known now of these early settlers of the Valley is Justin Hinckley Sisson.

Sisson, born in Connecticut in 1826, came to California as a '49er, mined in a number of the California diggings without spectacular fortune, and filed claims on government land in Strawberry Valley. He went back to Illinois briefly, married there and returned in 1861 to Strawberry Valley where he and his bride built a cabin on the site now occupied by the Mt. Shasta high school. The home was enlarged into an inn and became popular with travelers. Sisson also built a hunting and fishing lodge at a point some 20 miles away on the McCloud River. He selected a particularly scenic reach of the river in magnificent forest. It was called "Horseshoe Bend" because here the river makes nearly a complete loop.

A post office called Berryville came to Strawberry Valley, and when the railroad finally struggled up the canyon, the community was ready to boom. A full-fledged town was laid out in the vicinity of the inn. The Pacific Improve-

The Southern Pacific station at Sisson was replaced by the present smaller but more rustic structure near the turn of the century. Ample evidence of winter is shown. —CHARLES M. HAINES COLLECTION (BELOW) A Southern Pacific construction train in the Sacramento River canyon near Shasta Springs. —HUNTINGTON LIBRARY, SAN MARINO, CALIFORNIA

ment Company, a colorful venture with far flung interests, was responsible for the first formal real estate promotion, and its agent, one D. H. Haskell, sold the first lot in November 1886, practically coincident with the arrival of the railroad.

Two years later the pioneer was honored by the prospering village being renamed Sisson. The Sissons operated the dining room in the Southern Pacific depot in addition to their other holdings until the death of Sisson in 1893. The original inn, known by then as "The Tavern," burned in 1916, Mrs. Sisson passed away in 1917, and with the family no longer prominent in the eyes of the neighbors the town took its present name of Mt. Shasta City in 1922.

The Sissons provided the personality to start the village and add color to its past; the railroad gave it the economic means to grow and prosper. The Southern Pacific never established a substantial terminal or offered extensive direct employment here, but its arrival gave meaning to the forest that bordered the valley. Until the railroad came, the timber had little real usefulness; hardly more than did its vast extension to the east. The rails provided both a means for the products of the forest to move to markets where they could be sold, at a price that would not demand too great a share for the transportation alone, and a direct buyer for wood as well. We ordinarily think of a railroad as twin ribbons of steel, but those rails are laid on crossties that are cut from trees. The ties are greater in bulk and total length than the rails, by far; they just aren't as romantic a concept. They do mean money to their suppliers, as rails do to the distant steel mills. We think today of the locomotives of 1886 as "quaint" because they were so small and burned wood; their enormous appetite for wood might well have been the major concern of their owners. People could make a living cutting, stacking and loading wood for locomotive fuel, and Strawberry Valley was a logical place to add wood to tenders. Wood was close by, and the supply aboard the engine was substantially depleted after the hard pull up from Dunsmuir and out of the canyon.

The first sawmill was completed within about four months of the arrival of rails in the Valley, others followed. In contrast with the ill-fated ventures across the mountain, it was now possible for enterprises to grow and prosper here.

Sisson was the dreamer who loved the Valley and its surroundings and delighted in hospitality to others who could appreciate nature at its grandest, but economic development required men with another kind of vision. Partners George W. Scott and William W. Van Arsdale, who had ability to spend money to develop the resources that could make them wealthy, were the men most important to this story.

Early engineering graduates of the infant University of California, these men formed their first acquaintance in school. They added practical experience to their technical knowledge and by the time they came to Strawberry Valley they had the ability to handle men and machines and knew how to tap effectively the

Upton at the turn of the century. Electricity and railroads had come to the slopes of Mt. Shasta as evidenced by poles and wires in the foreground and a string of railroad cars across the field to the left. Downtown was largely obscured by foreground buildings. The few patches of snow far up the mountain show the season to be late summer. Nothing remains of this once-prosperous little settlement. —CHARLES M. HAINES COLLECTION

great natural resource that brought them. First associated here with the firm of Sisson and Crocker, they became the managers of the Siskiyou Lumber and Mercantile Company, leading enterprise of the Valley.

The Southern Pacific Company was far larger but its few miles across the Valley was only a tiny part of its total venture. Actually, the Siskiyou Lumber and Mercantile Company also did not confine its operations locally, but its principal store was located in Sisson, and its major mill at Upton, two miles to the north. Four other mills were under its supervision.

With prosperity favoring their store and mills, Scott and Van Arsdale looked beyond the current activity of helping keep the railroad wood yard full and sending the product of their mills down the canyon. Within a decade after arrival of rails, it was obvious that the supply of logs within easy reach was giving out, or was in the hands and control of other operators. In addition, the partners could see the ability of the market to sustain far larger sales. Expansion would be the answer!

The Upton location for the mill had been satisfactory, but did not have an adequate water supply to allow the growth contemplated. Although the parties involved can no longer verify the fact, there is evidence that Scott and Van Arsdale asked for a substantial donation of land in Sisson, where there was plenty of water, to establish the new mill. The citizenry was not ready to give up its property to entice a payroll; the partners were not ready to pay the going price. They were ready to take advantage of Friday George's failure.

Friday George had thought he held the key to success. He had imagination, access to a certain amount of capital, and a new technology. He had picked up control of thousands of acres of the finest timber, protecting himself from the shortage that would soon limit the Strawberry Valley operators. On his side of the mountain ten dollars an acre was considered a high price. Squaw Valley, barely ten miles to the east of Strawberry Valley and the railroad, had level land for a mill, a stream with plenty of water to support the mill and a village around it, and the forest was close in every direction.

The biggest problem was getting the lumber to the railroad, but the solution was Friday George's special vision. True, the spur of

15

George W. Scott

William M. Van Arsdale

Shasta that came between his valley and that of the railroad rose about a thousand feet, but he would conquer it with a steam engine. No, he couldn't afford a railroad, but he could buy locomotives that would run on the highway. Accordingly, he worked on the primitive grade that Justin Sisson had maintained to gain access to Horseshoe Bend, widening and smoothing it up to and past the Mountain House that had been built on the summit, and down the west side to the Southern Pacific.

The mill was built, the machinery installed, and the boilers were fired up. First, steam turned the saws in the mill, and then the wheels that would take the lumber across the mountain more efficiently than the legs of animals had been able to accomplish. Everything worked as it should, but the dream was not to be realized. The costs of maintaining road and machine, bucking the grade with its winter snows, plus all the other costs of getting the boards to the user, however beautiful the trees at the source, added up to ruin. Friday George found the bitter taste of bankruptcy and on June 10, 1895, the voice of the auctioneer was

raised at the mill where the shrill whine of the saws was stilled. The Bank of Shasta County salvaged its interest from the financial ruins by sale to Scott and Van Arsdale.

The Siskiyou Lumber and Mercantile Company could accomplish what Friday George could not. Just as steel rails meant the ability to enter distant commerce for enterprises in Strawberry Valley, so could rails open up the McCloud River side of the mountain for lumber production that would yield earnings instead of deficits. Scott and Van Arsdale would put down the steel. Furthermore, Friday George had selected his mill site well. It would be expanded and run again, and Upton and Sisson could be left to their own devices. The remnants of the village around the George mill were named Vandale* in honor of the new manager and action would commence forthwith!

Before the actual laying of steel is narrated, yet another look at unrealized dreams should be taken. It is no particular surprise that Scott

*Vandale was renamed McCloud in 1897.

16

and Van Arsdale were hardly original in contemplating a railroad to the McCloud country, but the fact that there was another motive, as well as a variety of routes, might not be obvious.

Logging spurs were built off the Southern Pacific in the timber country, and at least one of them aimed toward the McCloud River. The Red Cross Lumber Company had one mill close to the Southern Pacific 20 miles or so down the canyon from Sisson and another at Bartle's. A couple of miles of track were laid up a stream called Soda Creek away from the SP and in the general direction of Bartle's, but the mill at Bartle's was closed for the usual reason, and the buildings later collapsed under the weight of winter snow.

Timber was and is widespread in California, even if there are few stands to compare with that of the McCloud. Another resource of less common nature in the state, discovered not far from Bartle's, led to even higher hopes for a railroad. There is coal in the area, and a rich coal vein would surely bring rails. It is hard to realize today how concerned people were with railroads for their own sake in those bygone days. Perhaps the nearest thing to it today is the attachment we all have toward our own transportation, the automobile. In any event, to read newspaper accounts of the day, one might gain the impression that the forest around Bartle's was atop a vast coal seam, rich in quality and easy to work, just waiting for someone to command untold wealth by making transportation feasible. Evidently no one tried to transport coal out by wagon train.

Coal is there. Even though this area is largely one of lava flows, in which mineralization is not common, the presence of coal was not a false hope, and a little was actually mined and sent out over the railroad that came to move logs. Coal is used less generally in California today than a century ago, but perhaps when oil and gas become too expensive someone will remember that coal can be mined in the McCloud country.

If coal wasn't enough to excite the railroad magnates, the early editors said that there are iron deposits in the McCloud watershed, too. News reports were a lot less specific about the extent of iron ore than they were about the coal, but their efforts to provide an attraction for everyone became even more vague when they assured us that well known residents were prospecting the area for gold. No strikes came to light.

One thing we can depend on. There were a good many trees along the McCloud.

The first mill at McCloud. Built by Friday George and enlarged by Scott and Van Arsdale, this sawmill was considered both large and modern. Railroad tracks that spelled success for the venture are evident in the foreground. —CHARLES M. HAINES COLLECTION

2

STEEL
ACROSS THE MOUNTAIN

WHEN the spring sun cleared the snow from the lower slopes of Shasta in early 1896 Al Shearer of Yreka laced his high boots and started up the hill from Upton with rod and transit. He was headed for Squaw Valley and the George mill. Where his survey party pointed the way graders and tracklayers would follow. On July 3 man and machine began to alter the contour of the earth that had lain undisturbed since the mighty volcanic blasts built the mountain centuries earlier. William Van Arsdale was managing the new venture, with H. Cooley, formerly a division superintendent for the Southern Pacific, heading construction in the field and an important new investor as well.

The highway locomotive, or traction engine, had not been able to keep Friday George financially afloat, but Boss Cooley devised a new use for it by attaching strong plows and scrapers to the frame and turning it loose on the grading. Reports indicate that it could and did move earth at a "lively rate, tearing up ground filled with roots and small rocks as if it were a sandpile." The traction engine was brought over from the former George mill and work initiated from the Upton end because the railroad did not need to go all the way through to Squaw Valley before it could become useful. Logs were available here on the west slope and could be moved to the mill at Upton while the railroad was being completed.

Before the summer ran out Cooley had more than 300 men scattered out on the mountain clearing the forest, following the traction engine, cutting ties, making fills, and driving four-horse scrapers. Enough 50 pound steel rail to lay five miles of track showed up at Upton and was ready to go forward when needed. Temporary camps were set up along the grade, each housing some 80 men at a maximum. Other men were working in Squaw Valley framing the new sawmill and preparing for the arrival of machinery to expand the old Friday George operation.

Viewers of the activity up the slope wrote favorably of the quality of the effort being put forth on the new grade. It was laid out to a demanding four percent climb right from the mill at Upton and continued at this pace for about a mile and a half. After rounding Spring Hill, the climb eased briefly but then the four percent lift resumed for another run of two and one-half miles to the head of Big Canyon, terminating there but backing away in another direction by means of a switchback. Again climbing, but at a somewhat lesser rate, the grade lead to the summit near the Mountain House.

Use of the traction engine for a purpose quite different from its original ambition was but the first of a series of innovations in equipment and practices of this railroad that would give it particular interest. Another such "different" practice came into play building the grade even before any rail was put down. Most railroads of the era in hilly country were marked by spindly trestles across ravines; highly photogenic affairs that didn't appeal to management because of maintenance expense and fire danger. Crews were not usually too enthralled either with an ever-present vibration to remind men that once in a while one did collapse under load.

Instead of waiting until someone in management got tired of trestles and their problems and filled them in, this line was built without them all the way to Squaw Valley. Moving the massive amounts of dirt required to build a fill ordinarily is considerably more expensive than building a trestle, but these builders had another idea that worked. Instead of moving dirt by the sweat of men, animals and perhaps the traction engines, they let water, which worked for free, do much of the labor.

Anywhere this grade would run, higher ground leading up toward the snow covered cone was always adjacent, with watercourses bringing the snow melt down from above. Borrowing from the hydraulic mining technique practiced during gold rush days (before it was outlawed for doing exactly what this ingenious builder intended), when a fill was needed workers first built a small dam up the mountain from the fill. They then rigged a pipe from the resulting pond leading down to a nozzle or monitor called a "giant" in mining days, mounted to aim at a wall of the gulch or ravine just above the desired fill. In the meantime workers laid the necessary drain box where it would be covered by the fill, exactly as most fills are built with drain culverts today, except that in this case the drain was extended up canyon a bit farther than normal. Then a low dike was built across the bottom of the defile, level on top and perhaps three feet high, at the downslope end of the proposed fill.

With all in readiness a valve on the water line leading to the giant was spun open and a solid stream of water under high pressure from the drop of the lead pipe ripped into the hillside with the same devastating effect that exposed the gold in earlier days. The muddy mixture of dirt, stones and roots came cascading down against the dike. Here the heavy solids settled to the bottom and the water escaped over the top of the dike. When the new fill reached the level of the top of the dike the process was stopped, the pond above refilled, the dirt dried out a bit, a new dike built atop the first layer of fill, and then the giant turned on once again to repeat the process. Eventually the fill reached the desired height of as much as 40 feet, and the railroad had a well-compacted low maintenance section of line rather than an expensive nuisance.

Minority groups play a role in this history and the record starts with the grading of the line. The construction work force was largely Caucasian, but some 25 Chinese were also put to work in the first month, and trouble resulted. Ample precedent existed for the use of Chinese in railroad construction. These patient and efficient workers had furnished most of the brawn that pushed the Central Pacific a mile and a half high over the rugged granite of the Sierra Nevada and across endless tedious miles of parched desert eastward from California. Precedent there was for trouble, too. Hardbitten Europeans in the new land tended to think the primary right was theirs and used whatever might be necessary to get and hold what they wanted. Outnumbered Chinese soon learned to be docile and content themselves with leftovers.

The white majority of construction workers felt that building this railroad should be their exclusive privilege, regardless of wishes of management or the stipulations of law. Within a week after Chinese employees showed up there were conferences among the whites and a plan of action was worked out. On Sunday afternoon, August 9, a mass meeting was held in Sisson on a vacant lot. Discussions were quiet and no particular excitement was aroused amongst the local citizenry, who may or may not have been surprised to discover the next day that the Asians had departed.

The Chinese camp had been visited by a large number of the rival workers in the dead of night, who made the alternatives quite plain to the Orientals. The raiders had brought wagons along. Property was heaped aboard the vehicles and the men marched to the far side of Sisson and on to the next railroad station. A news report tells us that: "In routing the Chinamen only one or two were bruised or cut, and those not seriously."

Sheriff Hobbs and District Attorney Raynes hurried down from Yreka the next day to investigate, with no more positive result than might be expected. A public meeting was called at which manager Van Arsdale made a statement of his company's position that served both as an answer to the men who remained and a threat.

The majority workmen were concerned that they might lose their jobs to Chinese. Van Arsdale promised not only to keep all the present force who wanted work, but to hire more white men if any became available. He wanted as many as 75 Chinese in addition not only because of the need to get men working in greater numbers, but because the Chinese would do work that the whites refused. He stated also that it was of prime importance to him to get the road pushed through this year and that if it appeared impossible to do so because of labor strife, or for any other reason that would prevent the Squaw Valley mill from running next season, he was ready to abandon the whole project.

The property owners and business men of Sisson endorsed a proposition agreeable to Van Arsdale. They would encourage peaceable continuance of the railroad construction provided that no more than 75 Chinese were employed and that the company would ship them back to Red Bluff no later than November 15. When word of this agreement was circulated amongst the white workers it met with something less than enthusiasm, but reason prevailed and the compromise was accepted. Construction went forward.

By September 3 the survey party had completed its work, but no track had yet been laid. The advance grading crews had reached the summit of the line near Mountain House, with a "permanent" grader camp being established

there before the end of the month. Work continued through October and into November before snow closed activity down for the winter. Advance grading was in progress on the slope down from Mountain House toward Vandale, and the first few miles out of Upton had rails scattered along ready to be placed in position. Connection with the Southern Pacific at Upton was by means of a switchback, which was not installed until late October, when men were laid off from the mill because of its shutting down for the winter.

Machinery for the new mill at Vandale was dragged over the hill on logging trucks, with ten horses assigned the task of moving the bed for the mill engine. Much of the building was completed. Some activity of erection would continue during the winter in preparation for the summer season.

The manager arranged for a special car on the Southern Pacific to return the Chinese laborers to Red Bluff on the 19th, and five days later all the road work ceased and the remaining men were paid off. Snow had brought the project to a halt. Most of the grading was completed and rails were laid from Upton for some four miles to the Howard ranch on Cold Creek. Chief engineer Cooley came in from the field and departed to spend the winter with his family in the milder climate at Oakland. Where his subordinates scattered to we do not know, but solitude had returned to the mountain.

Although the new venture was being carried on by the owners of the Siskiyou Lumber and Mercantile Company, who also used the name Scott and Van Arsdale in some of their enterprises, they assigned a new name to the Vandale operation, one it would retain for more than 60 years. Enter the McCloud River Lumber Company. And, although incorporation would not come until the following year, the railroad was given a name of its own, too. The McCloud River Railroad Company now had four miles of track and ambition for more, even if it hadn't reached Vandale in this first year.

With all work on the actual line in suspense for the winter, its owners could devote some time to tidying up the paper details. On January 21, 1897, they signed articles of incorporation, which brought the new railroad into legal existence the following day. The incorporators

Engine No. 1 has been delivered from its former home on the California Railway far to the south of McCloud where it was No. 2, renumbered, painted with the name of its new owner and is in service. The very early stage of its career at McCloud is evidenced by the presence of the man with the oil can, who is engineer Bert Moran. He suffered the unviable distinction of being the second crewman and first locomotive engineer to lose his life on the McCloud River Railroad. The unfortunate accident occured in 1900. In this scene, his wife has joined the crew for this portrait, obviously taken before the fatal runaway. —CHARLES M. HAINES COLLECTION

were William E. Brown, William W. Van Arsdale, Daniel W. Earl, J. Dalzell Brown and George W. Scott. Scott listed his address as Alameda; all the others San Francisco. These men each subscribed for 132 shares of stock at the par value of $100 per share, a total of $66,000. The men constituted themselves the board of directors, with Scott as treasurer, who certified he had received the required ten percent minimum of the amount subscribed, or $6,600 in cash. The total number of shares authorized for the new corporation was 12,000, a figure that never has been changed.

Articles of incorporation are typically made rather broad in their description of proposed future activities of the corporation, the notion being that this charter should impose little restriction on just about anything the corporation decides to engage in through the future. The McCloud River Railroad articles provide a rather interesting contrast by being relatively restrictive in comparison to ambitions sounded in the public press. News reports would have us believe that the line would reach far beyond Siskiyou County, with Klamath Falls, principal settlement of south central Oregon, being reported again and again as a construction goal just months away. A transportation void did exist to the east, but talks of rails to Oregon, to Lower Klamath Lake where a steamer would connect at Lairds Landing for Klamath Falls, or even to Alturas, only settlement of note farther to the east in California, remained only talk. The talk also more modestly assumed that rails would reach the Fall River Valley, not far beyond Bartle, but they never got there either.

The incorporators did claim that their four miles would be expanded to reach McGavic (to the north of Bartle), to Ash Creek Mill with a spur from the McGavic line, and to Sisson with a spur from the existing four miles. All of these claims they meant, and did in fact achieve before long. They also prudently added a clause that they might "lease, purchase, construct, own, maintain, operate" to such points as "the board of directors of said company may hereafter from time to time determine to be necessary for the best interests of said road." Certainly then the articles would not appear to actually prohibit building to Klamath Falls — or anywhere else.

In addition to declaring where they would build, the incorporators described what they intended to build, which could be summarized as "a railroad," although they took considerably more than two words in the process. Even allowing that they specifically include a line of telegraph and telephone the language is somewhat elaborate.

Snow had not completely vanished from the lower reaches of the mountain when engineer Cooley returned from his sojourn in the South and decided it was time to get back to work. By April 15 he had rounded up 30 men and headed up the hill to lay track. A day earlier two other gangs of 30 men each had set out to establish two logging camps five miles up the road. The tracklayers under Cooley would have to hustle to get the mile of track laid before O. B. Neal's loggers would have timber to load!

On the other side of the ridge at Vandale, construction did not resume until arrival of the train. Much of the machinery was now in place, logging chutes built and the building enclosed in readiness.

The McCloud River Railroad had a locomotive, appropriately enough numbered No. 1, and a fleet of short log cars, which it didn't bother to number. The little Mogul was kept busy supplying steel to the railhead and logs to the mill at Upton, and its reach of operation steadily expanded as the track moved closer to the summit. In May the company provided some boarding cars for track layers and the surfacing gang which meant that they would live near the job instead of commuting out from Upton each day.

In early June the new venture faced an experience that must have shaped the careful attitude which continues to this day. A forest fire struck! It started near the logging camp, probably set by some careless action there, and proceeded to burn slowly until a strong south wind turned it into holocaust! Roaring flames foraged relentlessly ahead through brush and timber to the slopes of Black Butte, well to the north of Upton, rolling up great black clouds of smoke. Then the wind changed to the north and drove the fire devil to the town of Sisson, causing alarm not only from the approaching flame, but from hot cinders that the wind

The forest monarchs next to the tracks between Sission and McCloud had not yet fallen when these two photographs were taken, some time during the 1920's. The ever-curving nature of the line is readily apparent, as is the natural ballast. —BOTH W. C. WHITTAKER COLLECTION

dropped ahead of the actual conflagration. Mills closed down and men turned out to save the town, at which they were successful (a few years later much of the town was lost in another fire). The inferno swept on up the railroad grade, found extensive slashings left by the McCloud crews, and fed until the roar approached that of distant thunder. Van Arsdale led his employees in the fight, which brought the fire under control after nearly a week. With the wind remaining at high velocity, the crews did not relax until even the smoldering ceased.

When the excitement of the fire was over track laying resumed, and steel reached the summit in mid-June. Locomotive No. 1 now had ten miles over which it could roam, and climbed a total of 974 feet each time it made the run. E. F. Dean was the regular engineer and liked the prospect of continuing his employment well enough to build a new home for his family at Upton.

Although Vandale was not reached in 1896 as originally contemplated, tracklaying in this second summer continued downhill from the summit with little interruption. With more than a thousand feet of descent to accomplish in fewer miles than the climb from Upton, the grade on the east side was even tougher than the west slope. The maximum is listed as four percent, but old-timers snort acidly that it was a "civil engineers' four percent." By this, they insinuate that it was an actual seven percent, with dark suspicion that it could be even more. The official record is silent on this, but in the early years locomotives were purchased with stipulations as to their ability to perform on seven percent ascents, and four percent, an ascent of four feet for each 100 of forward progress, does remain today. Even so, to squeeze the line into the allotted space on the mountainside another switchback was needed, at Signal Butte, five miles short of Vandale.

Today the McCloud River Railroad has an impressive safety record, despite the heavy grades over which it continues to operate. Railroading was more haphazard everywhere in the 1890's, with mishaps of all sorts more or less taken for granted as part of the price of progress. The first wreck on the McCloud River line came before it was built to its original destination, in the form of a collision even though

Two lumberjacks fell a near perfect specimen near McCloud. Shortly a bucker will cut the felled tree into log lengths. The bucker had one of the worst jobs in the woods for he also had to clean up his slash (tops, broken branches, and all trash) after him. —CHARLES M. HAINES COLLECTION

Compared with the giant severed in the photograph shown above, the log suspended under the wheels is comparatively modest. Even so it comes thigh-high to the driver. The big logging wheels were a common method for moving logs from the point of cutting to loading areas where rail cars were boarded. The large dimension of the wheels enabled the suspended loads to be moved over irregular terrain without benefit of a prepared road. Horses were a popular form of motive power for many years, but bull teams, steam road locomotives, and, later, tractors were used as well. —CHARLES M. HAINES COLLECTION

it had but one train. Furthermore, locomotive No. 1 was safely tucked away for the night at Upton when the accident occurred on the other side of the mountain. A loaded flat car had been left at the summit on July 9, and somehow got loose on the downgrade to the east. The construction cars were parked at the end of track about two miles away. The runaway had enough room to attain terrific velocity, but held to the curves and tore into the standing cars with sufficient force to demolish several of them. Fortunately no one was hurt; perhaps the cars receiving the brunt of the impact were not occupied. In any event, the debris was cleared and work went on.

Vandale was reached on July 21, 1897, and the company announced that the new line would be open for regular business on August 1. Not only could the new railroad engage in its primary purpose of linking the Vandale mill with the rest of the world, but freight traffic moving across the mountain in wagons to more distant points would be transferred at Vandale rather than Sisson. The same transfer could be accomplished for passengers as well, and the announcement soon came that the Southern Pacific would sell tickets good on the McCloud River Railroad.

The SP also changed the name of the station just south of Sisson to Azalea, thus releasing its former name of McCloud. The change seems appropriate enough, for the wildflower can be found here, but neither river nor its namesake railroad are at hand. Van Arsdale must not have been anxious to perpetuate his name in his new townsite, for he promptly rechristened the eastern terminus of his railroad McCloud.

A stage line had been running on regular schedule from Sisson eastward through Bartle's prior to completion of the new railroad to McCloud, but the competitive relationship of highway transportation with the railroad prior to the development of the gasoline powered vehicle is shown by the news item that appeared within three months after the railroad opened for business: "George W. Levens (the stage operator) has removed the livery stock from his barn in Sisson and gone to Fall River Mills."

Complete supremacy of the locomotive across the mountain was to be brief. Henry Ford was already dreaming of his future, too.

As McCloud River Railroad rails reached further and further into the woods, the hungry locomotives were distant from their source of wood fuel. Enormous woodpiles were placed alongside the tracks in the woods to feed the ever-hungry locomotives. Slash in addition to wood which did not meet the high standards of the mill were used for engine fuel. —ROBERT HANFT COLLECTION

3

RAILS
INTO THE WILDERNESS

WHEN THE fledgling railroad linked the new mill that had risen from the ashes of Friday George's dream to the markets opened up beyond the mountain its primary function had been achieved. Today the modern Mc-Cloud River line still serves in this same capacity, but to explore the development of the road since 1897 it might be well to note that several transportation duties with rather different demands upon the railroad have been met. All four demands were present at the beginning, but the evolvement of each since then has been distinct.

The basic need, as already pointed out, was to provide a means to get McCloud lumber to market at a transportation cost the company could bear. Hardly less important to the railroad has been the movement of the primary raw material, logs, to the mill where it is processed into lumber. Log hauling has accounted for substantially more change in the plant and behavior of the railroad than has the more stable lumber traffic. The third and fourth types of service are both by-products of the first two even though they have survived the disappearance of log hauling. They are the transportation of passengers, and of freight of whatever nature offered by the general public, as con-

trasted to the specialized needs of the McCloud River Lumber Company.

In the early years publicity was largely about expansion to serve the general public; in other words, common carrier freight and passenger hauling to and from the largely undeveloped reaches to the east of McCloud. The fact is that the company never concerned itself particularly with building to serve all shippers. Its objective was to service the McCloud River Lumber Company, which meant extending its lines to new supplies of logs as the old ones were harvested. When a log line could add to income by engaging in common carriage for others this was done. Common carriage, passenger and freight, was never the primary goal of construction.

Considerably more mileage of track has been devoted solely to log hauling than to common carrier services as the record has slowly spun out over the nearly three quarters of a century that have elapsed since the first carload came down from Howard. More is known, however, about the lesser portion of the railroad engaged in common carrier activity than the parts used for logs alone. Even though the company preserves fine detail maps showing hundreds of miles of log spurs, comparatively little impor-

In the early days the McCloud River Lumber Co. used four wheel wagons to haul out the logs to the railhead. Log wagon wheels were sometimes boxed with board, as shown here, to keep mud from accumulating on the spokes. From two to six, and even ten oxen were generally used for draft purposes. —CHARLES M. HAINES COLLECTION

Log loading in the early days made use of either gravity or donkey engines to roll logs onto the rail cars. In this McCloud scene it appears a "Big Wheel" has just brought in a load as the team in shown on the left, and the donkey engine was where the photograph was made. —CHARLES M. HAINES COLLECTION

tance can be attached to the specific history of most of them. The life span of some of the log lines was hardly more than a week or two. They were hastily graded, tracks put down, the trees felled and the rails removed again, never to return. At the other time span extreme almost all the trackage east of McCloud today could be said to consist of logging spurs that have become permanent. This record of expansion is, then, largely the history of the longest-lived log trackage.

Even though logs were within reach of the original main line, which did perform its first useful haulage from the camp at Howard to the old mill at Upton, a short log line was built in the very first year of service to McCloud. Total length was only a couple of miles, and the exact location is lost. It could have found logs in almost any direction, for Friday George's bull teams had not reached far from the mill.

Once the original main line was completed Scott and Van Arsdale lavished effort and money on their new mill and the town around it for some months rather than in pushing the rail frontier along. They announced that the mill would be the largest and finest in Northern California and the town the most modern in the state. They may well have realized both these claims. Enlargement and modernization programs continued to improve mill facilities for many years, and the town was advanced for its era. When one visits McCloud today the wooden sidewalks that still remain in residential areas and gas lights along the main street give an impression of quaintness to the quiet little city composed entirely of frame buildings. On the other hand, those wooden sidewalks were laid down in an era when sidewalks of any kind were far from universal. The gas lights aren't quite what they might imply, either, for they are a very recent addition to the scene. The town was built with electricity in every home, again at a time when electric lighting was certainly not the usual method in out of the way locations. The lumber company installed electric generators for the mill large enough to supply all the homes as well, and did so at no cost to the user in the early years — even if the current was turned off at 11 p.m. That was time for sober working folk to be abed anyway.

Many of the company built houses in early McCloud still stand today, as do some of the board sidewalks, but the stumps in the middle of the street have long since vanished. Raw stumps also provide the only yard decoration in evidence, whereas today virtually all yards have nice lawns, shrubbery, and often sizeable trees. —T. E. GLOVER COLLECTION

An overview of McCloud, showing houses of varying sizes and the livery stable. Status in housing is clearly evident here, with the size of the dwelling not necessarily an indicator of the extent of the family. The sawmill and the planning mill may be viewed in the background. This illustration appeared on a postcard mailed in 1913 which would give an indication as to the circa of this scene. —CHARLES M. HAINES COLLECTION

The McCloud River Lumber Co. mill had expanded from the first structure shown on page 18. The stone block structure with the stack is the power house that furnished steam and electricity; the latter used not only by the mill but throughout the town, well ahead of general acceptance in communities isolated as McCloud. At this time logs were unloaded directly onto the ground alongside the mill chute. Logs then moved up the conveyor to the second floor entrance, passing through a sprayer visible just above the carload of logs. The spray removed dirt that could damage the saws. (RIGHT) A site is being cleared for a mill pond in order to eliminate the dry unloading shown above. The pond ended up as a diked in area and was used until 1970. Today the company has returned to dry storage and transfer to the mill conveyor. —BOTH CHARLES M. HAINES COLLECTION

At the right, a cut of log cars await unloading into the mill pond. The unloading ramp is just to the left of the trestle. —CHARLES M. HAINES COLLECTION (LOWER-RIGHT) The completed mill and pond in full operation. The chain of logs, sometimes called a boom, restrain logs from drifting aground in shallow water. The pond man leads the logs to the jack ladder which is the conveyor carrying the logs into the mill. —T. E. GLOVER COLLECTION

The company piped in running water and the houses were equipped with toilet facilities served by a central sewage system. With a large store, recreation hall, depot and post office, what more could any resident ask? The company built everything, owned everything, and turned usage of the fine facilities over to its employees at a most modest fee. A man living in the company dormitory could, for example, "enjoy all the luxuries" including an iron bed and use as much hot and cold water as he wished for one dollar per month. Excellent ventilation was claimed to be a special feature, which appears entirely plausible, especially during winter storms, and perhaps a necessity too, if the lumberjacks were a bit shy about using the free hot water to full advantage.

In these early years the railroad made no attempt to operate through the long winters, but rented a snowplow from the SP to clear out the last of the winter snow and open the line for the season of 1898. Regular train service did not commence until May 1, by which time snow problems were no longer important. Closing down for the snow season was a luxury later operators would envy!

The end of June found the new railroad faced with the necessity of informing the Interstate Commerce Commission, stern guardian of the public interest, just how it had handled its responsibilities. Among the tidbits of information, relevant and otherwise, that show up in this first report is the humble apology that the company had functioned in its duties to the public for only four months. In addition to the 660 shares of stock taken by the original incorporators, another 2,940 shares had been sold and $216,000 worth of first mortgage bonds had also been issued. A ready market for these additional securities was at hand, for William E. Brown, president and chairman of the board, William W. Van Arsdale, vice-president and general manager, and George W. Scott, secretary-treasurer, sold them to the McCloud River Lumber Company, of which William E. Brown was president and chairman of the board, William W. Van Arsdale was vice-president and general manager, and George W. Scott secretary-treasurer. The money was well spent, though; the 18.32 miles of railroad cost $530,350.58, plus $47,048.63 for the equipment that now included two locomotives, both fitted with train brakes hopefully capable of coping with the tilted terrain, a combination passenger car that cost $800, 47 flat cars, a tank car and a caboose, and two other road cars. The company built and equipped a shop that must have been something short of luxurious, since the total spent was $223.13. Even the bill of $4,073 for station buildings and their fixtures hardly shrieks of extravagance.

In this initial period the company took in $13,459.81 from hauling 7,937 tons of freight at an average charge of 9.2 cents per ton for each mile carried. A total of 380 passengers paid $333.80 at the rate of 4.7 cents per mile to ride in the combination car, with almost all of them making the full trip between Upton and Mc-

The McCloud River Lumber Company office building and company store at McCloud at the turn of the century. (BELOW) The first railroad station at McCloud. This building also served as an office for the railroad and lumber companies, general store, post office, express office, and town meeting house until additional structures could be erected. —BOTH CHARLES M. HAINES COLLECTION

McCloud River No. 4 was a Baldwin 2-6-2 built new for the road in 1898. In this scene she appears brand-new and has wood piled high on her tender for a trip with a mixed consist abbreviated to the minimum. Note that coach No. 1 has the front end lettered simply "Baggage and Express." While the photographer was capturing this scene on film, the express messenger cautiously peers around the door in the best tradition. The "U.S. Mail" and "Wells Fargo Express" captions had not yet appeared. —CHARLES M. HAINES COLLECTION At the right, Southern Pacific No. 1582 helps unload logs at the McCloud mill pond circa 1900. Records of leased motive power on the McCloud River Railroad are non-existant, yet this illustration is evidence that they were used. In this scene, a temporary power hoist operated by a steam skidder was used for the unloading of logs. The steam skidder may be seen between the log cars at the left of the view. —DON H. WARREN COLLECTION

Cloud. Most of the freight was lumber, 6,417 tons of it, although "manufactures, merchandise, and miscellaneous" are all represented.

It cost the company $8,219 to move the traffic, and after the interest of $4,960.80 on the mortgage bonds was turned over to the lumber company, a modest profit of $704 remained. To accomplish this end, the officers were as frugal in their parting with the income entrusted to them as they had been with the construction money. Starting with their own salaries of zero, the average daily wage of the 53 employees was $1.86. Engineers got $3.81, firemen $2.34, conductors $3.25, trainmen $2.05. The lone section foreman was rewarded with $2.45; his one-man gang got $1.25, which was 25 cents more than general laborers received.

The Southern Pacific made $30 from the loan of its snowplow.

The first full year of operation (save for the winter hibernation) saw no expansion of the line, although extension was in the plans, and $4,750 was spent in preparatory work, primarily grading. In the offing was a partial exception to the claim above that expansion east of McCloud was designed for logs. The first extension from McCloud was built to another new mill; one that proved to be short lived and thus more or less made its trackage a log spur by default.

Ash Creek Mill with Superintendent C. G. Gage in the inset. This new mill was equipped with all the most modern equipment available for processing logs, but did not have a pond, as evidenced by the dry log landing in the foreground. The entire operation was destroyed by fire in 1902. (BELOW) The Ash Creek general store where the loggers could buy everything from a pair of Levis to a bottle of Swamp Root. —BOTH CHARLES M. HAINES COLLECTION.

Evidently the McCloud River Lumber Company was not quite ready to put all its boards through one production facility as yet. Even while establishing McCloud and the mill there at a scale impressive for the day, the company decided to add another factory a few miles distant. This was the Ash Creek mill, 12.31 miles to the northeast of McCloud, reached by rail in 1900. Output at Ash Creek was less important than that at McCloud, evidently the showpiece of the company from the time it was built. Yet the Ash Creek mill was constructed with the most modern equipment available for processing logs, as was typical company practice. It was equipped with a band saw for the first cut, as contrasted with the older type circular saws then installed at McCloud. Ash Creek had to have railroad service, and it was provided.

Before Ash Creek added its figures to the total, the first full year of business reported freight traffic up to 43,737 tons, of which 40,-833 tons was lumber, bringing in $70,213.85. Passenger revenues were $1,350 from 1,933 rides. Express added $80, and telegraph another $59 to the coffers. With operating expenses just under $40,000, which included $6,835 for cordwood to fuel the locomotives and about $200 for tallow, oil and waste to keep them running smoothly, the officers were sufficiently pleased with their results to declare a dividend of $14,200 to the stockholders.

During the following year the Ash Creek line was completed, but was not opened to revenue traffic as yet. It cost $125,517.74, and was formally placed in service on July 1, 1901, after facilities there were ready for use. Construction was also aimed eastward from McCloud toward Bartle, with 6.83 miles completed when the winter snow once again brought the usual hibernation. In addition, the year 1900 marked the purchase of another railroad by the McCloud line. The logging trackage of the Red Cross Lumber Company, some two and one-half miles leading toward McCloud from Castle Crags to the south of Sisson, was sold to the company. The McCloud River people had no plan to continue the Red Cross operation or to extend this trackage, but only wanted the rail it contained. They had been experiencing difficulty in buying as much track metal as they

It appears the McCloud River Lumber crews are moving to a new landing, as their Best Steam Tractor may be seen snaking the donkey engine. The Best Steam Tractors which were built at San Leandro, California, were very popular on the southern slopes of Mt. Shasta. —ROBERT HANFT COLLECTION

Considerably less clumsy than the Best Steam Traction engine was the reliable Perry Log Cart. Shortly after McCloud Lumber Company took over from Friday George, the horses and wheels returned to various sections of the woods on the southern slopes of Mt. Shasta. —CHARLES M. HAINES COLLECTION

desired from the usual supply sources, and accordingly entered the salvage business long enough to remove the used rail. A gang went to work in August, and the rail was duly picked up for reuse.

As early as 1899 rumors were heard that Scott and Van Arsdale were considering sale of the McCloud properties, and that an English syndicate would take over. Nothing materialized from overseas save another rumor that the English capitalists had withdrawn because of involvement with the Boer War. In 1902 a deal was consummated that brought in a substantial interest by Minnesota capitalists. The north central states of Wisconsin, Michigan and Minnesota had been the scene of aggressive exploitation of a major forest resource to serve building needs both locally and to the east, but by the turn of the century many of the holdings were depleted and owners were turning westward to reinvest the capital they had accrued. The McCloud River operation provided a very solid outlet for investment with a long range future and immediate wealth to the present owners.

J. R. Wisdom, representing the new eastern interests, became general manager of the mill

McCloud's locomotive No. 6 was the great experiment in rail motive power. This double-ender built by the Baldwin Locomotive Works in 1900 was the only one of its kind. One engineer could drive both halves of this twin locomotive simultaneously. Because the cabs were joined back to back, wood and water had to be carried atop and alongside the boiler. —CHARLES M. HAINES COLLECTION

At the right, an aerial view of McCloud showing a section of town and the railroad yard. At the lower left, the roof of the depot. The structure just above the depot is the McCloud Hotel. At the center of the illustration is the roundhouse, car repair building, and other facilities. —T. E. GLOVER COLLECTION

and railroad in 1902, and in his first year the main line was shortened .52 miles by removal of the Big Canyon switchback. Although this act yielded a substantial improvement to operating conditions the switchback at Signal Butte remained and does so to this day. Thus, instead of trains being called upon to back only between Signal Butte and Big Canyon, since 1902 every train reverses direction at Signal Butte and backing up must be done for the balance of the trip either to McCloud or to the connection with the Southern Pacific. Until the coming of diesel power where a single engine crew could control enough tractive force to lift the train to the summit the backing up problem was neatly solved by placing locomotives at each end of trains, headed in opposite directions. Thus a train normally always had a locomotive on the front end aimed forward. The front end became the rear at Signal Butte, and vice versa. The short passenger train provided an exception when it used, as was customary, a single locomotive. Cabooses and coaches have been equipped with whistles to warn the

infrequent competitors for the right of way, and crews even now take their back up runs as a matter of routine, just as they do the very heavy grade. This is the way it is with their railroad and they make it effective, even if it is unique.

The year 1903 was an eventful and trying one. In midsummer an epidemic of typhoid fever was raging in McCloud. Death struck both the humble and the highly placed and brought down the new manager, who was succeeded in office by his son Charles. A concerted effort was made to trace the source of the disease, which was not accomplished before serious question about the entire environment had been raised. Human culpability and carelessness was found, sadly enough, to be responsible. A dairy supplying milk to the town was diluting its product with water taken from a source contaminated by effluent from the town sewage system. Once action had been taken to correct the problem the threat was over, but it was a long time before the natural confidence of the residents returned, and they once

again recognized that their town was an exceptionally healthy place in which to live. Visitors were hardly complacent, and others simply avoided becoming visitors, for some time.

The scare in McCloud had not completely subsided when, on August 26, fire broke out in the mill at Ash Creek and not only burned the mill to the ground but also destroyed the drying sheds, their contents and adjacent stacked lumber, together with nearby dwellings. The total damage was estimated to be in excess of $100,000.

The company decided after some deliberation not to rebuild at Ash Creek, but to continue expansion at McCloud and use part of the rail in the Bartle construction program. A section of about four miles of the Ash Creek line was retained as a log spur, and Bartle was reached in 1905 by adding an additional 6.75 miles to the partially completed line. In March the company brought in some 60 Greek laborers to work on the rail extension, again generating a certain dissension because of failure to reserve employment for those who by now considered themselves natives.

The shift to control by men with a Minnesota background became complete, as Scott and Van Arsdale left the company and J. H. Queal came in as president and general manager.

With 18.21 miles of new line between McCloud and Bartle the main trackage extended 36 miles, with an additional 18.75 miles of branches and spurs, plus ten miles of yard track and sidings. The railroad was now a million dollar enterprise in its own right; it had cost $1,097,825.34 by the end of 1905. Although the four general officers of the railroad drew a total of hardly more than $1,000 in wages between them for the year, they were not able to make

During the early years of operation, the crews would stop nearly anywhere on the line for a train portrait. While engine No. 9 had arrived on the roster in 1901, by the time the photographer captured this scene of the daily mixed train headed downgrade to Upton, the expanse across Big Canyon had been filled in hydraulically. —CHARLES M. HAINES COLLECTION

41

Three scenes at Bartle station, just 18.21 miles east of McCloud. The name was applied to the station in 1905, after Abraham and Jerome Bartle who ran cattle in the Shasta Valley and built a resort at what is the McIntosh place. In the view above, station agent Pete Miller in the chair, takes life easy while his children watch the photographer. The box car parked at the station platform is a long way from its native Texas. (BELOW) In this view, No. 12 has just pulled in with the passenger train. At the right, the passenger train crew joins with the station agent and family for a classic railroad photograph. Locomotive No. 12 shows the typical spic and span condition maintained by the engine crew. The combination coach now boasts affiliations with "U. S. Mail" and "Wells Fargo" painted on her sides. — ALL CHARLES M. HAINES COLLECTION

as impressive a financial showing as their predecessors had done. Profit for 1905 was a scant thousand dollars. Freight had brought in $140,251, passengers another $4,000, telegraph $130, and express $452. The problem was that expenses had risen even faster than income, leaving the bare thousand dollar difference between the two. Furthermore, the company now had a 192 foot trestle to maintain. Apart from that the new line to Bartle was not particularly difficult either to build or operate. A decade earlier when newspapers of the region were trying to build enthusiasm and entice a railroad the editors claimed that once Squaw Valley was reached additional construction would be a mere breeze. Perhaps so by comparison with the hill line, but the McCloud River Railroad never found any extensive flat land. The Bartle extension did boast a mile and one-half of level track, but also had 17 miles that weren't, including 28 ascents and 20 dips eastbound, with a total climb of 900 feet and 350 of descent. For the McCloud line this is straight trackage, too; there were only 64 curves between McCloud and Bartle.

Bartle is one of two already existing communities of any importance that the railroad would ever reach save at its western terminus. Hardly a bustling metropolis, the little settlement was perhaps more important as a transshipping point for a number of years than for traffic of its own. People and goods for the Fall River Valley and to a less settled but extensive area to the east left the comforts of rail transportation at Bartle and fought the dirt roads of the time. Westbound, of course, reaching Bartle meant one's transportation problems were over. Well, mostly, anyway.

Construction did not stop at Bartle, but continued on, turning northward, to the great ex-

McCLOUD RIVER RAILROAD--Upton and Bartle

FROM UPTON		Minimum Time	Distance from Upton	TIME TABLE No. 10 EFFECTIVE APRIL 23, 1906 At 6:00 A.M.	Distance from Bartle	Minimum Time	TOWARD UPTON	
4 PASS. First Class	2 PASS. First Class						1 PASS. First Class	3 PASS. First Class
P.M. LV. 6:30	P.M. LV. 1:00		.0	UPTON W	37.00	6	A.M. AR. 9:30	P.M. AR. 5:30
6:39	1:10	8	3.80	BURK	34.20	8	9:19	5:20
6:50	1:18	10	4.83	HOWARD W	32.17	8	9:11	5:08
7:00	1:28	8	6.83	Big Canon	30.17	10	9:03	5:00
7:15	1:40	13	9.57	PIERCE	27.43	9	8:52	4:48
7:25	1:50	8	11.84	Signal Butte	25.16	10	8:40	4:37
7:35	2:00	9	14.54	HOOPER W	22.46	12	8:25	4:27
P.M. AR. 7:46	2:15 2:30	10	17.79	McCLOUD W	19.21	4	8:10 8:00	P.M. LV. 4:15
	2:35	4	19.00	North McCloud	18.00	3	7:55	
	2:38	3	19.98	Ash Creek Junction	17.00	10	7:52	
	2:48	10	23.15	Esperanza W	13.85	13	7:40	
	2:59	9	26.79	Bigelow	10.91	7	7:20	
	3:08	8	29.19	Dry Creek	7.81	10	7:13	
	3:20	10	33.15	ALGOMAH	3.85	11	7:00	
	P.M. AR 3:45	12	37.00	BARTLE W	.0		A.M. LV. 6:45	

Water 1¼ mile west Algomah.
No. 2 will wait at Upton for S. P. No. 16 unless otherwise ordered.

Through passenger service to Bartle was new when this employees timetable was issued, taking effect just a couple of weeks after the great San Francisco earthquake. This schedule called for runs to originate and tie up in Bartle and McCloud rather than Upton. —MCCLOUD RIVER RAILROAD

citement of those who envisioned this line as the new route through to Klamath Falls, Oregon. The railhead got three miles beyond Bartle before snow closed it down.

Spike maul continued to follow the grader in 1906. The main line reached a new terminal called McGavic, 15 miles north of Bartle. More interestingly the company built a new spur to the mill of a rival producer, the Bridgeford-Cunningham Company at Algomah. This mill site was to the south of the Bartle line, adjacent to the McCloud River itself. Here was a shipper with excellent future potential for the common carrier. In addition Bridgeford-Cunningham decided to log by rail, but was content to have the McCloud River Company handle the arrangements under contract. This agreement was as close the company ever came to having a connection with the line of an independent logging operator, despite the extent of the forest it penetrated. Algomah was soon to meet the fate of Ash Creek, but not before it caused a new yet ordinary enough tribulation to the carrier.

The McCloud area did not feel directly the seismic disturbance which with its accompanying conflagration devastated San Francisco in early April, but the company had maintained its corporate headquarters in the city. It continued to do so in fact for close to another four decades until an economy move brought the main office to McCloud. All records of the company were lost in the fire; with them may have

vanished solutions to a puzzle or two, including details of the transition from Scott and Van Arsdale to the new owners, and of early equipment of the line. When it was apparent that San Francisco would rebuild, demand for forest products was high, and the saws whined unabated. It was becoming increasingly obvious that a railroad with intentions to run only from May to November was hardly adequate.

McGavic was as close as the company would come to Klamath Falls, which wasn't really very close at all, but evidently certain optimists may actually have used this route to connect Klamath Falls with San Francisco. A steamer plied Lower Klamath Lake from Klamath Falls to Laird's Landing, California, some 25 miles away on a straight line. Today much of what was once the steamship run is hardly more fluid than a marsh at best, and some is dry land. By road it is another 50 miles or so from Laird's Landing to Bartle, through as lonesome a part of California as can be imagined. Yet it appears reasonable to speculate that the company called the McGavic line a part of its common carrier operation rather than a log spur in anticipation of a potential northern traffic.

By 1907 log spurs were up to some 30 miles, a figure that remained remarkably stable in the reports for a number of years to follow. Our suspicions could lead us to infer that the company reached the eventual total of 32.18 miles of rail on inventory, which it put down and took up as demand indicated. Our best guess

High-drivered locomotive No. 7, only example of its wheel arrangement the line ever owned, seldom had a chance to demonstrate her capability for speed on the McCloud River Railroad. It took its turn towing logs, herding work trains and bucking snow as this and other photographs testify. Engine No. 7 was the first-built of the company's entire roster. She was built in 1886 for the Atlantic & Pacific (Santa Fe), later sold to the Weed Lumber Co. prior to 1897, and came to the McCloud River Railroad about the turn of the century. (RIGHT) Over sized kindling. Men and horses survey this tangle of logs, cars, wheels and rails, all thoroughly mixed. Fortunately, derailments on the McCloud River Railroad were not usually this complicated, suggesting that a runaway could have been the cause here, generating speed enough to scramble everything and leave the scar high on the tree in the middle of the mess. It took more than re-railing frogs to provide an adequate solution to this puzzle. —BOTH CHARLES M. HAINES COLLECTION

45

In the early days, logging camps were crude structures having few, if any, conveniences and the men who worked 12 to 14 hours per day were given very plain fare. Camp 1 of the McCloud River Lumber Company, located nine miles east of McCloud, was a sylvan setting for a primitive facility. Trout was readily available in the backyard for those who tired of cookhouse menus. In the old days, camps were numbered Camp 1, Camp 2, etc. as the location followed the cutting of the timber. (LEFT) Water boy, tank and motive power. Keeping a supply of this simple fluid available where men and beast needed it without needless interruption of work was an important job. The seriousness of this responsibility reflects in the expression of the young employee. —BOTH CHARLES M. HAINES COLLECTION

Human muscle and simple tools (axe, saw and wedge) felled the forest. Concentration and all the power he can muster to the swing are needed here. The logger is standing on a springboard, a tiny working platform fastened to place the logger at a proper level to focus his effort. —DONALD DUKE COLLECTION (ABOVE) A steam donkey crew pause for the photographer. This early and small version is mounted on skids. The single capstan is located to the right of the boiler. —WILLIAM WOODS COLLECTION

Wheels of this character could be used in a region where it was not possible to snake, or to use bummers (low-wheeled carts) without swamping out trails. They could be readily driven over light standing brush or in down timber with a minimum of swamping. The capacity of the wheels was one large log, or from three to four small logs. McCloud's wheels were from 7 to 12 feet in diameter and tires from 5 to 10 inches wide. In the view at the left, two wheels are about to be loaded. The drivers would back the team over the log. Note one driver has his chains in hand. While at the right, extra power has been added to this wheel in order to get it to the railhead. —BOTH CHARLES M. HAINES COLLECTION

The coming of the logging railroad changed the conditions of camps radically. With quick easy access to the outside world by rail, portable houses, tents, and house cars replaced the old logging camp. There was greater permanency and men could be moved greater distances to and from the felling and skidding operations as they were transported by wagons or log trains. All four photographs on this page were taken at Camp 1, located near Buck Mountain or Dry Lake. It was a practice for a camp to remain near the site of operation, then move completely when a new location was handier for its scope of operation. The camp number was generally retained regardless of the number of shifts in the woods in the early days. The appearance of the Shay geared locomotive in the lower scenes dates the views between 1911 and 1924. (ABOVE-LEFT) Logs are piled here to await loading on the log flats. One of the two teams here is driven by oxen. (CENTER-LEFT) A wood crew load a log flat with an old slide back loader. (LOWER-LEFT) With a full train of logs, Shay No. 17 rolls through Camp 1 en route to the mainline of the Mc-Cloud River Railroad. (BELOW) The crew of Shay No. 17 pause for a portrait out in the woods. —ALL WILLIAM WOODS COLLECTION

A train of logs en route to the mill at McCloud. Locomotive No. 8 poses with crew and logs on the trestle, since filled in, about two miles east of Bartle. The straight stack on No. 8 indicates her wood-burning days are over. —MILLER PHOTOGRAPH—CHARLES M. HAINES COLLECTION

would be that it didn't ever have more than 30 miles or so of log line in service at any one time. It could have had a good deal less on occasions, with the balance of rail piled up waiting for use, but without anyone bothering to change the reported figure. One thing is clear about the log spurs: they were somewhat more stable in the earliest and the last years rather than in the middle period, but the writer has not identified dates and mileages involved.

The force that gives rise to this claim is the method used to move the logs from the point of cutting to the rail car. Friday George used bull teams to harvest the logs, reserving his traction engines to get lumber over the mountain (he tried bull teams in this service too). The Mc-Cloud River Lumber Company used some nine traction engines and an unknown number of bull teams in the woods, but became primarily a horse and wheel logger. A pair of the great wheels would be placed straddling the downed log, which would be lashed to the back end of a bar centered upon the axle of the wheels and free to pivot around the axle but perpendicular to it. When the wheels moved forward the log rose to become parallel to the bar, which then could be secured at the other end as well, and log, wheels, motive power and driver proceeded to trackside. The number of horses used per axle depended somewhat on the size of the log and the nature of the terrain. The great diameter of the wheels enabled them to cover rough ground without a road, and they could well proceed a mile or more. A practical limitation to their use was the need for substantially more

An impressive array of wheels, teams, and drivers face the camera. Ear length on the animals reminds that the term "horses" should include mules when one refers to "horse logging." —CHARLES M. HAINES COLLECTION

Horses have maneuvered the wheels astride a log. The pole is not yet in position and fastened to lift the log clear of the ground with forward motion. Bill Ralph at the far right of this scene, oversees the loading. —BILL RALPH FROM TED WURM

50

Traction engines were used for transporting logs from the woods to the mill or railhead where the amount of timber to be hauled was not great enough to warrant the construction of a railroad, where the grades were unfavorable for animals or where timber of large size and great weight was to be handled. The scene above is another application of the Best Steam Tractor in the McCloud woods. This machine was adapted from farm use to haul pine for McCloud. (RIGHT) Sixteen horsepower bring in a wagon load of logs, with a traction engine directly behind towing a second wagon. —BOTH CHARLES M. HAINES COLLECTION

As the era of the 1930's approached, donkey loaders became larger and more sophisticated. A line of four donkey jammers has wintered in McCloud where machinery could be overhauled at leisure, and they are now ready to head for the woods. —CHARLES M. HAINES COLLECTION

In the early days bull teams dragged logs over skids (hence skidding) from the woods to the yard, or landing, or dump. Horses were used to some extent, both pulling logs on skids, and hauling the big wheels. This was called skidding or wheeling. About the time the steam donkey came into use, skidding became known as yarding. Hence the business of getting logs from the stump to the landing is yarding. (ABOVE) This donkey (yarder) was the subject of a company post card in a publicity effort showing modern equipment used in a bygone day. —CHARLES M. HAINES COLLECTION At the left, another donkey yarder in the McCloud woods showing the cables stretching out to yard in the logs. Behind the yarder is one of the large steam traction engines. —ROBERT HANFT COLLECTION

power if the logs had to be moved uphill. The result was that rail log spurs were located in the valleys and the wheels brought the logs down the slopes to them.

Long before the company discontinued horse logging entirely it was using donkeys extensively. Although named for the four-legged type, the McCloud variety were mechanical. The donkey is a semi-portable steam boiler with steam powered winch, usually mounted on the same frame. A tall tree near trackside was topped and a pulley hung high up on the remaining trunk, with the cable from the winch running through the pulley, with tongs or a hook on the far end. The slack cable would be fastened to a log, the winch pulled in the cable, and the log came along with it to trackside. Donkey logging worked about as well uphill as down, but 1,500 feet was a practical limit to winch capacity, if not awkwardness in paying out cable. The 1,500 foot limit led to the familiar herringbone pattern of trackage. Parallel access spurs were laid somewhat less than 3,000 feet apart, each leading off the logging main line. The access spurs were laid down as needed and taken up when their usefulness was finished; at any point in time only a few of the access spurs would actually have steel with most being either already abandoned or just planned for future building.

The third and final phase of railroad logging used "cats" (tractors) to bring the logs to trucks, which in turn carried logs to a reload or transfer point where they were shifted from truck to rail car. The rail haul assumed main line characteristics as the trucks gained increased range because of improved efficiency. With longer truck runs the need and cost of a temporary rail line to serve limited territory was eliminated. Eventually the cost of operation reached the point where the rail haul which had the inevitable cost of reloading to contend with could not compete with the truck at all. Exit railroad logging, but this explanation has left us ahead of the story, for the railroad was destined to move billions of board feet of logs over more than half a century.

At the other end of the line during winter and early spring of 1907 the company proceeded to accomplish a change of terminals that had been rumored for some time. The people of Sisson

These three scenes show the beginning of the present era in logging. Prior to 1922 the tractor fever gripped the whole logging industry, and the success of tractors in the woods was definitely recognized. The question naturally arose on the Mc-Cloud River Lumber Co. — why not use tractors instead of horses with the big wheels. A machine was connected to a big wheel, and the increased output was so astonishing that several tractors were purchased to replace horse work. This early experiment is shown in the scene above. The wooden wheels seemed impractical, so a 'caterpillar' salesman devised the idea of mounting a hydraulic pump on the rear of the tractor, and with a hose connection running to the arch above a steel wheel, have a hydraulically operated sheave take the place of the old slip tongue principle of raising and lowering the logs. At the right, two scenes showing this operation and the capacity of the steel wheels. —ALL CHARLES M. HAINES COLLECTION

54

who had decided a decade earlier not to give land to get a new mill did in fact donate land to get the McCloud River Railroad into town. A cutoff from the existing line east of town at a point called "Section 16" extended westward, then curved south and parallel to the Southern Pacific to reach the Sisson station of the SP. Opening of this cutoff was duly celebrated by a banquet of the Sisson Masonic Lodge on March 3, 1907, with the McCloud members arriving by special train over the revised trackage. The new line into Sisson is .94 mile shorter than the Upton route. It served a box factory at Sisson built by Scott and Van Arsdale, but cut off direct access to the Upton plant when the old line was promptly abandoned. Today no trace whatever of the once prosperous little town of Upton is visible to the casual passerby.

The lumber company completely controlled the railroad in 1907, with all the stock in its own name save for a nominal five shares apiece held by the directors to validate the corporate structure. The lumber company had, of course, furnished the construction money and now figured it was time to re-evaluate its corporate

relationship with the railroad, which was an increasingly important aspect of the company's function. Freight revenues had topped a half-million, 281 people were on the payroll, more than 15,000 passengers were carried, and the United States mail was under contract, in addition to Wells Fargo express.

The authorized but previously unissued 8,400 shares of common stock were entered on the books and turned over to the lumber company, bringing the 12,000 share official total into force. In exchange the railroad received title from the lumber company to all lumber company land over which the railroad had been built, which was most of the line east of McCloud. In addition the railroad agreed to pay the lumber company $1,200,000 for money advanced to build the railroad, including consolidation of earlier obligations incurred for the same reason. To raise the $1,200,000 a handsome batch, 1,200 of them, of thousand-dollar bonds were printed up as prettily as those issued by a transcontinental line, each bond bearing coupons clippable for $60 of interest per year, and the bond itself was redeemable in

50 years for the $1,000 it cost. Inevitably, the lumber company bought the bonds. It is not impossible to imagine J. H. Queal in his dual role as president of both companies solemnly presenting himself with an I.O.U. of $1,200,000 on behalf of the lumber company, handing himself 1,200 bonds, counting out cash to the tune of $1,200,000 for the bonds, then giving himself the cash and tearing up the I.O.U. In any event the bonds proved to be very good ones, with money always there to meet the interest payments even when the lumber company no longer owned the stock, and the principal was eventually paid off in cash. Most bonds never are; they are just reissued when due. The Mc-Cloud River Railroad has been exceptional in quite a number of ways.

The expansion program for 1908 was negative. The company decided that the McGavic terminal was serving little useful purpose and pulled up 3.5 miles, again making Slagger Creek the end of track. The real problem of the year was with the Bridgeford-Cunningham Company at Algomah. Instead of grateful appreciation for service provided in enabling its lumber to reach the market, the Algomah operators had the nerve to complain that they were being overcharged. Not only that, when the railroad refused to yield, the case was taken to the California Railroad Commission which agreed with Bridgeford-Cunningham rather than with the railroad. The railroad was charging $3.50 per ton to move lumber from Algomah to Sisson; Bridgeford-Cunningham asked for a retroactive reduction to two dollars plus $5,000 for its trouble and the insult. It further

Four flags beneath the headlight, white shirts and ladies with their Sunday hats, and a capacity load in coach No. 1 show a picnic special is in order on July 4, 1906. This train provided an opportunity to celebrate out of town in the woods, with the company usually furnishing a shuttle service at no cost to the riders. —CHARLES M. HAINES COLLECTION

56

claimed that the railroad had deliberately put on a high freight rate in order that it might buy out Bridgeford-Cunningham cheaply. The Commission neatly split the difference with a $2.75 rate, and the later fire solved the absorption problem. We may suspect that the McCloud operators knew full well what a high freight rate would do to this rival, but there is absolutely no hint of McCloud arson in the demise of Bridgeford-Cunningham.

By 1909 the railroad had seven trestles. An accident happened during construction of an eighth trestle south of McCloud on a log spur when one collapsed injuring two men.

Save for the constantly changing log spurs, the railroad remained in relatively stable position for a number of years. President Queal noted that the company had more than $120,-000 on hand in 1911, a condition of surplus cash for the first time in his experience, and asked the directors to declare dividend number one of $10 per share, payable December 1. With the early records destroyed, we may forgive the inaccuracy of his count. Dividend number one or no, it was far from the last.

In 1913 the main line was extended to Dry Lake, an additional .96 miles, also known as Engineer's Station 1629 plus 10. In 1914 another minor extension followed. The reason for these changes being classified as main line rather than log spurs is not apparent.

The track gang at work. This crew was equally versatile at putting 'em down or picking 'em up. In this scene, the track gang is taking up a logging spur and all ties and rails were saved for the extension of the next spur into the woods. Engine No. 7 provides the power. (BELOW) With the three flat cars loaded with ties and rail, the train is ready to be moved to a storage or new construction site. In later years power for this job was often a tiny Plymouth gasoline locomotive. —BOTH CHARLES M. HAINES COLLECTION

The Bartle's Hotel. Popularity of this rather rustic hostelry operated by the pioneer family is shown by the number of people gathered on the porch. Some confusion is generated by the fact that the Bartles ran the stage stop at Bartle, later built in McCloud, and then the railroad company owned a hotel in Bartle later on. — CHARLES M. HAINES COLLECTION

Although the railroad has not diversified over the years into very many ventures apart from transportation, it bought or built, probably the former, a hotel at Bartle, at a cost of $5,256.48, with $706.97 of furnishings. With its ever present eye toward modern conveniences $51.62 was spent for a toilet in the hotel, and the ICC was properly informed of this use of railroad cash. With $341,593.64 now coming in from railroad operation the $51.62 was probably not too much of an extravagance.

In 1914 the Bartle Hotel was leased to C. L. Middleton to operate for an annual rental of $35. Although this figure indicates a rather low rate of return on the investment of the year before, it did represent an income of $24.96 over the expense to the company of $10.04.

The high finance activity at Bartle involved more actual money, but another transaction worthy of note took place in the same year. The lumber company and the railroad were divorced! Or perhaps it would be more appropriate to say the parent turned the destinies of the child over to its own management. The analysis in these pages is a cautious yes and no in appraisal of the foregoing statement. The lumber company, which now held all but 25 of the 12,-000 shares of stock representing ownership of the railroad, did give them up, with only a minor string or two attached (it retained 283 shares at first, but did not keep them). The de-vice for parting with the railroad stock was simply to turn it over to shareholders of the lumber company at no charge, a perfectly valid device, since the lumber company shareholders already indirectly owned the railroad anyway. Now they did so directly. The virtue of this was that the lumber company could no longer be accused, or at least it would be more difficult to prove, of meddling unduly in the affairs of a common carrier railroad. If this had been done before Bridgeford-Cunningham's claim was aired, the $3.50 rate might have been retained.

"Mother McCloud," as the lumber company was more or less affectionately becoming known for its habit of providing all the legitimate needs of its employees, continued to extend its benevolence to the railroad workers as to its own. Despite the severance, railroad people lived in McCloud housing, shopped at the company store, and enjoyed charge privileges at Red Cloud, a suburb for entertainment purposes of a sort not provided in McCloud itself. Lumbering attracted rugged men with rugged tastes that had to be segregated from the more genteel aspects of a community.

To protect its interests in return, the lumber company asked that its shareholders pin their railroad certificates to those of the lumber company and not dispose of one apart from the other; a gentleman's agreement. Just in case

59

some of the shareholders were not gentlemen, a voting trust was duly established, to run through 1924, that would vote the best interests of all shareholders as the three members of the trust interpreted best, regardless of any divergent thoughts of the stockholders in the meantime. The three trustees just happened to be highly placed officials of the lumber company. The trust was renewed, but finally allowed to lapse in 1940, and by then the gentleman's agreement was no longer remembered or regarded as necessary.

Although the railroad thus became an independent property owner in the town of McCloud, it had one additional restraint placed upon any excessive exuberance. Default on any one of the lengthy list of conditions imposed in the indenture to the bonds could result in the

Two 1901 Baldwin built 2-6-2's in typical double-header style pause near Pierce (summit between Sisson and McCloud) for a crew photograph. —CHARLES M. HAINES COLLECTION (RIGHT) All 15 loaded log cars, the four-wheeled caboose and the wood-gobbling locomotive No. 8 are included in this pose on the trestle east of Bartle. The old print carries a date of 1905, just after this line was opened. —BILL RALPH COLLECTION FROM TED WURM

bondholders stepping in and taking over the railroad, and you know who held the bonds!

The first tiny storm cloud on the future of railroad service appeared in 1916 in the form of an announcement that Tom Davis' auto stage was now running two round trips daily from Sisson to McCloud, leaving from Kuck's Saloon. Davis promised courteous treatment to all, and would make special trips anywhere in the county on request.

In 1917 the last building in Upton, remains of the former sash and door factory there, was torn down.

World War I evidently had surprisingly little impact on the railroad. It had a new headquarters address, having moved into the Southern Pacific building in San Francisco, to remain for the next two decades, although without affiliation with the larger railroad. Patriotism to the war effort was evidenced by the purchase of $10,000 in Liberty Loan Bonds in 1918. More followed, including holdings of $34 in war stamps that appeared on the books in 1921. Some ten miles of line beyond Bartle was dropped, leaving 47.03 miles of main, plus 31 miles of spurs and 16 miles in yards and sidings. The road came under federal control during the war, but this meant little to the McCloud River Railroad, in some contrast with the problems of its larger brethren. It continued to haul logs to McCloud and lumber to

Sisson, generating more than ten million ton miles of service in the process in 1919. It made money too, with revenues close to half million dollars each year.

With the end of the war came a new arrangement for logging service. The railroad company dropped its reporting of log spurs and turned them over to the lumber company. From 1919 to the end of logging the McCloud River Railroad no longer operated in the woods beyond the limits of its main line and associated sidings. The lumber company leased rail from the railroad, but shuffled the steel around with its own crews, largely with the use of its own small Plymouth gasoline locomotives at the actual rail laying and removal operations. The Plymouths were also used for modest sized movements of empty and loaded log cars. The major trains in the woods were pulled by steam locomotives also leased from the railroad company, but operated by lumber company crews.

The next important venture of the McCloud River Railroad was one of its largest projects, but one that had very little to do with its primary objective of moving forest products. The Pacific Gas & Electric Company entered into an ambitious construction program for the generation of electric power along the Pit River, another tributary of the Sacramento River, larger than the McCloud and 23 miles away to the south at Bartle. To build its series of dams,

At the right, the Pit No. 1 powerhouse of Pacific Gas & Electric under construction in 1921. (BELOW) In this view, the powerhouse has been completed. Water is coming through the penstocks from the reservoir high above and escaping through the ditch in the foreground. Save for the touring car on the bridge and raw earth on the hill, this scene has changed little during the past half-century. — BOTH CHARLES M. HAINES COLLECTION

Locomotive No. 10 had been converted to an oil burner by the time this photograph was made. It left McCloud in 1925, and was less fortunate than its surviving sisters, No's 8 and 9, meeting the scrapper in 1944. —CHARLES M. HAINES COLLECTION

tunnels, and power houses PG&E needed cement, steel, and heavy machinery in considerable quantity, more than would be practical to move in by highway. The McCloud River Railroad was nearest to the construction sites; as a common carrier it would move everything needed as far as Bartle. Material began to come in during the winter of 1920-21, but plans were being firmed up to extend the railroad to the Pit and eliminate the awkward wagon teaming from Bartle. Surveys were made on snowshoes. The extension was not to be a common carrier; instead the McCloud River line became a constructor and operator under contract. Two small steam locomotives of its own are claimed to have been brought in by the utility and used in the immediate vicinity of the dam and power house construction sites. The McCloud River Railroad did everything else necessary to build and run the railroad.

The new line was officially the Mount Shasta Power Corporation Railroad. Mt. Shasta Power was a subsidiary of PG&E, and the new trackage was often referred to as the PG&E line or the Pit River Railroad. It was operated with McCloud equipment and crews. Speed in building rather than permanency was the word, and steel pushed forward in a hurry. Grading started as soon as weather permitted in early 1921 and the line was completed to the site of Pit No. 1 powerhouse on September 17, hardly more than three months from laying of the first rail. Track extended south from Bartle to Peck's Bridge on the Pit, 23 miles, then followed the river upstream for ten miles. A later extension was built downstream, making the new line resemble an inverted "T". A very twisty "T".

The new line actually left the McCloud main just east of Bartle, then used a 4.2 mile log spur belonging to the lumber company, which proceeded to rent it to the railroad for $99.50 per month. The railroad in turn rented the use of the spur to the power company for $99.50 per month. The railroad also agreed to build a new line at cost plus ten percent, and to rent locomotives at three dollars per hour, flat cars at 50 cents per day, box cars for one dollar, outfit cars for 25 cents, and snowplows and flangers for $1.50 per hour. Building the new line cost nearly a half-million dollars.

Railroads are forbidden to disclose traffic figures for any shipper, but a look at the inbound tonnage figures for a few years can give some notion of the importance of the Pit extension to the McCloud River Railroad. The company had line haul revenues to Bartle, and income under the contract beyond.

Year	Inbound Tonnage
1919	5,611
1920	17,315
1921	19,255
1922	25,711
1923	12,493
1924	47,278

A record of loaded cars turned over by the common carrier McCloud River Railroad to the contract operation of the McCloud River Railroad in the year 1924 is available. It shows:

Grain	4
Flour	5
Hay	25
Fruit and vegetables	10
Coal	5
Stone	1
Lumber	30
Ties and timbers	186
Petroleum products	93
Rail and fastenings	10
Structural iron, pipe and machinery	330
Cement	308
Brick, lime and plaster	3
Other manufactures	222

The Bartle Hotel was in the red for the year, though, despite all this new traffic past it. It cost $24.84 in expenses, and produced no revenue.

This new extension came closer to the established settlements and agriculturally productive areas of the Fall River Valley than did earlier trackage. In addition the ever-present optimists saw the east-west line parallel to the Pit serving as the nucleus of a new route. After

all, it takes only a little imagination to dream of terminals on the Atlantic and the Pacific if you just keep expanding an east-west line. More practically, D. M. Swobe, who succeeded J. H. Queal as president of the railroad upon Queal's demise in 1921, made negotiating with PG&E for the establishment of common carrier service over the new line an early order of business. The power company proved amenable enough, but the plain fact was that traffic to merit the service never materialized, even though diatomaceous earth deposits were found along the new line and the Mt. Shasta Silica Company was formed to mine them and ship carloads out over the new route.

When the power project was finished so was the railroad. In contrast to the fanfare of its building, not a single word of its ending was found in the original source material researched for this book. Dismantling probably took place in 1929, and rail may have gone to the expansion of the McCloud company. Between the completion of PG&E construction and tearing up the railroad, sporadic train service was provided by a small steam locomotive

The identification of early logging camps is difficult since many look alike in photographs. From the layout this appears to be Camp 1 located at Buck Mountain (1912-1913). Locomotive No. 8 rests beside the water tank for service the following morning. The sacks contain sawdust used to insulate meat and vegetables in storage. —T. E. GLOVER COLLECTION (BELOW) Hand-sawing a McCloud tree. Ethnic characteristics of McCloud loggers often did not fit the Paul Bunyan legend, but their output did —CHARLES M. HAINES COLLECTION

This illustration was taken from one of the lumber company promotional post cards. The scene appears to be Camp 5 east of Bartle shortly after its construction. —CHARLES M. HAINES COLLECTION At the right, loading at the end of a spur with a donkey yarder. —WILLIAM WOODS

Whether served and prepared in a tent or a rolling kitchen and commissary car, the food facilities of the McCloud River Lumber Company were noted for their better than average quality. The view above from a company post card appears to be linen on the tables, however close inspection will show one of the first uses of oilcloth. —BOTH CHARLES M. HAINES COLLECTION

brought in for this purpose, owned and run by PG&E. A more complete probe for these details is left to others.

The lumber company had followed a typical pattern for its logging camps over the years since its founding. A cluster of rather crude and temporary buildings would be established in the woods at a point of convenience. From this center the men who actually harvested the logs would move out to their work daily. Others, including cooks, saw filers, and clerks remained in camp for their duties. When distance to the timber became too great the whole camp would shift to a new location. Sometimes all of the buildings were mounted on rail wheels and a move could be accomplished with a minimum of disturbance. The McCloud River Lumber Company decided to try a new approach to logging camps in the form of a larger, more permanent logging community, one containing more of the comforts a family would desire, as compared with the minimums provided to the predominantly unmarried work force of an earlier era (four camps, two horse and two donkey, were running in 1920). Accordingly, the new model logging village of Pondosa was built in the mid-twenties. Logging railroaders, as well as loggers, headquartered here, and, of course, the logging railroad connected with the main line. This connection was at a junction named Car A for lack of any particular inspiration. Car A was eight miles east of Bartle, and had been reached with the shifting around of the end of main line during the previous decade.

With the practical cessation of traffic over the PG&E line, Pondosa provided a closer point than Bartle to transfer from railroad to highway for Fall River area traffic by some 13 miles, with fewer snow problems than were usually found on the highway between Pondosa and Bartle. In addition, the lumber company had built a new spur from Pondosa that connected with the power company railroad over a better route than the existing line from Bartle. To operate into Pondosa from Bartle the railroad made application for approval to the ICC and entered into a contract with the lumber company for trackage rights over the lumber line at an annual rental of one dollar. The ICC gave its blessing, and the railroad was accordingly extended 7.81 miles from Car A to Pondosa as of October 26, 1928, courtesy of the lumber company and one dollar.

In 1928 the railroad company decided to buy the bus line operated by Mrs. Davis, who had continued it after her husband died. Prudent negotiations kept the purchase price down to a mere $4,000, but the company never enjoyed much success financially as a highway carrier. The Bartle Hotel didn't do very well in 1928 either, with $168.25 of expenses and only $100 in revenue.

The year 1929 looked like one of great promise to the railroad, which had no crystal ball to forecast the great depression that did in fact materialize. Actually, so did much of the promise. In 1928 the lumber company had purchased 80,000 acres of timberland with more than a billion feet of harvestable logs from the Red River Lumber Company. The new purchase was known as the Whitehorse tract, and centered some 35 miles east of Bartle. The logging railroad was promptly extended toward the new holdings, and the junction point between common carrier and log lines established at Hambone, 50.17 miles from Mt. Shasta City.

Hambone was a logging camp and an identifiable community with a name, the first that the railroad had enjoyed as an eastern terminus since leaving Bartle behind. Hambone remains as the nominal east end of the railroad today, although little is left to show it ever amounted to anything. A crumbling water tank and even more decrepit ruins of a coach-depot are visible from the track and the auto road, but both bypass the site now. Legend has it that the name was given because of an identification sign placed along the main trail nearby. Hambone had a well and you could get water if you turned off the trail to the north at the point where someone had fastened a ham bone to a tree. The name stuck, even if the settlement didn't. The bone is gone now as well.

The present depot and general office building at McCloud was erected in 1929, at the same location as the original structure. The old building was wrecked in minimum time by putting cables around it and tugging at the cables until it collapsed. Alas for romance, evidently a locomotive on the adjacent track was not used to provide the force. The old building came down in May; the new one was occupied in September, but the record doesn't tell us whether or not the summer was mild enough that an open air terminal and office sufficed for the interval.

Visitors seeing this handsome and commodious structure today admire its harmony with the woodsy community and the snow-capped backdrop. They might well be amazed to know it was built for an outlay of but 18,-000 dollars.

The most important railroad development of 1929 for all California as well as for the local railroad was being arranged in offices far from McCloud, even though President Swobe's persuasiveness was a factor. The Great Northern Railway and the Western Pacific Railroad decided to join and in the process form a new

Hambone 1968. Ruins of the water tank and combination coach are virtually all there is.
—ROBERT M. HANFT

The original McCloud River Railroad depot at McCloud has been collapsed to make way for the present structure located on the same site. This 1929 view was made before removal of the debris remaining after the roof supports had literally been towed out from under the roof. —CHARLES M. HAINES COLLECTION

Two views of the present log style depot and headquarters building at McCloud. The view at the left shows the southerly entrance, while above the front showing the general offices and freight shed. —BOTH DONALD DUKE

north-south route. The Southern Pacific had long since completed its Siskiyou line between San Francisco and Portland, Oregon, and by 1929 had finished the alternate route via Klamath Falls that then became its main line. SP was about ready to put the finishing touches on a Reno-Klamath Falls cutoff. The GN had also reached Klamath Falls from the north, but President Jim Hill, the Empire Builder, had long had his eye on a bigger goal than Southern Oregon. When the gap between Klamath Falls and Keddie, California, on the main line of the WP, was plugged, GN and its connections would have a rail route from the Mexican to the Canadian borders serving the important centers of Seattle, Portland, San Francisco, Los Angeles and San Diego, independent of the rail monopoly the SP had long enjoyed.

The relations between SP and McCloud had been cordial enough over the years, but the smaller road had very little say and it didn't always agree that its connection had done everything just right. Accordingly, Swobe painted word pictures to the GN and WP management of many cars of lumber that would head to eastern markets over their route from McCloud if they just completed the Inland Gateway. Hill was not living to see the culmination of his dream, but his successors decided to push ahead, and made application to the ICC for permission. When the SP made the expected last ditch fight before the Commission to stop it the rivals were well prepared to quote past sins and shortcomings of the present monopolist, and their logic prevailed. Western Pacific would build northward, Great

Northern south, with a meeting just west of the little town of Bieber.

The McCloud River Lumber Company had, by then, pushed its logging line to Widow Valley, more than 60 miles to the east of Mc-Cloud and within a mile or so of the proposed GN-WP extension. The lumber company needed money too, and proceeded to work out a deal that would give it some and at the same time make McCloud freight available to the GN-WP, which was what those roads wanted. The McCloud River Railroad had actually anticipated this next move by extending its eastern terminus to Hambone, which had adequate water and enough level land for a yard, although the agreement eventually reached eliminated any need for the yard. The Hambone extension was accomplished by purchase of 6.9 miles of line from the lumber company for $1,000.

Next, the lumber company sold a line of railroad to the GN-WP extending from Hambone to the vicinity of Lookout, where a short connection would tie in with the GN main stem. The price was $250,000. The GN-WP gave the McCloud River Railroad trackage rights over the ex-logging line between Hambone and Lookout Junction, at a rental fee (7 cents per loaded car-mile) for use based on the actual traffic operated. Finally, the GN-WP asked the short line to run all of the actual train service as their operating agent. This is the arrangement still in effect today, except that the Western Pacific has turned its interests save for trackage rights over to the Great Northern without ever having operated a train north of Nubieber, its connection with the GN a few miles south of Lookout Junction. Thus, the McCloud River Railroad trains run between McCloud and Lookout Junction, 65 miles, but

do so east of Hambone over a Great Northern branch. The transition is not noticeable.

The Lookout extension generated a traffic that its builder and buyer did not anticipate. Logs moving to the McCloud mill and lumber eastward were about all that had been expected, but the new line also originated trainload after trainload of cinders. Great Northern people were inspecting their new acquisition one day together with McCloud officials when someone mentioned that the GN was going to bring in gravel from Oregon to ballast its new main. Roadmaster Haines of the McCloud remarked that the Hambone line passed near a hill composed of volcanic cinders which would make fine ballast. The inspection party went to Porcupine, location of the cinder mound, and Haines showed the probes he had made indicating extensive deposits under the outcroppings. The GN vice president leading the delegation was convinced and with the words. "I say let's do it," his railway cancelled plans for gravel ballast on the new line and spread the natural cinders instead. The McCloud River Railroad eventually ballasted its entire line with them, too.

The McCloud lumber people are very pleased to have the new connection. They now have a choice of eastward and north-south routes via Southern Pacific, Great Northern, or Western Pacific. About half the traffic moves to Mt.

Shasta City and the SP, the other half to Lookout. Car shortages and traffic blockades do not ordinarily occur simultaneously on all three routes.

The Hambone-Lookout line passes through a particularly desolate and lonesome country today. Part of the track is directly across a lava flow, all of it is undulating enough to preclude long stretches of straight and level right of way. Second growth timber is coming along in the forested parts, but inhabitants for the most part have either four legs or feathers. The former logging camp of Whitehorse is little more than a signboard and a passing track, although it sent many a carload of logs west in its time. At least the blat of the diesel horn as the nightly freight comes and goes doesn't seem quite as lonesome as memory's ghostly wail of a close-coupled prairie type slipping along with its trailing freshly cut forest monarchs smelling faintly of fresh pineapple.

In 1931, the year that the Lookout line was completed, railroad revenues were showing effects of the depression with a gross just under a quarter of a million dollars, hardly more than half that of some of the booming years of the 20's. Fewer than a thousand passengers were hauled, and about 65,000 tons of lumber products. Expenses were down also, and a modest $10,000 went to the profit column. This was the bottom year of the depression for the railroad in both receipts and profit. The Bartle Hotel had vanished from the accounts, but remained present in fact if not in use until in 1936 it suffered the same fate as the Ash Creek mill.

The railroad had assumed the form that it would hold through the booming years of World War II, save for minor details. Just to elaborate a few of those small changes using 1938 as an example: replacing stub switches with point switches at McCloud added .01 mile of track; reinstalling the balloon track at Bartle added .23 mile; a team track at Pondosa added .13 mile. An .18 mile spur at Dry Creek was taken up; mill track number five, .01 mile long, was retired; and .03 mile of lath shed spur at McCloud was retired. A railroad plant is seldom completely without change during any year.

Another problem arose to plague the railroad in 1934. As already reported, the railroad had

The cinder pit at Porcupine ballasted not only the McCloud River Railroad, but also much of the Great Northern (now Burlington Northern) in California and Oregon. Three of the cinder cars in this view are converted log flats. (UPPER-RIGHT) Portability even for rather large buildings in the camp could be gained by assembling several structures which could be loaded and moved on log flats in short order. Shown here at Whitehorse is the cookhouse and dining room. —BOTH CHARLES M. HAINES COLLECTION By 1968 little but the sign and the siding remained of Whitehorse. —ROBERT M. HANFT

One of the unique features of the railroad is a switchback, a series of zigzag levels whereby trains can ascend or descend back and forth to get over steep grades A switchback still remains today on the McCloud River Railroad between Mt. Shasta and McCloud, but trackage reversed itself by this means at several other locations in the past, especially on logging spurs. The switchback pictured above is in the woods on the now abandoned log line west of Pondosa. The scene at the right was photographed just a few feet away from the view above. Generally on a switchback operated line, a locomotive is positioned at each end of the train to facilitate easy operation. —BOTH ROBERT M. HANFT

leased rail for the logging spurs to the lumber company. The rent was $8,404.24 per year, and the lease, which was to run for five years, contained an agreement to take an inventory every year. Rail found to be unfit for further service would be returned to the railroad and replaced with new rail, with the rental adjusted to take account of increased value of the new rail.

Once the lease was made evidently everyone forgot about the fine print it contained. The lumber company paid the railroad a welcome $8,404.24 every year, and if the woods train crews complained more and more about derailments they were given little heed. After all, a certain amount of static is expected around a railroad. Thus, it took 15 years before someone's plea that the rail was junk aroused sufficient alarm to cause the first annual inventory to be taken. The railroad had the leased rails on its books for $115,658, but the ensuing inventory report stated tersely that there had been a considerable decrease in both quantity and value. If quantity refers to length rather than weight, one may be entitled to wonder just what happened to the balance. Whatever the reason, the lumber company didn't desire to spend any more lease money for rail that existed only in the ledgers, and a lot less, if anything at all, for the puny steel it did retain.

The railroad was in the unhappy position of having to dicker for anything it could get, knowing full well that the lumber company could buy all the good relay rail it wished for less than a penny a pound in this depression year. The nice $115,658 figure on the property accounts was due for a substantial alteration.

The purge wasn't as drastic as feared, however. The negotiations were lengthy, but the lumber company finally agreed to pay full rental to September 30 of $5,233.47 and to purchase the rail as of October 1 for exactly $64,-766.53, provided that the railroad would apply the $70,000.00 total to retirement of railroad bonds held by the lumber company. Thus the lumber company got out of paying the lease money, but the railroad also no longer had to pay $4,200 in bond interest. If the lumber company wanted to upgrade the quality of its line, it was now up to it to buy new rail. With our memories of the year 1934, perhaps we may be forgiven for suspecting that the problems of

the lumber company train crews were not solved overnight and that they would get considerable exercise for some time to come carrying rerailing frogs.

The rail lease wasn't the only oversight of the decade. In 1939 the railroad commissioner of the State of California hauled the railroad into Superior Court and informed it that it was about to be fined for violating the law and overcharging its customers. Shades of Bridgeford-Cunningham, except that this time no shipper was in sight, only the State of California! It appears that the regulatory agency had ordered less-than-carload rate reductions and the railroad dutifully complied — but forgot that long ago it had once filed tariffs from such stations as Burk, Howard, and Signal Butte, from which no traffic had ever moved other than carloads of logs in earlier years. The company had filed its new legal rates from all points where traffic was found, but the sharp eye of the law spotted failure to comply none the less since Burk, Howard, and Signal Butte were being discriminated against, if a shipper *did* show up. President Swobe was greatly relieved to find that nobody had actually been overcharged, made haste to correct the oversight, and asked the commissioner to forgive and forget under the circumstances. The commissioner was reasonable and suggested that a compromise settlement out of court of $150 would be agreeable. Swobe didn't agree that the $150 was reasonable, but the alternatives open to the railroad appeared even less so.

The great depression was largely over for the railroad in 1939, as the war in Europe brought increased demand for building materials and with it greater freight traffic and revenue. The company received more than a half million dollars for its services, the first time that figure had actually been exceeded. As detailed elsewhere in this book, the company was modernizing and expanding its equipment roster, which proved to be foresighted indeed with war shortages just around the corner.

The voting trust agreement expired in 1940 and was not renewed. The railroad stockholders, of whom there were now 109, were free to run their railroad as they pleased.

The World War II years saw no important changes in the facilities of the railroad, but the most intensive use ever of what it did have. The increased traffic was reflected by revenues nearly half again those of 1939 and almost triple those of the depression lows. In peak 1943, for example, ton-miles of revenue freight service topped 27.5 million, with well over a half-million tons of logs moving from the woods to the mill pond on the company flat cars. A total of 5,739 loaded cars of lumber either zig-zagged through the switchback at Signal Butte or crossed the lava flows on their way out to contribute to the nation's mighty war effort. The railroad employed 172 people, 37 of whom worked on the trains. We can only speculate about the far-flung uses of McCloud pine, but it may well have spread into all corners of the world where Americans worked and fought.

Curiously enough, even though McCloud lumber was indeed in the heart of the war, and railroader, logger and mill worker alike concentrated successfully on getting out more production than ever before, the McCloud companies never received an "E" award. With "E" signifying excellence for effort, these certificates and the corresponding pennants that flew from corporate flagstaffs were handed to war industries that turned in superior performances in support of the military services. But, as one lumber company official growled: "We were so busy turning out lumber we just didn't have time to fill out all the paper and go through the ceremonies involved with an award." Award or no, the contribution was a proud one, and perhaps made even more so when we are reminded that their personal participation was direct in the case of those railroaders who served in the armed forces. As in World War I, the company made investment in war bonds part of its contribution.

President Swobe did not live to experience the satisfaction of knowing that his company's part did indeed help in a successful conclusion of the war. His successor, in 1943, was M. P. Madison. Madison's personal involvement with the railroad appears in retrospect to have been quite limited, by comparison both to his predecessors and the next two presidents who have followed. These two, P. N. Myers and Flake Willis, became very concerned with the day-to-day affairs of running the railroad. Although the formal term of office of Phil Myers was to

be only five years, under the Madison regime he came close to being the president in fact if not in title. Myers was on the scene in McCloud, with Madison headquartered in San Francisco.

The McCloud River Railroad for most of its existence has adhered to a policy of treating its employees at least as well as those working for the larger connecting systems. Big road wages have been paid; the men belong to the same unions. In 1943 railroaders, tired of the long hours and what appeared to be scant rewards to themselves for their contribution, called a nation-wide strike to bring more meaningful attention to their complaints. Because such a strike would be intolerable to the war effort, President Roosevelt took over the McCloud River Railroad at 7 p.m. on December 27 and made the Secretary of War responsible for its continued operation. While he was at it, the President also seized control of the connecting Southern Pacific and Great Northern, and their connections in turn.

Perhaps it is a bit drastic to infer that the McCloud line was the key to the nation's railroads, but certainly it was important enough to warrant the necessity to keep it functioning too. Suffice it to say the Secretary of War did not show up in McCloud to pull the throttle on a locomotive, nor did any of his troops. Myers remained in actual control, even if he now reported to two bosses instead of one. The trains ran without interruption. After three weeks the problems of the men were adjusted on a nationwide basis and on midnight of January 18, 1944, the Secretary of War ended his brief tour of duty as head of the McCloud railroad.

A respite from the wartime peaks and tensions may have been welcomed, but the company was hardly inactive after international armed conflict ended. In 1948, 21.5 million ton miles of service were performed, and total revenues topped more than three quarters of a million dollars, thanks in part to freight rate increases coming along in the post war adjustments. Although the next major line change did not appear until 1950, a program of improvements was started soon after war's end. Ballasting six and one-half miles of main line east of McCloud got under way with an appropriation of $6,500 in 1946. Tie plates and rail anti-

The mountain looking down on the McCloud River Railroad facility at McCloud has not changed, but the railroad has. The roundhouse for the steam locomotives has been replaced by this diesel enginehouse and repair facility with an imposing array of Baldwin diesels. — McCLOUD RIVER RAILROAD

creepers were purchased and installed, rail was gradually improved, and the first diesel locomotive showed up on the line in 1948, to the distress of interested rail enthusiasts devoted to steam power. This acquisition also presented an increased need for aspirin to company officials until they learned to live with it, as will be related later. At least the improvement program also included an air conditioner to cool off aching heads in company headquarters.

The railroad had decided some 20 years earlier to abandon a route that gave it access to Pondosa from Bartle without going to Car A. In 1950 it built the present line that once again turns south at Bartle to reach Pondosa. As usual the trackage involved considerable cooperation with the lumber company. For the first 5.3 miles out of Bartle a new line was constructed by the railroad to a point now known as Curtis. The lumber company built a section of logging railroad from Curtis to Bear Flat, which was only .47 mile from Pondosa upper yard. Trackage rights over the lumber company rails from Bear Flat to Pondosa upper yard rendered the Car A to Pondosa line surplus to the railroad. It then proceeded to sell the no longer used rail to the lumber company to take up and relay as needed.

Flake Willis came to the railroad as its president, replacing P. N. Myers, in 1952, and

served in that capacity until 1969. Early 1952 was another season of heavy snow in the Mc-Cloud country, and it may not be a mere coincidence that Myers took a position with the Trona Railroad in that year. Snow is not a problem to the Trona. Flake Willis pushed through the modernization started by Myers and has added more than a few embellishments of his own. Dieselization was completed on schedule, together with suitable new service facilities highlighted by the present modern shop building. Two-way radio made instant contact between train crews, enginemen and the dispatcher a reality. Less noticeable but highly important has been the track renewal program that got under way in 1953, with the end result that the entire line is now ballasted, with heavy steel laid on long-lived treated ties with tie plates and anti-creepers, luxuries hardly heard of in earlier times. Nearly all the rail is 90 pound, save for a few miles where the replacement program still continued in 1968.

The railroad system of the United States reached its peak mileage more than 50 years ago, with gradual decline ever since as unneeded segments were pruned and few extensions were found necessary. The McCloud River Railroad was involved in one of the last important additions to the national system when the Northern California extension came through from Klamath Falls to Keddie, yet the

connecting link from Hambone to Lookout did not bring the operations of the McCloud company to its maximum mileage. Completely new common carrier railroad extensions (most new rail lines in modern times have been relocations, as was the Pondosa construction of 1950) were virtually unheard of in the decade of the 1950's, but this unusual railroad went ahead and built one anyway.

The town of Burney, 61 miles to the southeast of McCloud, had long sought a rail outlet. Burney was hardly ten miles from the old PG&E Pit River line, but could not then generate enough traffic to keep the power company railroad open. Burney shippers trucked to Pondosa and loaded rail cars there, while continuing to hope for better service eventually. The never ending appetite of the McCloud mill for logs was to get it for them as the result of negotiations between lumber company and railroad that began to firm up in 1953.

The Fruit Growers Supply Company, primarily a maker of boxes for the citrus industry, owned 82,000 acres of prime timber land in the Burney basin with more than a billion board feet of pine ready for harvest, and another half-billion feet of fir also available. With an increasing substitution of paper cartons for wooden fruit boxes, Fruit Growers was ready to work out an arrangement with the McCloud River Lumber Company to cooperate in harvesting and milling the pine lumber. After careful consideration of the transportation alternatives available the lumber company decided that rail transportation still offered the most economical method of getting the logs to McCloud, even though a completely new railroad would have to be constructed for 20 miles, and part of some existing trackage revamped and upgraded. At anticipated rates of harvest the traffic would continue for some 50 years and amply repay the cost of investment in rail facilities. Logs were the inspiration for the proposal and would be the mainstay of traffic, but as long as the line was to be built anyway it might as well be extended just a bit to serve the town and other shippers while it was about it. Thus it would be an advantage to all concerned for the railroad to build the Burney extension as a common carrier rather than a long lumber company log spur.

The railroad had long since paid off all of the original $1,200,000 it had borrowed from the lumber company years earlier and now had no direct financial ties whatever with its former parent. To induce the railroad to proceed, the McCloud River Lumber Company again offered to provide the bulk of the money that would be needed, up to 1.5 million dollars. A rather unique repayment schedule, whereby, in effect, the lumber company guaranteed the traffic to repay the loan, was worked out. The lumber company asked three and one-half percent interest for the use of its money, a rate that would certainly appeal to borrowers today, with payment of principal based on the traffic actually moved over the railroad. For each thousand board feet of logs hauled over the new line the railroad would repay the lumber company $1.50. For each carload of freight other than logs $15 of revenue would be applied as a payment on the loan.

To insure that only traffic actually generated by the new line would obligate the railroad to repay the lumber company the railroad company won a stipulation that only shippers not already shipping by rail from Pondosa would be counted in the $15 per car payments. Thus, if the lumber company decided not to use the railroad after all, and no *new* traffic came along that the railroad didn't already have, the lumber company could wait forever for any repayment of the loan. If all proceeded according to plan, hauling a billion board feet of logs would exactly repay the principal. To restrain the railroad people from overwhelming enthusiasm for borrowing, the lumber company stipulated that the railroad could make no additional loans from any sources until it repaid this one — unless the company consented.

By late 1953 the railroad had quietly acquired options on property not owned by the lumber

The McCloud track gang lays new rail on the Burney extension near Lake Britton in 1955. Company forces had years of experience at this work on log spurs and the line to Lookout. —MCCLOUD RIVER RAILROAD

company that it would have to cross. In the following February the contract with the lumber company was signed and the railroad was considering how to get across the Pit River, which had been backed up by one of the dams the railroad had helped build years earlier. This particular part of the problem was solved by hiring a bridge engineer to draw up plans and to supervise execution of a contract with a professional bridge builder. Except for the bridge the company decided to build the new line with its own forces.

The new line could actually have been laid on the old grade used in the 1920's from Pondosa as far as the Pit River, or more correctly now, Lake Britton crossing. It did not do so, because the 1954 extension was built for permanence rather than to get logs moving at the earliest possible date. Once again a log spur of the lumber company provided a nucleus for the new line. Even this part, the first ten miles, known as spur 400, reaching from the common carrier Pondosa route at Bear Flat to Ditch Creek, was extensively overhauled to bring it up to main line standards. An eventual operating speed of 35 miles an hour was set as a construction requirement, which meant substantial cut and fill work predominating through the rolling terrain. Apart from the big bridge across Lake Britton, the only other span of importance to the builders was a highway overpass practically adjacent to the water crossing.

In late August rail reached Cayton Valley, a bit of country open and level enough for the company to set up a side track and loading facility, and in October it was receiving revenue freight there. The usual winter storms caused a suspension of the construction activity on the part of the railroad. The bridge contractor continued to work on the seven-span crossing of Lake Britton, but experienced a severe setback in early December. When placing the main center span of the new bridge in position mind or muscle must have been betrayed, for there was a slip and the steel assembly plunged away from its setting and into the inky frigid depths below. A man went with it.

In addition to the life, the bridge cost more than a quarter of a million dollars and a lawsuit against the railroad. The railroad was eventually held blameless, for it had turned responsibility

along with the work over to the contractor. In mid-March the railroad crews pushed the remaining snow aside and the track laying resumed.

Formal opening of the new line took place on July 3, 1955, with ceremonies befitting an event unique to the times. Three special passenger trains came to Burney, one hauled by the remaining serviceable steam locomotive, which charged through a paper barricade with the sound and smoke effects only a steam engine can generate, to symbolize breaking the transportation barrier that had long isolated Burney. Dignitaries were present in force, along with interested lesser mortals, and spikes of precious metals were driven in the last tie. Tie and spikes were carefully retrieved after the excitement died down, all in good tradition. The last tie is something of an oddity, for it is redwood rather than the pine typical of the McCloud country.

The Lake Britton bridge had been completed early in this 1955 construction scene, but track-laying equipment was still at work pushing rail toward Burney. Note the rail crane at the far end of the bridge. —CHARLES M. HAINES COLLECTION (RIGHT) The grand opening of the Burney Extension was the biggest thing to happen in the Mt. Shasta region in years. On July 3, 1955, the crowds turned out to watch the first train into Burney. The throng lined the track as old No. 25 crashed through a paper barricade to officially open the new line. —BOTH MCCLOUD RIVER RAILROAD

Last tie and last spike ceremony at Burney was unique in railroad history in that it took place at the end of the line, not where rails were linked midway. Various railroad and civic officials had a chance at tapping the last spike. The tie and plaque are preserved today in the company general offices in McCloud.
—MCCLOUD RIVER RAILROAD

It was donated by the oldest railroad in California, the Arcata and Mad River, to this, the newest line, as is so stated on a neat bronze plaque. With this warm sentiment, and a representative of the donor present at the ceremonies as well, no voice was raised that a redwood tie was out of place in the pine country. The tie reposes in a pine framework, for it remains on display at the company offices in McCloud.

The town of Burney furnished one of the four last spikes, two of which were gold, the other two silver; three came from a San Francisco area railroad club responsible for one of the three special trains. Nobody tested the spikes with a sharp knife to see whether or not the gold and silver were solid.

Tappers of the last spikes included President Willis, Burney civic leaders, and, suitably, Asa Lakey, a Burney pioneer, who had waited a long time for the iron horse. President Whitman of the Western Pacific observed, as did President Phil Myers of the Trona Railroad, who may have felt reasonably secure about returning to the McCloud line in July. Lesser titled representatives from other railroads abounded.

President Flake Willis of the McCloud River Railroad on the left chats with President Fred Whitman of the Western Pacific at the Burney ceremonies.
—MCCLOUD RIVER RAILROAD (RIGHT) Commemorating the completion of the Burney Extension was the colorful stamped cachet. —D. S. RICHTER COLLECTION

The largest crowd of people in the history of Burney is claimed for the golden spike celebration. At the left, many swarm around No. 25 and its special passenger train. — MCCLOUD RIVER RAILROAD

For its starring role in the Burney festivities No. 25 was painted and polished to a state of perfection fit to dazzle all viewers and amaze those used to more prosaic days in the woods. The smokebox and trim were of gold, and the tender was extensively decorated. The heavy Pullman train called for strenuous effort as the train left Burney and later crossed Lake Britton. —BOTH MCCLOUD RIVER RALROAD

Although principal attention was lavished on the main line into Burney, work with considerably less fanfare went ahead on branches expected to deliver more revenue. An eight mile log spur was built into the heart of the timber tract, with a change of relations between the lumber company and the railroad once again. Railroad crews were used to man the log line trains instead of lumber employees as had been the practice for so many years.

Another spur was built to reach the Scott Lumber Company mill on the west side of Burney. Rather than going through the town from the station, a longer track to reach the mill was built from a connection north of town. For 5.13 miles this spur was jointly owned by Scott Lumber and the railroad, except that Scott owned rail and fastenings. An additional 2.5 miles belonged entirely to Scott. All was built by the railroad.

Also in this momentous year of 1955 another shift of ownership between the railroad and the lumber company was under way. This procedure gave the railroad undisputed title to the line all the way from Mt. Shasta City to Burney. When the railroad reached Pondosa via the present route from Bartle, it had done so in part by trackage rights over a bit of lumber company line. The railroad had some good steel left over from the Burney extension, and proposed to swap it for title to the trackage rights section between Yellow Post (Curtis) and Pondosa upper yard, 8.15 miles. The railroad actually owned 25/85 of the rail in this 8.15 mile stretch already. The lumber company and the ICC were willing. While the dickering was going on the lumber company also agreed to add another hundred thousand dollars to the railroad's construction loan. Building a new railroad was even more expensive than anticipated.

In considerable contrast to the drumbeating that accompanied new rail service to Burney, the railroad quietly opened a truck route paralleling the rail branch. The new railroad was fine for trainloads of logs and lumber, but hardly as convenient as the highway for Burney merchants.

Thus the McCloud River Railroad reached the form it has today. The main line extends from Mt. Shasta City to Burney, 76 miles, with a four mile branch from Obie to Pondosa, 13

This carload of logging machinery was the first revenue load into Burney. McCloud Vice President J. C. Orlowski, left, and President Flake Willis, right, pose with officials of the Scott Lumber Co. —MCCLOUD RIVER RAILROAD

miles of main from Bartle to Hambone, and 34 miles between Hambone and Lookout operated over the Great Northern. The long spur into the Scott mill at Burney is still used, but all lumber company logging trackage has vanished. Minor changes to the line continue to take place, with relocations in the Ditch Creek area and west of Bartle resulting in fewer curves and smoother operation. A short log loading spur for an independent operator, the Kalpine Plywood Company, served for a while to haul logs away from McCloud, quite a reversal from the customary procedure. Access tracks have been laid to new mills at Mt. Shasta City and Burney, and the Pondosa branch exists to serve a mill there rather than the logging camp activity for which the town was designed.

PG&E had provided a tremendous impetus to McCloud railroad traffic with the great hydroelectric project on the Pit. Forty years later it again was a mainstay of the railroad, but this time the other half of PG&E's business was responsible. A monster pipeline was snaking over the lava beds enroute from the gas wells of Alberta to the cookstoves and furnaces of San Francisco. Steel pipe in sections three feet in diameter and 40 feet long was loaded at the mills onto flat cars and headed out to the field. For a long stretch in northeastern California the field headquarters was at Burney. A trainload of cars arrived at Burney every day, seven

Two box cars accompany a string of logs en route north from Burney to McCloud. The Lake Britton bridge in the background no longer rumbles to the passage of logs, but consist of todays freight is sufficient to operate on a daily schedule. (BELOW) A string of just a few more than 1,000 cars of 36-inch pipe moved into Burney in 1960 by the railroad for the PG&E pipeline. —BOTH MCCLOUD RIVER RAILROAD

days a week, until a string of the giant pipe more than a hundred miles long had been received. At Burney the pipe was coated and moved by truck to the arrow straight trench cut across the wilderness. Each carload meant a $15 payment toward the $1,600,000 owed to the lumber company.

Yet another PG&E project came along in 1963, with a dam and diversion tunnel constructed on the McCloud River south of McCloud town. For two years the railroad moved supplies over the hill to McCloud, but this time trucks wheeled everything from McCloud to the construction site and the abandoned logging spur that extended much of the distance was not reactivated.

In connection with its program to improve the railroad with heavier rail, cinder ballast and

treated ties, the company also has installed anti-creepers (rail anchors), another luxury it never considered in earlier times. Forty-eight thousand of these little fasteners came from the Bamberger Railroad in Utah, an electric interurban line that had been abandoned.

The year 1963 was one of the most important in the history of McCloud and the railroad, despite the fact that physical appearances were hardly altered. The U. S. Plywood Corporation had moved into California, and looked over McCloud. In 1963 U. S. Plywood offered the McCloud River Lumber Company some 40 million dollars for its properties, town, mill, land and trees, and the balance due on the railroad construction note. The offer was accepted.

Ownership of the railroad was truly independent by this time, with a fair number of the 12,000 shares in the hands of its own employees through a stock purchase plan. USP management decided it wanted to own the railroad and made a cash offer of $85 per share to the holders, more than double the usual price when shares had changed hands in recent years. For an additional million dollars USP found itself owning a railroad. Not quite as completely as Scott and Van Arsdale had almost 70 years earlier, however, for there was one lone holdout who did not sell his shares to USP. Thus the McCloud River Railroad is co-owned for the time being, even if hardly co-controlled.

USP ownership has meant rapid change from the old ways. It is not interested in being a landlord, and promptly sold the town to the John W. Galbreath Company of Columbus, Ohio, retaining only the mill properties. The Galbreath firm specializes in disposing of company towns, acting as landlord only until suitable sales can be arranged. "Mother" is no longer associated with McCloud. The buildings are still there, but today the occupant is usually an owner instead of always a tenant. The gas lights have been added, along with pride of ownership and some hesitancy over independence that has by no means worn off yet. Somehow the mill management is no longer as close and personal to the town. People are well aware that their destiny is shaped by a remote board of directors, even though it no longer is present in the very walls within which they live.

For the railroad, new ownership meant prompt and total abandonment of log hauling. USP liquidated its rights to Burney tract logs to raise its cash position which had, of course, been lowered with the McCloud purchases. The last log train rolled to the mill within a week of the formal takeover of the railroad in early December. There were heavy hearts and misty eyes as the end of an era was witnessed.

Now the railroad was released from the $1.50 per thousand foot payments on its note to the lumber company, but once again the transaction was purely internal, since USP owned the railroad for all practical purposes. In addition to the windfall from PG&E, the railroad common carrier traffic over the Burney line exceeded expectations and the debt has been paid off in full, log traffic or no.

Although USP control has brought significant change it also generated a move that is a curious part of the record but which now appears to have had virtually no real meaning. Another California property of USP was located near Samoa, off a feeder line of the Northwestern Pacific Railroad. The Samoa plant was serviced by its own spur track connecting with the NWP, and USP decided to include the Samoa trackage in the McCloud River Railroad corporate structure. With this arrangement the McCloud River Railroad was to have an isolated segment hundreds of miles (by rail) removed from the rest of the system. Before anyone got used to this new notion of the McCloud actually running trains over at the coast, USP turned its switching there over to the NWP and later got rid of the Samoa mill entirely. To the best knowledge of the writer, no equipment at Samoa was ever marked with the name proposed for it.

USP went through another merger that gave it a longer name; U. S. Plywood-Champion Papers Inc. Although the new company uses its full corporate title, the abbreviation "Plychamp" is sometimes heard, if unofficially. Actually, the abbreviation has been preempted by a minor subsidiary. U. S. Plywood-Champion Papers Inc. is well aware that it has a railroad among its far-flung properties. What it does with that railroad depends on what the railroad does for U. S. Plywood-Champion Papers Inc.

McCloud No. 18 assists No. 26 as they double-head a freight near Bartle bound for McCloud back in the days when steam locomotives and railroad log-hauling were the order of the day. —JOHN KRAUSE

4

LOCOMOTIVES
MOVE THE FOREST

TO THOSE WHO follow the steel rails either for a living or for love — and the number who have combined both is and always has been substantial — the essence of it all is the locomotive. Steam is the quintessence of locomotives. He is to be pitied who has never known the quickening of pulse that comes in the still of the night when the whistle cries of its passage across the land, or the thousand and one sounds that form the accompaniment to the mighty soloist thundering defiance to tonnage and gradient as it accelerates into Wagnerian cresendo. This symphony of steel has given full voice on the four percent across the mountain at McCloud, and an intriguing remnant may yet be heard by the fortunate. Truly, the glamour of railroading is with the engine, and here in this chapter the writer remains mindful of the special treatment to be accorded the nearly 40 stars of this show.

Appropriately enough, the first, and briefly the only, locomotive on the line was numbered No. 1, a trim little Mogul, the only example of this wheel arrangement* on the line. This engine had proved its mettle on the Califor-

nia Railway running out of Oakland before coming north to the mountain line. Most McCloud power was purchased new, but the company has not been adverse to picking up a bargain in used engines from time to time. The engine was No. 2 on the California Railway roster, and as changed to No. 1 for the McCloud line the pattern of serialization was established.

The Baldwin Locomotive Works had built this machine in 1891, which meant it was fairly new as locomotives go when it came to Upton.

The fate of the first locomotive is not explicitly recorded. To work in the high fire hazard forest country the one spot lost its straight stack and received one of a typical expanded type used on wood burners. A substantial screen to arrest sparks without unduly impeding the draft is the reason for these bulges in the smoke system. All McCloud locomotives had them in

---

*The "Mogul" has six driving wheels, led by a two-wheeled pony truck. It has no trailing wheels. In the Whyte system of identification acording to wheel arrangement a Mogul is identified by "2-6-0."

Locomotive No. 1 may be compared with an earlier pose of the same machine as California Railway No. 2. In the scene above, McCloud's No. 1 all wooded up for a run to Upton. Obviously the spark arresting stack and an automatic coupler have been added. —CHARLES M. HAINES COLLECTION (LEFT) California Railway No. 2 shortly before its sale to the McCloud River Railroad. —GERALD M. BEST COLLECTION

the wood burning era. Engine No. 1 was to receive other important alterations to its front end, due to its involvement in sticking its nose somewhere it shouldn't have. It was rebuilt with a shortened smoke box and was renumbered No. 12 in the process. At least there is no other explanation for the appearance of No. 12 on the roster and the vanishing No. 1. A careful scrutiny of available photographs of engines No. 1 and No. 12 does not provide completely conclusive evidence as to whether or not they are the same engine. Unanswered, of course, is the question of why the company would bother to renumber. A story that No. 1 was a jinx and

that it was renumbered to throw off the hex would be welcome, but not forthcoming. The official record is gone, and minds of living men do not reach to the answer.

No. 12, probably the reincarnation of No. 1 was successful enough and served faithfully for many years, usually on the passenger train, for it was the least powerful engine the company owned. The scrapper caught up with it in 1932.

Scott and Van Arsdale were well aware that one locomotive would hardly be able to move all the anticipated freight. They went shopping for more motive power. With the workout an engine receives lugging loads up and over moun-

tains, something unusual was needed, and No. 2 was definitely not conventional.

To cope with heavy grades trunk line railroads turned to brute strength that came with sheer size of their locomotives. With size came high initial cost for the machine itself, plus the need for a high quality roadbed to support the additional weight and power. Small railroads sought an alternative. A machine that proved successful when speed was not essential was the geared locomotive. Built for power, not speed, these engines came in three principal varieties. All shared the concept of imposing a system of gears between the piston rod and the drive wheels to realize an extra thrust. It functions much as an automobile uses high engine speed to get power in low gear. The geared locomotive never shifts away from low gear.

The McCloud River Railroad bought such a machine from the Stearns Manufacturing Co. in 1897 and assigned it No. 2. The locomotive

Certain railroad historians believe that McCloud No. 12 is the reincarnation of No. 1, however, early motive power records are lost to the ages. Sufficient differences are apparent when No. 12 is compared with the earlier photographs on the opposite page to leave the viewer less than completely certain they are the same engine. In any case, No. 12 and coach No. 1 make a nifty train at McCloud some 65 years ago as the consist stands by the McCloud depot. —CHARLES M. HAINES COLLECTION

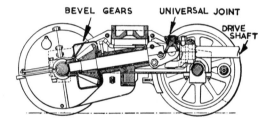

BEVEL GEARS   UNIVERSAL JOINT   DRIVE SHAFT

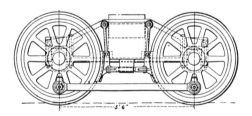

The only known service photograph of three truck Heisler No. 2 was discovered in a Los Angeles museum, thus authenticating its actual use on the McCloud River Railroad. Although publicized for its ability to pull lumber up the grade between McCloud and Upton, No. 2 was in log train duty when this photograph was taken. The third car from the locomotive is a wooden water tank car of a type commonly used to provide a water supply to men, animals and machines in the woods where adequate source was not always convenient. Note the link 'n pin coupler still in use on the McCloud. —ROBERT HANFT COLLECTION On the left, scale drawings of the Heisler truck. The top view gives a longitudinal section of the bogie showing gears and universal joint. The center shows the side elevation of the bogie, while the lower view shows the plan of the bogie with the bevel gears. —AL BARKER COLLECTION

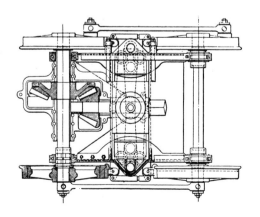

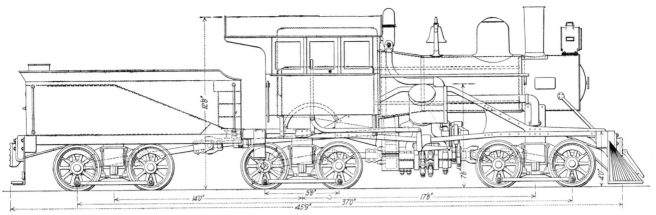

TWELVE-WHEEL GEARED LOCOMOTIVE; McCLOUD RIVER R. R.
Charles L. Heisler, Designer. Stearns Mfg. Co., Builders.

McCloud No. 2 was the largest Heisler geared locomotive designed and built at the time and received
wide publicity in *Engineering News* and *Scientific
American* magazines. The 60-ton engine had three
driving trucks, one under the forward end of the
boiler barrel, one under the firebox (which is above
the frames), and the third under the tender. The
cylinders were just forward of the firebox. Its maximum speed was 15 miles per hour empty, or from 5
to 7 miles per hour with a train. (BELOW) A cross
section of the Heisler showing the cylinders in rela-
tion to the gears. —BOTH AL BARKER COLLECTION

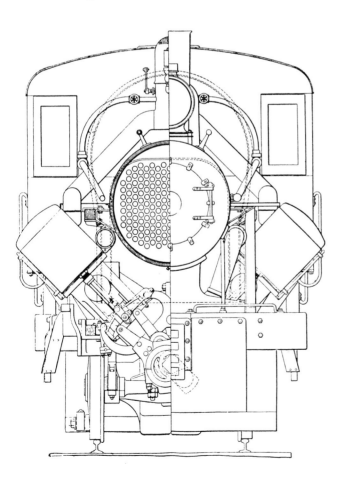

was called a Heisler and was distinguished
from the other types of geared engines in that
the Heisler had cylinders on each side of its
boiler inclined so as to directly drive a single
shaft underneath the boiler. The shaft was hor-
izontal and was connected to an axle of each engine truck by gears. An external connecting
rod for each wheel linked it to its adjacent
wheel in the truck to complete the power train.

If this description makes the machine seem
unwieldy, appearances are hardly more reassur-
ing. Geared engines looked clumsy, and sounded
as if they were tearing themselves apart while
accomplishing little. Actually, they have done
exactly what their designers intended; move
loads disproportionately heavy for their size
over dubious trackage. No. 2 weighed 60 tons,
the heaviest Heisler yet built for any railroad.

Students of locomotive history have long
been puzzled as they considered the nature of
the McCloud River Railroad locomotive No.
3. Later on the company often bought engines
in pairs, and one early narrative of the exploits
of the Heisler on the mountain uses the plural.
A more affirmative record was not forthcoming
and the case of No. 3 was to be left as a complete mystery in this work. A partial solution
was provided by an authentic old photograph
unknown to the McCloud collections until re-
cently.

A smaller conventional appearing Heisler of
perhaps 45 tons weight is shown to have served
concurrently with the larger and more publicized No. 2. The smaller machine had but eight
wheels, compared with 12 under No. 2. It was

The success of Heisler No. 2 inspired the McCloud River Railroad to acquire another Heisler for logging service. Heisler No. 3 was a two truck machine acquired secondhand from the Weed Lumber Company a few miles north of Upton. This view, also located in a Los Angeles museum, shows No. 3 with a 13 car train of logs somewhere on the Ash Creek line. —ROBERT HANFT COLLECTION (BELOW) Conventional 2-6-2 No. 4 poses for a Baldwin Locomotive Works builders photograph in 1898, prior to delivery to the McCloud River Railroad. —GERALD M. BEST COLLECTION

also built to the same plan of exchanging speed for power, even though it could not match the output of a larger machine of the same design. The photograph of Heisler No. 3 shows it in log service between woods and mill rather than engaged in the heavy climb over the mountain with a lumber train, but then, so does the only photograph of No. 2 actually coupled to a train.

The Mogul could take four cars loaded with lumber up the long grade from McCloud at six miles per hour, provided the rail was dry. If rain or snow was on the track three loads was capacity. The large Heisler, with 12 drive wheels gripping the rail instead of six, walked a full six loaded cars up the mountain, maintained the same speed as the direct connected engine, and actually consumed less wood in the process. When the rail was wet the Heisler still kept its adhesion and dragged the customary six cars to the summit.

Even if this performance was exactly as described, management must not have been entirely convinced that Heislers were the ultimate in performance, for No. 4 was a more conventional direct connected engine. No. 4 was the first of the 2-6-2 or Prairie wheel arrangement to appear on the line. The year was 1898.

Prairie certainly is a misnomer as far as the Mc-Cloud line was concerned.

To maximize adhesion on the rail as much weight as possible is placed on the drive wheels of a locomotive. All of the Heisler's weight, including fuel and water, was on drive wheels. The Mogul had a guide or "pony" truck ahead of the driving wheels, and separate tender. The Prairie had an additional pair of small wheels behind the drivers. With even less weight proportionately on driving wheels than the Mogul, No. 4 could handle no more cars, and in wet weather two was often the limit. Adding the extra set of "pony" wheels did provide a guide for the drivers when backing up, which was certainly a consideration with the switchback operation.

The four-spot stayed on the line for more than 40 years. Heislers No. 2 and No. 3 vanished without trace, almost surely before the records were lost in the 1906 fire. They may very well have moved only a few miles off the line, to the Weed Lumber Company. Two things are certain: they did not have a long and illustrious career at McCloud, and the design was never reordered. The virtues proclaimed above must have been diluted in some fashion.

Pride and hope of the Baldwin Locomotive Works at the turn of the century was this compound double locomotive. No 6 was two identical locomotives of the 0-6-0 wheel arrangement hooked back to back.
—GERALD M. BEST COLLECTION

The next locomotive for which the record is certain is No. 6, which arrived at Upton in 1900. Still more power than that already on hand was required and rather than rent locomotives from the SP or buy another Heisler the company turned again to the Baldwin Locomotive Works for help. The proposed solution to the McCloud problem was another innovation.

A little locomotive was obviously too puny for the rugged climb and the increasing traffic of the McCloud River Railroad. Even gearing down to gain power at the sacrifice of speed was not the answer. A monster of an engine would not work because of the sharp curves and uncertain steel. However well constructed for a short line, the McCloud River Railroad never attempted the standards set by Southern Pacific main line. To cope with the sort of problem that the McCloud faced, builders had proposed a solution different from gearing; build a locomotive big, but spread that size out over an extraordinary number of wheels in order that undue weight would not come against the rail at any single point.

Two principal types of locomotives, large yet not unduly heavy per axle, had been developed, the Mallet and the Fairlie. Mallets had a single huge boiler, but two separate sets of driving wheels (a few had three). The rear set of drive wheels and its power mechanism was rigidly connected to the boiler frame; the front set of drivers was free to pivot separately from the boiler in order to negotiate curves. Twelve or 16 drive wheels under command of one crew

could exert considerably more thrust than either a conventional or geared locomotive. The Fairlie principle was to mount two virtually complete locomotives back to back on the same frame. One engineer could operate two engines simultaneously with either Mallet or Fairlie. Each engine had its own steam supply in the case of the Fairlie, and a single boiler served the Mallet design.

McCloud River No. 6 came close to being the Fairlie type, but was somewhat simpler. Two identical locomotives, both of the 0-6-0 wheel arrangement, were hooked back to back. The basic connection between them was an ordinary tender drawbar, made somewhat heavier than usual. A metal plate covered the gap in the floor between the two engines, while the cab roof of one engine had an extension from its top that overhung the other to provide shelter. The most important problem was that of simultaneous control of both engines by one man. To accomplish this the throttles were connected by a link mechanism that ran between the locomotives beneath the floor plate. One problem was overcoming shifts in position of the "slave" throttle arising from the linkage being compressed or expanded as the locomotives went around a sharp curve or from slack action during starting and braking. To overcome this difficulty, the connecting throttle mechanism was carefully centered and the coupling between locomotives made as rigid as possible. As completed the design allowed the engineer to operate either throttle separately or both simul-

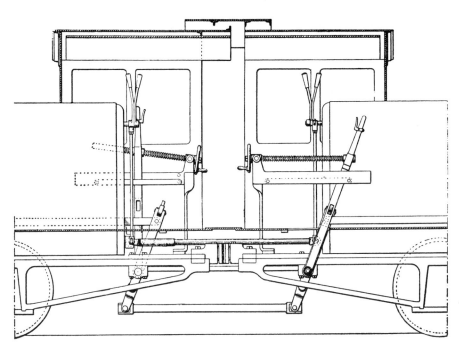

Locomotive No. 6 was designed with a view of meeting the same operating conditions as the well-known Mallet articulated locomotive. The object was to obtain simplicity of construction, low selling cost, and at the same time obtain maximum efficiency. The Baldwin Locomotive Works issued a special *Record of Construction No. 22* featuring these drawings. The drawing above shows the reversing mechanism of the two locomotives, while at the right the throttle lever rigging. (BELOW) The ordinary draw-bar connection commonly used between engines and tenders except that it was made of great strength compared to the work required of it. —GERALD M. BEST COLLECTION

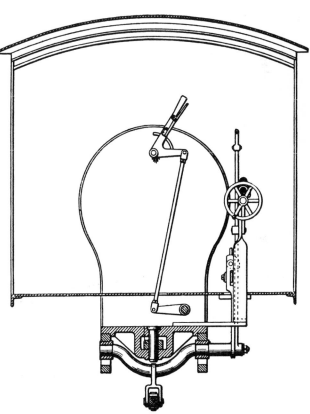

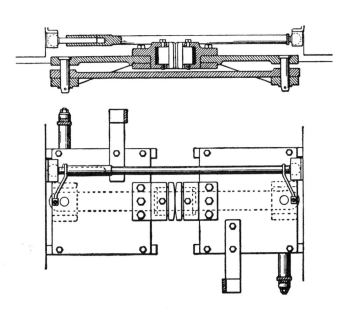

tanously from either unit by means of a simple interlocking lever.

The reversing mechanism was screw controlled, again with a linkage that connected the two halves. This apparatus could not be turned separately for each engine, and one may hazard a guess that activating two reverse gears and a connecting system meant quite a workout for the cranker. The locomotive engineer traditionally moves this stiff control, known from time immemorial as the "Johnson Bar," but visions of men spinning *both* controls of this contraption rather than one man turning *either* wheel appear plausible.

The locomotives were equipped with Le Chatelier steam brakes for the locomotive drive wheels, and conventional Westinghouse air brakes extending through the train. Brakes could be set easily enough from either half, but the very fact that no mention is made of a dual control for engine brakes leads one to the suspicion that each half had to be braked independently.

With engines back to back there was little room at the rear for a conventional tender supplying fuel and water for the boilers. Instead, a water tank was mounted in saddle fashion over the right side of each boiler ahead of the cab and a wood rack on the left. In running order the combined locomotive thus showed a wood rack and a water tank on each side.

Builder Baldwin guaranteed that its Siamese twins could pull 125 tons in addition to their own weight of 82 tons including wood, water, sand and not too corpulent a crew, up a seven percent grade. Just why this guarantee was considered necessary for a line that did not exceed a four percent incline is made clear only if there is substance to the accusation that the civil engineer's survey level slipped a bit. On flat terrain at least, the twins could exert a tug of more than 17 tons against a following train, substantially more than geared rival No. 2.

To cope with a burning hunger for wood, especially when working upgrade, each half was fed by its own fireman. Oil burning locomotives were beginning to appear on the Southern Pacific shortly after the turn of the century and the McCloud men, not to be outdone, referred to their fuel as "lump oil." The "lumps" were toted by hand from the side rack to the firebox inferno, and there was precious little time to enjoy the scenery with a heavy hand on the throttle and 125 tons coming along behind. The thought that the more the fireman worked the farther he had to run out into the woodbox was not always happy either. Too, each chunk tossed into the fire meant a replacement had to be loaded at the next wood stop.

The twins were Baldwin's answer to the Mallet and the Fairlie, and the manufacturer advertised them extensively, only to watch them fizzle out in one derailment after another on the hill. Their ability to pull had been guarantied, but no promises made about the machine staying on the track.

The Fairlie failed to catch on, too, but Baldwin consoled itself by later building thousands of Mallets. The McCloud River Railroad never again participated in an experiment with an unconventional locomotive — neither did it ever buy a Mallet.

One of the selling points of the twins before they became recognized as a mistake was that either half could easily be operated separately if one unit was disabled. Since the team failed to perform, the railroad decided to try the engines as individual machines. One half was renumbered No. 5, which is hardly a very adequate answer to why the twins were both numbered No. 6 in the first place.

The separate halves had something of a penchant for going aground, too. At least as individual engines they seldom did so at the same time. Management was hardly overjoyed at this new development, but decided to adjust the counterweighting of the machines and

Locomotive No. 6 not long after the divorce. Little change is evident here apart from boarding up the open rear of the cab, changing the coupler and adding a footboard. —CHARLES M. HAINES COLLECTION

The other half of No. 6 became No. 5, photographed shortly after entering switching service. Apparently the engine has just been wooded-up as wood is stacked high on the other side and is visible by the steam and sand domes. The reason for the ladies in full dress and the children on the locomotive is not known.
—MCCLOUD RIVER RAILROAD

found performance vastly improved. They didn't test their luck to the extent of hooking the halves back up and trying the combination once again!

Instead of providing the answer to moving heavy trains over the mountain, the two 0-6-0 s settled down to a long career as the mill switchers at McCloud. The No. 5 was sold to the Weed Lumber Company in 1919. From Weed it went to the Lystul-Lawson Logging Company and disappeared from view. The No. 6 not only outlasted its twin on the McCloud, but went on to gain a bit more of the spotlight before it closed out a career that spanned almost a half century.

With changing technique of lumber handling a full-time switcher was no longer needed at the mill, and the Guy F. Atkinson Construction Company could use a small but sturdy yard goat type to bunt cars at the Pardee dam building project. The No. 6, long since converted to burning oil, but still a compound* in an era when compounding had largely been given up, went to Pardee, some 300 miles south of McCloud, and acquitted itself well enough that its new owner decided to retain it for further use.

The next project No. 6 participated in was even more venturesome than Pardee dam. San Francisco was finishing a pair of tremendous bridges and decided to celebrate their completion with a world's fair, the Golden Gate International Exposition of 1939. Fittingly enough, the Exposition site was to be right in the middle of San Francisco Bay. The San Francisco-Oakland Bay Bridge paused briefly at Yerba Buena

*"In a compound locomotive steam from the boiler goes first to a high-pressure cylinder, does its work and then enters a much larger low pressure cylinder to be used again. Most compound engines were converted to simple (steam used once and then released to the atmosphere), because the increased efficiency in steam use was more than offset by higher maintenance costs. The 6 had a high and a low pressure cylinder on each side. Its style of compounding was called "Vauclain," after the inventor.

island in mid-bay; this island is small and steep, but shallow water surrounded its north side and could readily be filled in. A flat man-made extension to the island was built and this became the Exposition grounds. An access road curved down from the bridge to the fair. When the Exposition site was under construction the bridge was not yet completed; accordingly construction materials were barged out to the island. Once on the island short rail spurs provided the means of movement for heavily laden cars of the material that were part of the Exposition. Locomotive No. 6 was the moving force on Treasure Island, as the "annex" to Yerba Buena Island was aptly named.

The No. 6 was not the first locomotive from the McCloud River Railroad to become involved in an Exposition. Although it could with some justice claim to be the locomotive that built the fair, that sort of thing receives little widespread attention, and it was no longer heralded as a McCloud River engine. Almost a quarter of a century earlier another McCloud River locomotive visited a San Francisco fair, that time as an exhibit for the public to admire directly. The McCloud River Lumber Company was one of several California pine lumber producers to pool resources for a display at the Panama-Pacific International Exposition; the Exposition for 1915 that celebrated the opening of the Panama Canal.

The No. 6 probably was not regarded as sufficiently glamorous for the 1915 fair, and continued to shuffle cars around the mill back home in McCloud while its newer sister preened for the admiring crowds. Selected for this glamour role was 2-8-2 No. 18, painted and polished until it looked more like an ornament than a locomotive. A jewel of a locomotive, surely! To accompany the engine, caboose No. 15, also fancied up to a stage where its customary occupants could only shake their heads in amazement, went along, together with two flat cars loaded with especially selected logs and a lumber car.

Locomotive No. 18 and its log train may have caught many an eye at the Pan-Pacific, but some of No 6's work still stands on Treasure Island, which has been converted to a Navy base in the years following the Golden Gate International Exposition.

The wood-carrying side of No. 6 is evident here, with more than a little of the load overflowing right into the cab. The cab has been modified to get rid of the overhanging roof. —W. C. WHITTAKER COLLECTION

The problems are obvious, even after the two halves of No. 6 went their separate ways. Whatever went wrong here with No. 5, she was patched up and ran again. —CHARLES M. HAINES COLLECTION

Closing the fair, or, more accurately, completing the fair, did not mean the end of the long career of No. 6. It was transferred to another construction company, A. D. Schader, and finally sold to the U. S. Maritime Commission, where it wound up doing war work. A vast shipbuilding complex was constructed at Richmond, across the bay and to the north of the Golden Gate. Again a switching locomotive was needed and the No. 6 filled that need. It may not have been the only Vauclain compound to work in the war effort during World War II, but was certainly one of the oldest and smallest.

When World War II was concluded, most of the Richmond complex was torn down. Locomotive No. 2515, originally half of McCloud River No. 6, met the scrapper's torch in 1949, one of the last Vauclain compounds anywhere.

Engine No. 6 was a considerable disappointment in its early days, despite its eventual success as two separate halves. Whether or not the failure of the No. 6 influenced a decision is not known, but No. 7 was neither new nor unconventional. It did, however, bring a different wheel arrangement to McCloud. It also brought another riddle to this story, for neither its specific original nor ending careers are known.

Permanente Metals No. 2515 had been fired up for the last time when this portrait was posed at Richmond, California, in 1948. She still carried the unique smokebox door it had when built as McCloud River Railroad No. 6, and was no doubt the last Vauclain compound in the nation. —ROBERT M. HANFT (BELOW) The railroader beside the driving rods brings attention to the tall drivers of locomotive No. 7. The 57-inch diameter of these wheels was greater than those of any other McCloud power and meant she could scamper fast enough if given the chance. First-built of the McCloud roster of steam locomotives, she was several years older than the railroad, and the only 4-6-0 wheel arrangement on the pike. —CHARLES M. HAINES COLLECTION

No. 7 was a Ten-wheeler, a 4-6-0. It was erected by the Baldwin Locomotive Works a full decade before the McCloud line came into existence, thus making it the first built of all McCloud power, even though not first on the line. At the time this engine first went into service, the Atchison, Topeka & Santa Fe Railway had several separate operating subsidiaries within the state of California. The Santa Fe purchased locomotives for each of these roads built to a similar design, and one 4-6-0 was later to become McCloud River Railroad No. 7. It may have come to McCloud by way of the nearby Weed Lumber Company, and it may have left by way of Weed as well. The date of departure is somewhat more definite — 1917. In any event, it too was involved in dam building after leaving McCloud, for it was used in the construction of the Hetch-Hetchy Railroad. The Hetch Hetchy was the railroad used to build the high Sierra water and power complex that supplies the city of San Francisco.

In 1901 two identical new engines arrived from the Baldwin Locomotive Works but without any special provision for teaming them. No's. 8 and 9 were 2-6-2's, only slightly larger than and quite similar in appearance to their predecessor Prairie, the No. 4. Later in the year

The hillside was denuded of timber as Scott and Van Arsdale moved east from Upton toward McCloud several years prior to the taking of this photograph. In this scene, locomotive No. 8 takes its turn posing with the mixed train on Big Canyon fill. —CHARLES M. HAINES COLLECTION

a third 2-6-2, identical with No's. 8 and 9 save for additional power gained through higher boiler pressure, came along. The total expenditure for the three locomotives was $41,-246.49.

One of the distinguishing aspects of the McCloud River Railroad is that a comparatively high proportion of its steam locomotives are still in existence. The No. 8 is the first to be so favored. It had an entirely routine career for a quarter of a century, with its share of ups and downs, such being the nature of the railroad. By 1925 it was marked for disposition because more powerful and efficient engines were on the line, but it was by no means worn out. It stayed on for another 14 years, still capable of hard work when needed, although the call did not come as regularly as had been the case before the new arrivals of 1924 and 1925. In the later years all the 2-6-2's were basically logging locomotives assigned customarily to lumber company duties.

Locomotive No. 9 vies with No. 19 for the title of wildest roaming McCloud engine. Shown in the view above, No. 9 just four years after she was built by the Baldwin Locomotive Works in 1901. —CHARLES M. HAINES COLLECTION (LEFT) The engine was sold to the Yreka Western in 1939 where it worked during the World War II years. In 1944 she was sold to the Amador Central and joined sister No. 8 at Martell in 1946. No. 8 was renumbered No. 7 as shown on the left and freshly painted but not professionally lettered. From the Amador Central No. 9 went to the Nezperce & Idaho Railroad, finally to the Mid-Continent Railway Museum at North Freedom, Wisconsin, where she was restored to service in 1970 after years of standing idle. —BOTH ROBERT M. HANFT COLLECTION

Two locomotives were added to the roster in 1938. Scrap prices were high in 1939, and No's. 4, 8 and 9 were sold and left McCloud for the last time. The No. 8 went to the Amador Central Railroad at Martell, California, where it was renumbered to No. 7 and went right to work in duties similar to those it had performed at McCloud, hauling lumber. Lumber from Martell moves downgrade, so perhaps it had an easier life there. Certainly it must have been satisfactory to the Amador Central people. It not only closed out the steam age on that line, but when time allowed for its use in standby protection of the diesel run expired it remained as a pet, placed on a pedestal for admiration of passers by. It waits out the years in Ione, a pleasant village on the eastern slope of the Sierra Nevada, perhaps more securely than the railroad that brought it south from McCloud. More than a half century has elapsed since the No. 18 went on display the single summer at Pan-Pacific, and No. 8 is slowly catching up with it on the number of visitors who have paused to gaze at a fine machine. The sheen on the No. 8 today is hardly as polished as was the case with the No. 18 at the San Francisco Pan-Pacific Exposition, however.

No. 9 is also still in evidence but has pursued quite a different career from its twin after an almost identical history at McCloud. From Mt. Shasta City in 1939 it was towed north to the nearby Yreka Western Railroad where it was relettered but not renumbered. Before long YW, a little line perennially plagued with financial difficulties, decided it would be better off with money than the No. 9. The Amador Central was sufficiently enamoured with No. 8 to take on the No. 9 as well, and the deal was consumated. Amador Central never got around to changing letters or numbers on the No. 9. When it dieselized one twin was surplus. If nothing else, the No. 8 now Amador Central No. 7 had correct identification for the Amador Central, and the No. 9, which did not, was dispossessed.

From the warm slopes of the central Sierra the little 2-6-2 went north again, far beyond its former homes at McCloud and Yreka, to the Camas Prairie country of Idaho and the Nezperce & Idaho Railroad. After serving three lumber railroads in the California mountains, No. 9 was now called upon to haul wheat in the rolling Idaho grain region. The locomotive had been too small and light to be of much further use to the McCloud River Railroad. For the Nezperce & Idaho No. 9 was too big and heavy for the roadbed. A solution was found in the form of a tiny gas locomotive of the Plymouth type. The No. 9 was unceremoniously shoved out into the weeds to be scrapped or sold later if the price was right. The Nezperce & Idaho dropped the "and Idaho" from its name, but that didn't matter much. It never had afforded paint to change the herald on No. 9 from Yreka Western.

The No. 9 was not worth much when it last saw service, and time and vandals did it little good as steel slowly changed to rust. Eventually the steam locomotive became cherished again with the passage of time Nezperce had the hulk of a once trim and graceful 4-4-0 keeping the 2-6-2 company along with the birds that sought them both as shelter for nests. First, someone remembered the American or 4-4-0 type, one of a few of that once highly popular locomotive classification. The 4-4-0 left the remote Idaho shortline and was restored to its earlier main line appearance as Northern Pacific No. 684.

No. 9 dozed on, but railroad enthusiasts were aware of it, and its turn to ride out to restoration finally came along in 1968. A group of Wisconsin hobbyists had long sought an operating museum of steam railroad equipment. After the usual frustrations in the form of large dreams and small capital that accompany such ventures, the group wangled an abandoned branch of the Chicago and North Western Railway and a considerable assortment of obsolete paraphernalia with which to equip its railroad. The assemblage is titled the Mid-Continent Railway Museum, and its operating base is North Freedom. Wisconsin. It is a non-profit group, a status never difficult for small railroads to achieve, but this one has done so by design. It attracts thousands of visitors during the tourist season, extracts a modest fee for rides and souvenirs, and fights the battle of decay and maintenance with any surplus funds. Part of the game is to get as many treasures as possible into its horde, and the No. 9 came all

A 43 year career was ahead for No. 10 when the Baldwin Locomotive Works proudly posed this builders photograph at its Philadelphia works. —GERALD M. BEST COLLECTION (BELOW) This classic railroad photograph was taken after a number of modifications had been made to No. 10 at McCloud, principally the substitution of an oil tank in the tender built as a wood box. Change of fuel also meant a revision of the stack. —CHARLES M. HAINES COLLECTION

the way from Nezperce to join the fleet. Blessed with skill and fondness, if not with extra cash, the Mid-Continent people actually expect to restore the remnants of the No. 9 from junk to a functioning machine taking its turn in passenger service. It has been a long time since No. 9 towed a coach filled with riders.

Third of the trio of 1901 vintage 2-6-2's, the No. 10 did not last as long on the McCloud line as its sisters, and fell far short of survival through the avenues followed by the others. The McCloud Company was glad enough to make a deal when the Yreka Railroad Company offered $5,400 for it in 1925. The McCloud line was somewhat strapped for funds right then, with six new engines purchased in 1924 and 1925. The Yreka Railroad is the predecessor of the company that bought the No. 8 and No. 9 later, thus could not have been sufficiently displeased with its purchases from McCloud so as to boycott further dealings,

especially for nearly identical machines. The No. 10 remained at Yreka until 1944 before finally meeting the scrapper's torch.

Locomotive No. 11 also came new from the Baldwin Locomotive Works; arriving early in 1904. A 2-6-2 wheel arrangement was the same as its 1901 mates, but No. 11 was 20 tons heavier and a Vauclain compound. The compound arrangement was identical with that of the earlier No. 5 and No. 6 combination, and it, too, used a comparatively high 200 pounds steam pressure, 20 pounds more even than No. 10. The high pressure cylinders were smaller in diameter than those of the No. 10 and No. 11 had slightly less power than the No. 10 when it was running in compound to gain efficiency. To maximize power at low speed the engineer could admit high pressure steam to all four cylinders. This had to be done sparingly, because too much steam would slip the drivers, and if the engine ran "simple" in this fashion very long the boiler couldn't replace the steam used fast enough. The engine was well liked because of the extra power it had when needed, both

One of a kind and sole addition to the McCloud locomotive roster in 1904, No. 11 was a Vauclain compound as was No. 6, but had the 44-inch drivers and 2-6-2 wheel arrangement of Nos. 4, 8, 9 and 10. Engine No. 11 was photographed behind the mill on a hazy day after it was converted to an oil burner.
—CHARLES M. HAINES COLLECTION

on the hill and in the woods. It took six cars of lumber over the hard pull unassisted. It wasn't such a hit with the management on maintenance, a typical problem with compounds that often led to their being rebuilt simple. No. 11 stayed compound, spent most of its time in the woods after bigger engines came to the main line, and was sold in 1926 along with No. 10, but to a different party, W. S. Zimmerman of Portland, Oregon, who paid $6,500 for it. It evidently was not scrapped until 1939, but what use was made of it in the interim is not clear. A picture taken in 1937 shows it out of service in a northern junk yard, still lettered for the McCloud River Railroad and still a compound. Photographs also indicate that its cylinders were inclined slightly, a fairly common practice in early-day engines, but not ordinarily seen in Vauclain power. Why this was done in the case of the No. 11 is not apparent.

Although "lump oil" continued to be the customary fuel for struggling firemen, by 1906 the No. 12 was burning oil. Perhaps its regular assignment to the passenger train gave it special privilege. The renumbering preceded the change of fuel, for photographs of the No. 12 using both fuels remain as proof. With the end of regular passenger service between Mc-Cloud and Mt. Shasta City the No. 12 was declared surplus and scrapped in 1932.

The No. 13 was never used. Superstition may have penetrated the mountain country, and there was little to be gained by straining luck that had not been excessively capricious so far.

Internal combustion power was used early in the McCloud operation. The lumber company used small gasoline locomotives both around the mill and in the woods. Of less importance has been adaptation with flanged wheels of ordinary automobiles to run on the

Oil-burning No. 12 heads the regular passenger train at McCloud. She was the first locomotive to eliminate the wood-tossing chore, when converted in 1906. — CHARLES M. HAINES COLLECTION (BELOW) McCloud No. 14 was 33 years old when she was photographed taking water at McCloud in 1940. The device atop the stack was a screen for spark arresting. Popularly referred to as a hat, the spark arrester was worn during fire hazard season. —GUY L. DUNSCOMB

Elbow grease and light oil had been used to polish No. 15 just prior to this photograph with caboose *Shasta*. This shack was the only known piece of rolling stock on the McCloud equipment roster to have been officially named. Speculation has it that No. 15 had just come from the shops after conversion from wood to oil burning. —CHARLES M. HAINES COLLECTION

railroad, a practice established in 1906 with the ordering of a 50 horsepower Thomas Flyer for use by manager S. O. Johnson.

After a three year lapse in the parade of newly acquired locomotives following the arrival of No. 11, during which period the major change was the renumbering of the original engine to No. 12, Baldwin delivered two new machines in 1907. The Nos. 14 and 15 were conventional enough as locomotives go, but were the first of their wheel arrangement, the 2-8-2 or Mikado type, to reach McCloud. Bigger in every respect than their Prairie predecessors, with eight drive wheels, these engines could each exert even more tractive force than the combined effort of the tandem tug of No. 6. They were the first McCloud River power built as oil burners.

These 1907 arrrivals spent their entire career working logs, lumber and whatever other traffic was offered in and out of McCloud. That they were eminently successful is evidenced by their lasting to the diesel era, when all steam was vanquished, before meeting the scrapper's torch.

The purchase of two new oil-fired locomotives in 1907 may have portended the end of the parade of "lump oil" into McCloud fireboxes, but this exercise was far from finished for the local stokers of the flames. While chunk wood was in adequate supply as a cheap by-product of the lumber manufacture that then demanded a particularly high grade raw material, and while labor used to cut, pile, load and stoke was also priced low, there was no particular rush to eliminate wood burning locomotives. As a matter of record the company decided that it had underestimated the availability of cordwood and converted one machine from oil back to wood. Comments of the firemen have not been preserved, but may well be imagined.

Four years elapsed before another major change took place in the equipment roster, when another pair of virtually identical locomotives showed up in McCloud. A different builder from the favored Baldwin Locomotive Works was involved, in addition to a completely new design. Engines Nos. 16 and 17 were built by Lima Locomotive Works to the

A trestle is a braced framework of timbers, piles, or steelwork for carrying a railroad over a depression. No matter what their construction, trestles had appeal for the photographer of the McCloud River Railroad. This mid-career illustration of No. 15 shows the more modern headlight of its later days, but the combination coach of the east-end mixed run is one of the original pieces of passenger rolling stock. —CHARLES M. HAINES COLLECTION

104

Shay geared locomotive No. 16 with crew a few miles east of McCloud. Mt. Shasta appears as a marshmallow Sundae above the engine tank. The absence of wood leads to speculation that its conversion to oil might already have been made, yet the big wood stack and tender railing remained. —CHARLES M. HAINES COLLECTION

More successful than the earlier Heisler geared locomotives, the Shays were considered special purpose machines and were not retained on the roster after logging the Black Fox area was completed. In this scene, Shay No. 17 appears all wooded up for another run into the woods for loaded log flats. —WILLIAM WOODS COLLECTION

Shay patent. Shays were geared locomotives, designed as were Nos. 2 and 3 to pull heavy loads at low speed over the uncertain track typical of logging railroads. Shays had their drive mechanism on the right-hand side of the boiler, which was offset to balance. The Shay was by then a well proved machine, and the company bought them for a particular purpose. Logging in an area northeast of McCloud called Black Fox, the lumber company did not own all the land needed to build its woods lines to moderate grades, but instead had to climb steeply with tight curves and switchbacks. The four percent main line grade between McCloud and Sisson was still there, but evidently the company was well enough pleased by now with the performance of its direct drive locomotives, especially Nos. 14 and 15, that the Shays were never seriously considered as main line power. Perhaps management had recognized by then that the true measure of steam locomotive efficiency was the ability of a boiler to make steam. The Shays were a special purpose machine, at which task they performed well, but when that chore was ended, so was their prime usefulness. With Black Fox logged off, Nos. 16 and 17 were sold to another California operator in 1924, the Fruit Growers Supply Company, at Susanville. From the sale of these Shays $29,500 was realized. Fruit Growers used Shays extensively on its three operations, and the two former McCloud engines fit the needs of their new owners closely.

Locomotive No. 18 was both quite ordinary and quite special. The Baldwin Locomotive Works built it to rather standard specifications, just slightly larger than Nos. 14 and 15, and with the same 2-8-2 wheel arrangement. It was to have a brief career as a showgirl before settling down to a more mundane existence with its companion power. Some questions remains as to whether No. 18 came to McCloud first or went directly from Baldwin to San Francisco, but, regardless, she was part of the Panama-Pacific International Exposition of 1915 and her pristine splendor at that display is obvious even in the news photographs that record the occasion. The locomotive cost $16,851.79 plus an extra $2,000 for servicing.

Locomotive No. 18 and all engines subsequently purchased stayed on the line until displaced by diesels, and No. 18 is another survivor. The Yreka Western bought it for use in 1956 and still has it parked out of service at Yreka. YW mangement is well aware of the current demand for steam locomotives and may well sell it for repair and operation. Certainly it is not in immediate danger of the fate met by most engines in the great slaughter of a decade ago.

When No. 18 arrived at McCloud the use of wood fuel was rapidly declining. In 1918 less than 1,000 cords were burned, and Nos. 7 and 9 were the only road locomotives still using "lump oil." The 1919 consumption was 382 cords, 175 in 1920, 40 in 1921 and none during 1922 or thereafter.

No. 18's fireman never had to contend with tossing wood. When brand-new it was displayed at the Panama-Pacific International Exposition of 1915 at San Francisco. It survives today as No. 18 of the Yreka Western Railroad. —CHARLES M. HAINES COLLECTION

The brooding, eternal silence of the Mt. Shasta countryside is shattered by a whistle and the sound of five steam locomotives breasting the Signal Butte switchback which will carry the tonnage from McCloud to Sisson. The two locomotives above will cut off and run around to the head-end and take the train on to Sisson. The three pushers shown below will drop back light to McCloud for further service. —BOTH CHARLES M. HAINES COLLECTION

Locomotive No. 19 known as *Pancho* shows little evidence of its turbulent Mexican career on the United Mining & Smelting Co. railroad line in this sparkling portrait. This Baldwin Locomotive Works 2-8-2 was built in 1915 for the Caddo & Choctaw Railroad. —CHARLES M. HAINES COLLECTION

The stable of 12 iron horses, Nos. 4, 6, 8, 9, 10, 11, 12, 14, 15, 16, 17, and 18 kept traffic moving through World War I and were considered adequate enough until 1923 when another 2-8-2 joined the fleet. Surprisingly enough the new arrival was practically the twin of the No. 18. McCloud River No. 19 was built for service in Arkansas, where it was No. 4 of the Caddo & Choctaw and the Choctaw River Lumber Company. It was built a few months after No. 18 with virtually the same specifications. The No. 19 had also spent some time in Mexico between the time it left Arkansas and came to California. Its career below the border for the United Mining & Smelting Company, where it carried the No. 2069, was during troubled times. On arrival at McCloud it bore a few holes and dents here and there reported to have been the result of being on the receiving end of revolutionary bullets. In

consequence it was given the nickname of *Pancho*. Named engines have not been particularly common in this century, and *Pancho* was hardly official, but the No. 19 also had a formal name in its earlier career, when it carried the title of *R. L. Rowan* in addition to its number. Despite its more extensive service, the price of locomotives had risen. *Pancho* cost close to $25,000.

Once on the McCloud River No. 19 re-established the custom of twins on the line, and wound up being sold in 1954 to the Yreka Western and is preserved there with the No. 18.

Sale of the two surplus Shays in 1924 provided a substantial down payment toward the cost of two more new locomotives from Baldwin. Numbers 20 and 21 were also not designed for main line service, but rather for log runs on behalf of the lumber company. Accord-

The only turntable for locomotives on the railroad identifies the McCloud location for the portrait of No. 20, taken as World War II began to rumble in Europe. —TED WURM

Shortly after its 1924 arrival from Alco-Schenectady Locomotive Works, No. 20 starts logs on their way to the McCloud mill. Felled timber may be seen in the foreground which will provide future loads. —CHARLES M. HAINES COLLECTION

ingly, they reversed the trend toward larger and more powerful engines, and used the same 2-6-2 wheel arrangement of the early direct-connected engines. This pair of engines remained until dieselization.

The performance of these 1924 modern Prairie types was sufficiently sparkling by comparison with the earlier models built before the days of piston valves and superheaters that more were promptly in order. In 1925 not merely another pair, but two sets of twins — four locomotives in all — were added.

Save for the geared locomotives the Baldwin Locomotive Works had been the sole builder of McCloud River power. The railroad had no particular intention to switch, but it did give the American Locomotive Company a look at its plans for more 2-6-2's. ALCO offered to build all four for less than $90,000 as compared with the $55,000 for Nos. 20 and 21, even though two of the new four would be larger than the Baldwin engines of the year before. ALCO got the contract, and the engines arrived in due time.

Snow not only obscures most of locomotives No. 22 and 21, but most of the load these engines are expected to move. The situation is hardly an uncommon one on the McCloud River Railroad. The real trouble began when a load would derail, for even finding the derailed wheels would be a major project. —CHARLES M. HAINES COLLECTION

The locomotive in this scene is No. 25 and it is on the rails of the Pondosa branch where trackage connected with the Burney line. This photograph appears to be a regular freight, but the train is a passenger special on its way from Burney to McCloud on June 22, 1963. No. 25 had just been restored to service after seven years of dormancy. Its first duty was on a special with borrowed passenger equipment, followed by this excursion as a psuedo-freight called the *McCloud River Rattler*. The train consisted of box car carried, fare-paying hobos armed with cameras, tape recorder and memories of the good old days. —KARL KOENIG

All the 2-6-2's numbered in the 20 series remained to the end of the steam era. One, No. 23, was sold to the Arcata & Mad River Railroad at Arcata, but the deal fell through and it never saw service in the redwood country. The No. 25, a participant in the festivities that opened the Burney line in 1955, did not join the exodus of steam from McCloud. Instead, it was pushed to the rear of the new diesel shops, ostensibly to be held for standby, for a steam generator, or for possible future donation as an exhibit somewhere. It is not entirely impossible that a certain amount of sentiment prevailed at McCloud and all concerned really wanted to keep a souvenir of steam. Be that as it may, No. 25, after years of inactivity, was lovingly restored to service and in 1971 still provides the wail of the whistle and the beat of well-timed exhaust to echo against the slopes of Shasta.

Along with No. 25, Nos. 22, 23 and 24 pictured on this page represented the first straying from the Baldwin fold for McCloud motive power save for the special purpose geared engines. These Alco-Schenectady built log haulers served well but were not to survive the onslaught of diesels as did sister No. 25. In the scene above, No. 22 is on the turntable at McCloud in 1939. —TED WURM Locomotives No. 23 and 24 were photographed in 1947. At that time No. 23 was based at Pondosa and assigned to log runs. (BELOW) In this view No. 24 appears to be freshly painted as if she had been pulled out of the shops at McCloud. —BOTH GUY L. DUNSCOMB

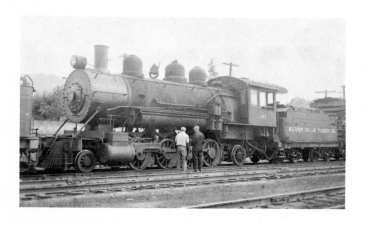

The seemingly endless snowfall of the winter of 1937-38 placed considerable strain on the finances of the railroad, and helped point out that more horsepower on the rail would be useful, even if difficult to afford. President Swobe declared that the high cost of snow removal would have been substantially less if more big locomotives had been available. With depressed prices still prevailing in the used locomotive market, a husky 2-8-2 of approximately the same size and vintage as the Nos. 18 and 19 was purchased from the Silver Falls Timber Company, at Silverton, Oregon, for less than $10,000. Curiously, when the Silver Falls locomotive was given a new number along with superheater units and a general overhaul, the McCloud River number did not continue the serialization pattern so long in effect. Instead, it became No. 16, taking over the slot originally held by the first Shay. Second No. 16 wasn't a twin, either, but was another Baldwin locomotive.

Swobe had located three used 2-8-2's, and the directors agreed that the company might as well get the other two, while they were at

Second No. 16 is about to make its first trip over McCloud rails. It has arrived at Mount Shasta from Silver Falls, Oregon, still lettered for the Silver Falls Timber Company its previous owner, and will be towed to McCloud for rehabilitation. —CHARLES M. HAINES COLLECTION (BELOW) The same locomotive, nearing the end of its career, is readied for work on a spring day in 1948. —ROBERT M. HANFT

it — and 88 cars, too. This equipment, and removal of all that snow left the company a bit pressed for cash, even if bargain prices prevailed. A bank loan of $150,000 at two and one-half percent interest was arranged. With that low cost for money there wasn't even any necessity for the railroad to call on the lumber company with hat in hand.

The other two locomotives were twins again, and also had been built by Alco rather than Baldwin. Formerly Copper River & Northwestern Nos. 72 and 73, the question of how to identify them on the McCloud River posed a minor dilemma. Silver Falls No. 101 took up one of the two numbers vacated by the Shays; only one was available. Going backwards to No. 13 or No. 12 would have been necessary to keep 2-8-2's in the 10 series. The Alaska veterans, displaced from their northern habitat by exhaustion of the rich copper deposits they had hauled down to salt water, got Nos. 26 and 27, highest assigned to steam power. They were also the heaviest steam engines ever owned by the McCloud line. They weren't the most powerful; the Shays could exert more starting pull with their geared system. They weren't the last steam engines acquired, either; one more came along to fill in that second No. 17 vacancy on the roster.

Ten years after its arrival in McCloud, No. 26 was equipped with a new tender acquired from the Southern Pacific. A 1938 purchase, No. 26 and its near twin No. 27 had spent the previous 28 years in Alaska hauling copper on the Copper River and Northwestern. With exhaustion of the high-grade deposits, the Alaska short line was torn up and the components sold. Although they were the highest numbered McCloud steam power, the pair were not the newest, the last acquired, or most powerful. They were the heaviest, but most of the other 2-8-2's exerted as much tractive effort, and the two Shay geared locomotives had substantially more. They served until displaced by diesels, but neither survived. —HAROLD F. VAN HORN

McCloud River Railroad No. 26 as it looked before relettering, with its original tender, as Copper River and Northwestern No. 72. —T. E. GLOVER COLLECTION (BELOW) The last number on the steam locomotive roster was No. 27. Here the locomotive bearing those digits poses for the camera of Robert Hanft at McCloud. The year was 1950 and No. 27's future was perfectly clear.

All the 2-8-2's lasted until displaced by diesels, but the rectangular tenders with which Nos. 26 and 27 were equipped wore out and were later replaced with the more cylindrical "Vanderbilt" type typically used by medium sized SP power.

The last McCloud River steam locomotive was added in 1943, at the height of World War II fury. It was the oldest engine ever to be acquired, being a contemporary of all the other 2-8-2's. Baldwin had outshopped it in 1916, nine years after Nos. 14 and 15, thus it saw 27 years of service before arriving at McCloud. The railroad bought 2-8-2's for 36 years from 1907 to 1943, but all were actually built within a ten year span. Well worn or not, any additional help was welcome during the war rush. Because it was not a twin of anything else, it would fit logically into the vacant No. 17 spot, which it was assigned. Second No. 17's tenure at Mc-Cloud was, of course, briefest of any of the locomotives remaining to dieseldom.

The end of steam came at a director's meeting in 1947. Once again the company was short of power, and the newest locomotive on the roster was now 22 years old and a logging engine at that. The newest 2-8-2 had been fighting tonnage and gradients for 30 winters and

The last steam locomotive to join the McCloud roster was No. 17, and the second to bear that number. This engine rather than No. 27 was the 27th steam locomotive on the 27 engine list. Purchased from the Pacific Portland Cement Co. in 1942, second No. 17 had seen 27 years of service before crossing the mountain to McCloud. It was compatible in age, capacity and dimension with the other 2-8-2's there, and was actually the newest of them all despite its extended service elsewhere. Once the diesels came, age and condition of the steam locomotives meant little. No. 17 was photographed at Mount Shasta in 1946. —ROBERT M. HANFT COLLECTION

Baldwin Locomotive Works diesel demonstrator No. 1501 shares honors with 2-8-2 No. 15 on the line between McCloud and Bartle. —KARL KOENIG COLLECTION (BELOW) At home in McCloud, No. 28 the road's first diesel moves a tank car past the depot. The general offices of McCloud River Lumber Company are in the background. —CHARLES M. HAINES COLLECTION

all the other seasons as well. Diesels were now the very latest thing. Vice-President Myers was authorized to rent whatever power he needed to tide the company over, but a study of diesel utilization was authorized and a delivery position with the Baldwin Locomotive Works was sought. Baldwin still had an inside track at McCloud.

Diesel locomotive studies seldom were prejudicial against them, and the inevitable firm order followed. In a way the engine purchased placed the railroad at the forward edge of progress once again. By this time diesel power in general was well tested, but the brand-new model chosen was big for 1947 by any standard, with few on the road anywhere, let alone on a small operation. President Myers was mindful of the proven fuel savings and high availability of diesels; he also was hopeful that a really powerful version could achieve substantial wage savings in moving tonnage across the mountain. That four percent pull still had to be faced daily. Accordingly, although diesel builders offer their wares as a package subject to only minor modifications, rather than custom built to user's specifications as was typically the case with steam, the model Myers evidenced advanced thinking and faith in the builder to deliver the performance hoped for. Few were around who had witnessed the experiment with No. 6 a half-century earlier, but the problem and the hope for a solution were basically the same, as was some of the risk. New diesel electric locomotives are not cheap; this one cost more than the six newest McCloud 2-6-2's, and not much less than the outlay for all eight 2-8-2's. In late 1948, the 1,500 horsepower machine arrived dead in a freight train at Lookout and was towed over to McCloud without incident.

After an appropriate amount of fuss and preparation, the diesel was revved up, tied to the Mt. Shasta City turn and given a highball. A new era on the McCloud River Railroad was launched with a roar and a honk.

Pride of the accompanying brass in their new diesel jewel soon turned to ashes. The new No. 28 seemed to demonstrate exactly the same foible No. 6 had evidenced so long ago — no particular desire to go where the rails led. It was aground before really leaving the town behind. At the first sharp curve the locomotive was de-termined to follow its head rather than the track. Not only did rails spread at curves, but they turned over on the straight stretches, too. The maiden run never got to Mt. Shasta City, for it was obvious that to continue would be farcial. Steam helped retrieve the recalcitrant diesel and its loads, and the engine was set aside while strategy was considered.

This time, by contrast with the No. 6 episode, the problem was not entirely unexpected. Design engineers by now knew not only what output to expect from their machines, but what stresses they would create and what was needed to cope with those forces in terms of rail size and roadbed quality. The McCloud conditions were sufficiently dubious that No. 28 had been built several tons lighter than customary for that model in order to reduce stress. It wasn't enough.

On the roundhouse turntable not long after its arrival from the Baldwin Locomotive Works, No. 28 would soon do away with both the roundhouse and the turntable. —CHARLES M. HAINES COLLECTION

The McCloud roundhouse was a sizeable structure for so small a railroad, but the amount of power required in steam days kept the rails shiny. At the right, Nos. 16 and 19 face their berths across the turntable.
—B. H. WARD

Who is missing? All nine stalls are filled, and each locomotive carefully spotted for the portrait shown above. Each locomotive has been brought out of the roundhouse a little way to register well in the photograph. Diesel No. 28 seems out of place here but it was the company's pride and joy. Soon it would have similar bedfellows and only No. 25 would have a home at McCloud. This 1949 vintage illustration provides evidence that not all the twins were identical.
—MCCLOUD RIVER RAILROAD

This was the sort of classic denouement over which steam enthusiasts loved to gloat, but the outcome was no different than for diesel problems elsewhere; the diesel was here to stay and whatever it took to make it function properly the locomotive was going to get. Roadmaster Haines took his lumps because the roadbed wasn't up to par, even if it had held the steam locomotives more or less adequately. The company had planned to lay some heavier rail soon anyway. Solid ties and tight spikes help, even when the rail is light.

Although No. 28 was purchased specifically to cope with the hill, the writer was told that a trial trip was also attempted and actually completed to Pondosa, but with results no more auspicious than for the Mt. Shasta test. What might have taken three hours proved to be a three day nightmare before weary men and equipment finally returned to their vacant beds in McCloud. Time after time the rails spread and the locomotive dropped to the ties. Heavy rerailing frogs had to be placed in position again and again to lift the 146 ton monster back onto the rail.

Although Baldwin could hardly be faulted for this initial fiasco, discovery of a design change led to a refund of $2,500 to ease the general condition of pain around McCloud. That was enough to pay for a secondhand caboose added to the roster, if not for the trackwork.

If a roadbed is good enough for one diesel, it can be used for two. Little more than a year after arrival of the No. 28, the order was sent to Eddystone for a twin. The inauguration of the second diesel took place without the trauma of the first.

By 1952 complete dieselization was being considered, and President Willis pointed out that payments on additional new diesels would very nearly be covered by fuel savings alone. The decision to add two new diesels in 1953 was made. A 1,200 horsepower diesel somewhat smaller than the original machines, for general road and switching use, plus a unit of 800 horsepower to operate on logging trackage, would earn their keep now and were ordered from Baldwin. These engines each had eight wheels, all powered, compared with 12 on Nos. 28 and 29. The pair arrived in late 1953.

Not long after its 1955 arrival, No. 22 the 1,200 horsepower diesel waits for an assignment at McCloud. —CHARLES M. HAINES COLLECTION At the left, No. 32 has just finished an all night battle with a snow blockade. —KARL KOENIG

In early 1954 the company was 100 percent dieselized, with the four Baldwin diesel-electric locomotives providing the entire service. By then the Burney branch was in the offing, with heavier traffic anticipated later in the current year as well. A pair of 1,200 horsepower Baldwins, if ordered soon enough, could avert the necessity of calling out the dead steam power. An all diesel road should have all diesel facilities, too, which meant the end of the old roundhouse and the erection of a modern shop especially equipped for diesel locomotive servicing.

Another single locomotive was ordered from Baldwin, and its arrival was looked forward to as usual, when a misunderstanding arose. According to company records, doubt was cast on the ability of the machine to meet dynamic braking demands as anticipated. This feature, a mighty useful accessory on the McCloud grades, allows the electric motors to function as generators on the down slopes and hold back the train. Willis summoned the builder's representative to appear before the directors, and, perhaps to keep events lively, asked the General Motors diesel representative to make a presentation as well, with emphasis on dynamic braking. The Baldwin man carried the day with a persuasive argument that Baldwin not only had a working dynamic brake, but also many major components identical with those already

on engines No. 28 and No. 29. The railroad went for an extra locomotive while it was at it.

Locomotive No. 30 served the railroad for only a decade, becoming the first diesel to leave the roster. The No. 30 wasn't exactly surplus, nor was it worn out. It wasn't as powerful as Nos. 28 and 29, and it didn't have the dynamic brakes of Nos. 32 and 33. It didn't match No. 31, with which it usually shared the Burney assignment. The only important difference between them was that No. 30 had a supercharger, but McCloud mechanical forces preferred to avoid maintenance of the pressurizing device. A more suitable locomotive was available from the Southern Pacific, and a market was found for No. 30. The purchaser wasn't completely satisfied with the condition of No. 30, but a $7,000 reduction in the original agreement led to soothed feelings all around — especially when the SP was prevailed upon to part with its used engine for $12,000 less than expected.

What probably will be the last Baldwin locomotive ever purchased by the company came on the scene in 1963, well after the exit of Baldwin and its successor corporation from the locomotive construction market. By this time all the engines on the roster were old as diesels go, and maintenance was a problem. Master mechanic Carter wanted more parts, and a substantial inventory of used parts was added all at once in the form of former SP engines Nos. 5204 and 5207 that had many components identical with those in McCloud River power. The Chrome Crankshaft Company owned the locomotives, which had been sent to the Oroville dam construction project. The dam operators changed their minds and decided not to use them on the project. Carter got them at bargain prices. With typical McCloud ingenuity, his men were able to put No. 5207 in running condition at little expense, and painted it up as McCloud River No. 35. The No. 5204, still lettered Southern Pacific, was parked behind the shops and is still there in 1970, showing evidence of the expected cannibalism. The No. 35 remained in regular service into 1969 with No. 28, the original diesel, no longer used, but near enough to running condition that a few visits behind the shop for more parts could restore it. In addition to ordinary wear it had sustained a few unexpected bruises.

Motive power was a well recognized problem in 1968. The all-Baldwin roster had served faithfully, but there were limits to what swapping of used parts could accomplish. With old locomotives there is a tendency to skimp, which only aggravates the problem. The test of time had showed Baldwin diesel locomotives generally unable to compete with present day rivals, but the special circumstances of the McCloud

Three Baldwin diesels, Nos. 33, 32, 31, team up to a drag freight moving out of Pondosa in August 1964, bound for McCloud and then over the big hill for interchange with the Southern Pacific at Mount Shasta. —DON HANSEN

River Railroad may have been nearly ideal for them. The McCloud line did not overload its motive power with either tonnage or speed, and under these conditions they kept on running with comparatively unsophisticated maintenance. With the end in sight, management could opt for a rebuilding of the old machines, find other used units, or switch to another variety. The choice selected was to purchase three powerful new General Motors model SD-38 engines, which are as modern as they come. The trio arrived in McCloud on Friday, May 9, 1969, and were coupled to trains the following Tuesday. Numbered 36, 37 and 38, they continue the serialization tracing back to No. 1 of 1897. The three have been handling all the work accomplished by the former roster of seven. With no more than two trains on the road at one time, they turn the trick nicely. If they should prove inadequate, the No. 25 is still there! Locomotive crews and Carter's mechanics alike are finding the SD-38's compare with the old Baldwins about as a 1969 V-8 does with a vintage four cylinder automobile, but the experience shouldn't be as trying as it was with locomotive No. 28 some 21 years ago.

As contrasted with the earlier departures from the Baldwin fold, this time there will be no return, for Baldwin no longer supplies locomotives. No one has yet faulted these successors on their ability to perform.

Brand-new General Motors diesel No. 36 poses in January of 1969. Three such 2,000 horsepower machines pack all the wallop needed to move present traffic — except for pleasure outings with No. 25. —DON HANSEN

Flavor of the mill pond operation is captured here, as pond-man maneuvers logs from the rail unloading ramp to mill intake. The pond kept going for trucked logs after rail log hauling ceased, but it too, has been outmoded. —UNION PACIFIC RAILROAD

5

ROLLING STOCK

BY CONTRAST with the study of locomotives in the previous chapter, a look at the other equipment needed to stock a railroad could appear anticlimatic. Records are not as detailed and nothing inanimate around a railroad has personality to compare with that of a locomotive — especially a steam locomotive — even to the point of occasionally rivalling the human characters for attention. Even so, there is a bit more to the support equipment story than just keeping the record straight.

To open the road, the company acquired 47 short flat cars, a caboose, a tank car, a combination baggage-coach, and two other freight cars in its first year. The record is silent on details of this early rolling stock, but the combination coach may very well have been No. 1, which survives to this day parked near Dunsmuir and is still on wheels. It is the only passenger car used during the first half century of the railroad that remains reasonably intact. Early flat cars did not carry numbers and were typically short lived under the battering received in log service.

In 1899 two freight cars and a tank car, not otherwise identified, were added to the roster, but in 1900 a substantial contract totalling 40 freight cars and one passenger coach was let to John Hammond and Company at San Francisco thus nearly doubling the inventory of rolling stock.

Car purchases have continued to be important throughout the life of the company. Log loading is one of the roughest kinds of service, and the fleet was replenished, rebuilt in part, or added to virtually every year while logs were being carried. The early log cars were 26 foot bob-tail flats. Later standard 40 foot flats were used. Evidently, gondolas, skeleton racks or disconnected trucks were never used. Movement of the latter over common carrier portions of the line would have been outlawed in any event. In early 1904 the company let a contract for 100 cars to the Redding Iron Works, interesting primarily in that this bidder was a local concern less than a hundred miles removed from McCloud. The builder did not use this order as a springboard to national

McCloud rail log hauling was done exclusively on flat cars, with 26-feet the standard length in the early days. This load appears to be almost as high as it is long. (ABOVE) Photographs of McCloud River Railroad box cars are rare. This partial view of No. 3031 was hardly deliberate. (BELOW) Both 26 and 40-foot logging flats are evident in this consist. Note how the logs too long for a 26-footer are cradled on two such cars. —ALL CHARLES M. HAINES COLLECTION

Locomotive No. 25 has exchanged empties for loads at the switchback in the woods west of Pondosa, and is drifting downgrade toward McCloud. —ROBERT M. HANFT

prominence as a carbuilder, as no further orders appear to have been placed with the firm.

Shop men on small railroads are often called upon to make up with ingenuity and diversity of talent for the more extensive equipment enjoyed by their counterparts on larger lines. That the McCloud people had attained such skills is evidenced by the 1905 completion of a homemade caboose-coach designed for service east of McCloud, where it would trail behind the log trains. Passengers were primarily loggers and other hardy types enroute to and from the operations frontier.

President Queal was not ready to have his shop men create the latest in luxury rolling stock for his own use. In an era where business leaders were not considered wholly successful without a chariot of the rails at their personal disposal, Queal was not to be outclassed. He ordered an executive car from the Pullman Company that could roll along as fast as that of any other tycoon. Numbered 100, this bit of elegance graced the McCloud River Railroad roster for the rest of Queal's lifetime, but totalled most of its mileage on foreign rails. Even its home terminal was more literally Oak-

Shay geared locomotive No. 17 has an unusual consist. Car No. 1001 is a flat car rigged up as a fish tank. The train stopped at stream crossings and men emptied trout overside into the brook. At one time railroads enjoyed a substantial business of this nature from state fish hatcheries. (BELOW) Prairie type No. 25 was well photographed prior to its passenger carrying days. In this scene its train is led by a water car of somewhat more orthodox design than the wooden boxes used earlier. Although the car was conventional enough, the pumper atop it is hardly a typical design. —BOTH CHARLES M. HAINES COLLECTION

land than McCloud, and the SP was very co-operative about providing the necessary services and parking facility there, what with all those carloads of lumber coming across its interchange up north. The No. 100 did show up on fairly frequent occasions at McCloud, either as a special movement or behind the coach on the regular passenger run. Presence of the private car and its cargo of human royalty was a special event to town urchins, who extended near-deity status to the porter in hardly lesser measure than to the president. Black men were a rarity in McCloud before World War I, and this porter had a flashing smile and an occasional tidbit for small boys that made him rather definitely their favorite visiting celebrity.

The president enjoyed bringing in guests aboard this deluxe vehicle and often included the ritual of making a stop at a particularly fine specimen of sugar pine growing close to the track shortly before arrival at McCloud. Visitors were assured this standing tree was representative of the timber that went into McCloud lumber. Had this tall tree been cut, more than one head doubtlessly would have been severed along with it. Even after Queal's death, the tree was spared as a kind of living monument to his memory.

When Queal died his car went with him. By then restrictions on interline use made such vehicles less attractive and his successor promptly sold the car to the SP. Nothing to compare with this rolling palace frequented McCloud for some four decades, until a Western Pacific observation-lounge car was used on an excursion and parked at McCloud. Available for a comparative song, management passed up the opportunity to purchase it and revive the luxury era of rail travel. Practicality may have been recognized with some reluctance.

Fifteen new logging cars were added to the fleet in 1907, plus 25 lumber flats. The latter purchase is worthy of a special note, because these cars were purchased for "on line" use, rather than for interchange beyond Sisson. The railroad has, with recent partial exception, always depended on cars rented to it by other railroads for the export of lumber beyond its lines. In 1907 enough lumber moved between mills of the lumber company, and to other points on the line such as back to the logging camps, to warrant a fleet of cars for this service. To offset the new additions, 30 worn out flat cars and one combination car were retired.

In 1914 the company reported 40 train miles operated by motor, a situation that brought the attention of the ICC, which promptly called for explanation. Unfortunately the record of the explanation is not sufficiently complete to determine now just what did happen. First thought of the writer was that this figure represented a leased passenger rail car, but the best guess now appears that it represents trips made by a seven ton four-wheel dinky owned by the lumber company and built by the Milwaukee Locomotive Works. After all the curiosity this report evoked from the ICC, the railroad probably learned to restrain itself from mentioning any further excursions of lumber company power onto railroad company trackage, leaving us with only surmises as to whether or not such usage ever did recur.

More than 100 new flat cars were added in 1925 to match the new power arriving that year, with 96 cars being taken off the roster. The modernization of those remaining older cars continued with 146 short 26 foot logging flats rebuilt to 40 foot length in 1925 at a total cost of almost $75,000. At the end of the year the company had 251 of the 40 foot flats in logging service. During this year the first automatic highway crossing wig-wag signal was installed.

Since the company had to protect the highway, it must have felt inclined to use it, for it got into the bus business in 1927, purchased two more buses to bring its fleet up to three in 1929, then turned its highway operations over to the wholly-owned subsidiary McCloud Transportation Company. Eight years later the parent again absorbed the subsidiary, adding two more buses at the time. The cost of less than $1,000 each did not strain company finances particularly.

The depression and war years saw few additions to the equipment roster. Three steel underframe flat cars were added in 1934, nine the next year, plus a water car.

The year 1952 witnessed another indignity somewhat comparable with the fiasco of the first diesel run.

As detailed in a subsequent chapter, the company had long used push plows for snow removal. A Jordan ditcher-spreader could not only handle snow removal more effectively than the existing plows, but is versatile with a wide variety of right of way maintenance chores. One of President Willis' very first acts in his new capacity after replacing Phil Myers was to ask for the purchase of one of these $35,000 machines. His wish was granted and the pristine new gadget with its impressive array of attendant paraphernalia arrived in December and was sent out for a test in a few inches of snow. To the horror of those responsible for the shepherding of the machine, it proved even more contrary than No. 28 had on its maiden run. The Jordan plow not only left the track, but twisted sideways to the line and buried its nose deep in goo alongside the rail. Plainly, rerailing frogs wouldn't do; the big hook had to be called for. When the mud was cleaned off and the dents fixed up the Jordan was no longer brand-new.

Alas for romance, just as the diesels were not to be denied by temporary setbacks, the older snow removal equipment was not in the same league with the modern machine, either.

Good braking is a necessity on a mountain railroad, as the McCloud line occasionally was reminded. Automatic air brakes were used even in logging when they would not have been required by law. However, in 1952 the ICC decreed that type AB brakes were sufficiently superior to older styles to make the use of AB equipment mandatory, including use on cars that did not venture beyond the trackage of the owner. This ruling caught the railroad with some 300 cars that had to have new brake sets, costing about $100,000, and which would have to be added within a year. The McCloud River Railroad joined the ranks of those appealing to the ICC for a bit more time to accomplish the mission, at least; preferably to exempt logging cars entirely.

Log cars remained a perennial problem, with the company ever alert to replacements, especially those with braking systems that would not be frowned upon by the ICC. In 1956 a new scheme was tried out successfully. The Western Pacific had surplus livestock cars, equipped with AB brakes, which it would sell for $650 each. The McCloud shops could remove the slotted bodies at comparatively little expense and quite acceptable log flats would emerge. Sixty WP cars were purchased, and the conversion went so well that another 40, all WP had available, were ordered.

A three year extension of time by the ICC for conversion of the braking systems also provided a welcome breather. So did another 110 stock cars that the WP decided were surplus and sold to Willis for conversion.

When one railroad uses cars belonging to another, a rental fee known as "per diem" is paid to the owner. The McCloud River Railroad had always paid per diem for cars outward bound from its line rather than owning any such cars. It had to pay this rental fee only for the time a car was actually on its trackage, and most of its lumber traffic wound up far from the origin. It did prefer to own the cars that stayed on line rather than leasing them through the per diem device. With rising per diem charges Flake Willis became interested in ownership by his company of some cars that would be used in interchange for lumber loading. Then, proposed Willis, the McCloud River Railroad would not have to pay high rent for each car while it was on the McCloud line, and would instead receive high rental fees for every day

Locomotive No. 7 and caboose No. 2 with a backup light nearly as big as the caboose. —D. S. RICHTER COLLECTION

the car was away from home. High per diem rates are an incentive to car building and ownership; low per diem charges have helped aggravate chronic car shortages that have plagued the industry. After extended consideration in 1952 and 1953, management decided the return on investment still would not make a car fleet worthwhile even at the new higher per diem charges. Instead, the company settled for a new bus and a radio communication system.

For years the railroad used hand-me-down cabooses, several of which were discards from the Great Northern. Banging around on the end of freight trains was hard on wooden cabin cars, boards and frame of which were typically vibrating out of synchronization before they made even their first run across the mountain. More durable steel cabooses were coveted, but the used steel caboose market was hardly as active as the worn-out wood caboose availability of earlier years. Shelling out $20,000 apiece for new steel doghouses was quite a step up from the previous provision for the train crews, but two such palaces were ordered.

The new steel cabooses led in turn to a much more important innovation. A vice president of International Car Company made delivery of the new vehicles in person and had lunch with Willis. Willis took the occasion to complain about the inadequacies of ordinary box cars for lumber loading and on a paper napkin sketched his idea for a superior type of car. The car builder representative was sufficiently interested and impressed with the practicality of Flake Willis' idea that designers were put to

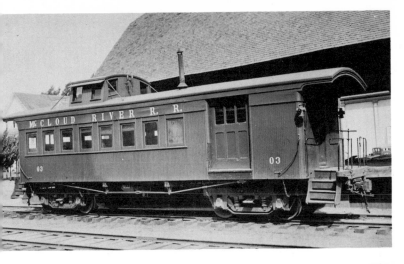

No. 03 was neither caboose nor coach, but a caboose-coach. The passenger car trucks provided a comfortable ride behind a freight drag. Note the whistles on the cupola for passing signals to the engine crew. —GUY L. DUNSCOMB (BELOW) Caboose No. 05 didn't have much capacity, but plenty of style. The four wheel trucks provided a rough and jerky ride behind a fast moving log train. —W. C. WHITTAKER

Caboose No. 027 shown above, came to the McCloud from the Great Northern. The airhorn on the cupola was used for the passing of signals. (RIGHT) This caboose with passenger and baggage compartment was built for service between McCloud and Mount Shasta. —BOTH W. C. WHITTAKER

International Car built several of these first class cabooses for the McCloud River Railroad. These shacks were more luxurious than found on a main line railroad. —ROBERT M. HANFT

The genius of Flake Willis, former president of the McCloud River Railroad is reflected in the all-door car, two of which are shown here at their home base in McCloud. With doors closed the lading is fully protected, as with a conventional box car. However, with an ordinary car loading into the ends is seldom possible except by slow and expensive hand stacking in the case of lumber in lengths longer than the car width. With an all-door car any section of the car may be fully opened to the side, for any section of the car sides will telescope another and get out of the way. A fork lift truck can deposit its burden directly on the car floor anywhere in the car. In the photograph on the left, the left half of the car has been loaded; the right half is ready for another load of fresh lumber. —BOTH ROBERT M. HANFT

work. The result was a prototype, followed by an order for 100 improved copies of an all-door car. The entire side of each car could be opened for easy loading and unloading. Each side is divided into four sections or panels, each of which will telescope with its neighbor. Substantial reduction in the labor required for handling the loads has resulted; as much as 90 percent in some circumstances. The higher cost of the car itself is compensated for by reduced labor in use. The new cars also require somewhat more maintenance than a conventional box car, with proper lubrication being a key to smooth functioning of the door mechanism. The McCloud car shops are the home maintenance base, a chore that does not call for as extensive an operation as did the servicing of log flats under the abuse of that lading.

The new all-door cars illustrate a problem and a solution. They obviously are highly desirable to lumber shippers because they provide the weather protection of a box car and the loading convenience of a flat car. If they are handled in conventional fashion, a railroad having one in its possession could turn it over to one of its own shippers rather than sending it back to the McCloud River Railroad. The using railroad would have to pay per diem, but this user charge is proportionately low for special equipment. The quite possible end result would be that the McCloud River Railroad would own 100 cars especially designed to give its own customers superior service, but which it would

never be able to provide because the cars never came home.

To avoid this dilemma U. S. Plywood is the actual owner of the cars. Because it is not a railroad it can control the use of its own property in a fashion that a railroad cannot. Anyone wishing to use a U. S. Plywood car must lease the privilege to do so by special contract. A car loaded at McCloud will be returned there because it is of no use to another railroad that happens to have it in its possession — except to provide transportation as purchased and directed by U. S. Plywood. In effect, then, the railroad has one of the most modern car fleets in existence — but only indirectly. It will also be interesting to see whether additional units will be purchased not only by U. S. Plywood, but also by other operators if receiving customers demand this extra convenience.

The actual inventory of rolling stock owned by the railroad is at its lowest ebb in years, consisting largely of seldom used maintenance cars. With rail logging discontinued, most of the log flats have departed the McCloud scene, leaving a forlorn few that might be used for miscellaneous movements, but aren't. Lumber shipments are the mainstay of traffic, but are made either in rented cars or the U. S. Plywood all-door vehicles. About the only two McCloud River Railroad cars to keep shiny wheels are the steel cabooses. Perhaps the next most important use is by the present passenger car fleet, but that is another part of this story.

Under a rolling cloud of oil smoke, No. 25 with an excursion train whistles for Hooper as it works the steep grade between McCloud and the summit at Pierce. —DONALD DUKE

6

PASSENGER SERVICE

PASSENGER transportation has never been a major source of revenue to the McCloud River Railroad. No more than three coaches have ever been on the roster at one time. Yet the limited passenger carrying activity of this railroad, while quite typical for many years of a line of its size serving no population centers, has enjoyed a revival hardly in keeping with general trends. The turn of events again shows the unique character of this company.

Although built for freight, primarily lumber, the railroad did carry people from the very beginning, with a passenger car included in the first batch of equipment along with locomotive No. 1. The reported revenue of $334 from passenger hauling in the first year compared with $13,500 from freight establishes a pattern that has prevailed most of the time since. Yet passenger service has added some money, and certainly a lot of color. There have been years, all too many, when it almost surely cost more to carry people than they paid for the privilege of riding. This less pleasant consideration was no particular problem in the early years, and now

people once again contribute something to net for their passage over the line.

Passenger carrying is a by-product of freight movement with rare exceptions, and the McCloud line fits the usual pattern. People movement has its own by-products in turn, for baggage, mail and express carrying usually go along with the passenger train even though including these aspects with passengers has been more of a custom than a necessity. Perhaps McCloud practice could be regarded as something of a compromise. The head end traffic moved in passenger equipment along with the people—even to the extent of sharing the same combination coach — but, more often than not, the passenger train consisted of the multi-purpose coach tied to the rear of a string of freight cars, the ultimate in diversity of lading.

Wells Fargo Express found its way to Mc-Cloud in the first year with A. L. Sobey as the McCloud agent, and in the first complete annual report to mid-1899 the movement of some 400 express units was included. That is, $79.88 was received for express, and the rate was 21.5

cents per unit. Just what a unit consisted of isn't detailed. The arithmetic doesn't come out quite even, either. At least the express revenue went a good way toward meeting the annual expense of $113.60 required to service the passenger car. Even at 1898 prices one might wonder how much 30 cents a day could buy in terms of keeping the little combine neat and clean, let alone greased and painted. The first addition to the fleet of one came along in 1898, as part of a contract for 40 freight cars and one coach awarded to John Hammond and Company of San Francisco.

The first account of a special passenger train appears in 1900. On September 22 the trainmen held a grand ball in the company dining room at McCloud and specials ran from both Upton and Ash Creek. The railroad contributed to the spirit of the festivities by donating free passage to all those who held tickets to the ball. The whole affair was regarded as a great success, save for a number of would-be participants who expected the Upton train to come into Sisson for passengers as the Sisson paper had promised. It didn't show up.

By 1901 the 2,000 passenger per year mark was exceeded, with almost that many dollars of revenue and with a double daily passenger train running between Upton and McCloud during the summer. Continuing expansion saw the $3,000 mark exceeded by 1903, and $4,000 in 1904, with more than $500 coming in from baggage and "miscellaneous," which may very well have meant express. The company by then received 28.5 cents per 100 pounds of express carried.

When President Queal's private chariot came to Mc-Cloud added to the regular combination coach consist the result was an exceedingly handsome passenger train. Pride in maintenance is evident in these fore and aft photographs of the two-car train. That the rear car was ever available to ordinary fare-paying mortals is highly doubtful. Car No. 100 was not ordinarily kept on its home rails, and when Queal passed away his car no longer visited McCloud. The wooden body and truss rod suspension would soon have limited its ability to roam in any event as steel cars came into general use. — BOTH CHARLES M. HAINES COLLECTION

Locomotive No. 8 and coach No. 1 make a Fourth of July picnic special in the wood-burning days. Shuttle service from McCloud to a picnic site in the woods was a common practice on holidays in simpler times. —CHARLES M. HAINES COLLECTION

The first "homemade" coach for revenue passenger service went into service in 1905 on the line east of McCloud.

With extension of the line, by 1907 more than 9,000 train miles were operated in passenger service, plus another 36,000 of mixed trains, to bring in $13,273.75 from 15,319 passengers, who paid an average 4.6 cents per mile. The company now had a mail contract, for which it received $1,593.45. Wells Fargo added $763.80, and extra baggage $68.15. Even with all this surge of traffic the equipment was not exactly overloaded, for the average number of passengers on board at one time was only six. This year also saw the first coach retired from service. Unfortunately no details of the circumstances appear, nor do the numbers assigned to early coaches or other cars. Mountain railroad-

ing was hard on all equipment — especially if it parted company with the rail after going on unscheduled romps down the hill.

Identification of the typical McCloud railroad passenger at this stage of development is not difficult. He was an employee, would-be employee or ex-employee of the lumber company. Lumberjacks were notoriously unstable in their job relationships and few spent their entire careers in the woods. Mill people were more apt to remain on the job, but virtually all men of either category came to McCloud in a combination coach across the switchbacks. Most left the same way. The railroad was also the ordinary means for those who remained to sample the metropolitan delights beyond those afforded by McCloud. Going on to San Francisco might be a rare and important event for a mill family, but even Sisson had an extensive red light district to entice loggers who tired of Red Cloud and felt the pressure to dispose of any residue from pay day after the account with the company store was settled. For lesser celebrating, rails provided the access between the lumber camps and McCloud. We may suspect that a substantial part of this latter traffic never appeared in the record, with rides bummed on the logging train, or miles trudged slowly by foot. Train crews did not argue with lumberjacks about the niceties of fares on log trains, for these people were reputed to be more than ordinarily persuasive in debate.

Apart from the comings and goings of the people who made their living from the activities centered in McCloud, lesser movements were those who would continue their journey through the wilderness beyond railhead. The railroad provided a link in the best route to the Pit and Fall River valleys, a region sufficiently developed to have a stage service before the coming of the railroad. As the railroad extended eastward, horse drawn stages continued to meet trains for through travellers. As already pointed out, passengers could venture to southeastern Oregon via McCloud and some must have. The number could hardly have been impressive to rail management, who left the dreaming about increased development in that direction up to the editors.

A third type of passenger, least of all in number but possibly more courted by management was the wealthy estate owner. Best known of this group was the flamboyant William Randolph Hearst.

Long before the coming of the white man the lower McCloud was a favored retreat for the Indian, who probably had his own appreciation of the beauty of the forest and the tumbling river, as well as for the bounty both contained. Here was a region to escape both the blistering sun of the lower valley and the penetrating chill of higher altitudes.

When the Southern Pacific followed the Sacramento River into Strawberry Valley a few San Franciscans with means discovered what Justin Sisson and the Indians had known all along about the virtues of the lower McCloud and decided to capture it for themselves. Even more important than the dollars needed to wrest the property from its natural owners was the possession of leisure time to enjoy a mountain hideaway. The Indians' favorite site at Ah-di-nah was picked up, as were other attractive locations along the river. Today Ah-di-nah has once again reverted to public use, but other estates remain in private hands.

McCloud is the nearest rail point to the McCloud River estates. The rail journey and the wagon road or trail beyond was easy enough to make the area attractive, yet difficult enough to add a flavor of remoteness more genuine than possessed by the spas closer to the city. The close-in retreats were left to the larger numbers of the less exclusive.

An attorney, Charles Stetson Wheeler, bought Sisson's modest resort at the big bend of the

The daily passenger was the pride of the McCloud River Railroad and conductor Haines. In addition to passengers, the combination coach carried mail, perishable foods, express and the company payroll. The only hold-ups were of later day excursionists and were just for fun. In this view the train rests between runs at the McCloud depot. —CHARLES M. HAINES COLLECTION

McCloud, some seven miles south of town, and built his own hideaway there. Among his guests who became enamoured with the region was Phoebe Apperson Hearst, who asked Wheeler to sell part of his land. The attorney was reluctant to do so, but finally agreed to lease some of his property to Mrs. Hearst, who proceeded to build a castle thereon in 1903. Her famous son, William Randolph Hearst, shared her fondness for the property as well, and later built a Bavarian Village that remains in the family along with the balance of the Wheeler estate, which he purchased. Hearst's proclivity for building lavishly and incorporating European art and features is best exemplified in his tremendous castle at San Simeon. San Simeon was his favorite, and its public availability makes it better known today, but he did use the McCloud property extensively as well. This northern estate is called *Wyntoon* for its original owners, the local Indian tribe. A little extra glamor is added even in the name, for the earliest reference to the natives that came to attention of this writer refers to them as Wintu. Wintun, Wintoon, and *Wyntoon* follow.

Hearst was acquainted with most of the great Americans of his day and brought numbers of them to *Wyntoon*. The thought of some of the nation's wealthiest and most famous people cozily sharing the combine with more homespun talent returning from a rip-roaring drunk is intriguing. It probably never happened that way, however. More to the point is the appearance in the old records of rental fees paid by the railroad to the Pullman Company for the use of its sleeping cars. Three dollars was the rate for a standard car for a day, one dollar for tourist. The 18 mile trip from Sisson to McCloud hardly warranted a sleeper in its own right; rental reports almost surely represent the comings and going of Personages. Not only special cars, but even exclusive special trains were run in this service. The first so reported was in 1905, chartered by Phoebe Hearst.

Hobnobbing may well have been part of the motive for President Queal's purchase of the deluxe No. 100 in 1907 in addition to his desire for a bit more luxury than offered by the combine, even the *new* combine added along with the No. 100. The new private car was often used by the Hearst family and guests. Perhaps the

The Hearst castle at Wyntoon was built by Phoebe Apperson Hearst in 1903 and destroyed by fire in 1930. Attorney Charles Stetson Wheeler built a country retreat overhanging the big bend of the McCloud River. It was acquired by William Randolph Hearst and stands today just above the upper end of McCloud Reservoir, but is inaccessible to visitors. —BOTH CHARLES M. HAINES COLLECTION

most famous guest to visit *Wyntoon* was Herbert Hoover, who later became President. His trips there were not publicized and details are lost. At least there is the chance that the little railroad included a President of the nation on its list of riders, even if not one in office at the time.

Queal's car No. 100 was wooden, which restricted its use in later years, and perhaps led to its demise not too long after his own and its disposal to the SP, where it had spent most of the time anyway.

With the general decline of passenger patronage as detailed later, Hearst turned away from the railroad along with the rest of the public. He had long since discovered the automobile, but used instead a new toy as a substitute for the rails in long distance travel. He was an early air traveller, and had his personal liner almost as soon as did the budding air lines. Instead of the McCloud depot, the Wyntoon terminal became Mount Shasta airport.

Even if the Hearst family did not participate directly, a certain amount of contrast both in equipment and riders was evidenced between the nifty little train serving McCloud and Sisson and the snoose-stained vehicle that followed log flats to and from the cutting frontier. Yet this less glamorous run was to far outlive the conventional passenger train.

The first people to ride special trains were typically residents of the area, either workers or their local families and friends enjoying a gala occasion, and in lesser numbers the estate owners and their guests. A 1905 special train evidently was the first of many that catered specifically to outsiders. On June 20 ten Pullman cars carrying some 200 members of the Nebraska Lumber Dealers Association arrived at Upton and were given a treat. Their sleepers were parked on a siding and the lumber people changed to five open cars fixed up with seats and plenty of Mt. Shasta air and sunshine. After being treated to the magnificent scenery across the mountain the visitors were fed at McCloud, then continued to the end of the railroad beyond Bartle to the model logging camp identified as Camp One. They witnessed actual felling, trimming, wheel carrying and car loading. At 8:35 p.m., which would be just about nightfall at that time of year, the visitors returned to

Upton and their more conventional train.

The trip was reported as greatly enjoyed by the visitors. When one considers the contrast between the great forest backed by the enormous glistening white cone and the treeless and endless plains of Nebraska the visitors could have been considerably awed. The natural air conditioning of the train must have been a welcome contrast to the blistering heat of home as well. Of course the visitors had also been exposed to certain other charms of the West, for they had attended a convention in Portland. One could expect these people did remember the trip on the McCloud River Railroad for the rest of their lives, regardless of what happened before or after it.

A solid precedent was established by this group, as thousands since have found their way to the slopes of Shasta to take a very special train ride. Even though most of those who followed did not visit a logging camp as well, especially one that used the house-high wheels to move the forest giants to railside, greatly enjoyed is the typical reaction and somewhat of an understatement. Open cars remain popular, too.

Evidently two years were to pass before another special train ran for a large group of outsiders, but 1906 specials included a Fourth of July train as part of the celebration. This one ran to Slagger Creek, where picnic grounds had been prepared for the occasion, even though the railroad hadn't quite reached there. Tracklaying crews did their best to remedy the problem, working all night of the third and right up to the arrival of the special train, but were still about a quarter mile short of the objective. Teams were hastily hitched up and manager Johnson had his automobile at trackside. No women or children were forced to walk. Fourth of July trains were part of a McCloud tradition for many years, until, as manager Johnson had done in 1906, people drove their own automobiles. Eventually community picnics largely vanished from the scene.

Some of the picnickers had hardly recovered from this revelry when the new opera house in McCloud was dedicated a week later. Once again the special train from Sisson (Longspur) left many of its intended riders behind because of a misunderstanding, but on this occasion it

The mixed train on Big Canyon fill is headed by No. 9. A locomotive on each end of the train pointed in opposite directions made the switchbacks somewhat less upsetting to purist notions that engines should head trains. —CHARLES M. HAINES COLLECTION

returned for another trip. Those who got a late start in the festivities because of this delay may not have felt too slighted, for the grand ball that climaxed the occasion continued all night and the return trip did not require lights for the sun was well up in the sky at the 5:30 a.m. departure time. Evidently not all the rugged people of the time came from McCloud itself.

Although the eventual winner in the race for the affection of the traveller was already chugging its uncertain way along the dusty, muddy or snow-rutted trail that passed for a highway 60 years ago, the growing passenger statistics gave little hint of the threat in the early years. Almost 21,000 passengers rode in the year reported July 1, 1909, which required 51,841 car miles, not counting 236 by sleeper. A year later the rider count neared 25,000.

That the ICC noticed the reports was evidenced by correspondence following the 1910 version. It asked the company to: "Kindly advise conditions under which mixed train miles can exceed mixed locomotive miles." The railroad had reported 19,816 miles by mixed train, but only 19,710 mixed train engine miles. Unfortunately the reply is lost, for it would be interesting to know if the 106 mile discrepancy represented crews letting the coach coast down the hill by itself, or runaways after it parted company with the engine.

The half-million passenger mile mark was exceeded in 1913, with more than 28,000 riders. About 26,000 passenger train miles were run, and 17,000 in mixed service. A combination car was added to the fleet, for a total of three such vehicles in addition to the official

car. Special train mileage was only 165, which included the "biggest passenger train that had ever pulled into McCloud." A group of teachers visited McCloud by rail in late September, this time using six Pullman cars right into Mc-Cloud. The visitors toured the mill and inspected the Italian settlements with considerable interest, for the Italian mill workers retained much of their old country culture. Other visitors drove out to the river, using rides furnished by the town automobile owners, of which there were more each year.

The year 1914 saw a modest downturn in passengers, although more than 27,000 rode, with the half-million passenger mile figure still exceeded. The following year riders slumped to 21,380, with $20,763.98 of passenger train revenue and 436,308 passenger miles of service.

The most readily apparent reason for decline in passenger figures is evidenced by the 1916 ad: "Automobile Stage — Sisson and McCloud. Leaves Sisson every day at 12 o'clock noon and leaves McCloud at 1:30 p.m." The railroad had finished off horse-drawn stage service, but competition was back again with gasoline-fed horses under the hood. At this time few were paying much attention to the real winner in the battle for riders.

Tom Davis' jitney that promised "equal treatment to all" and "special trips to all parts of the county" was not unnoticed by railroad management. Whether "equal treatment" was a back-handed slap at the railroad for carrying a favored few in the private car, or an excuse for the rigors of the highway trip isn't made clear. In any event, railroad reaction was the all too sadly typical one used in the face of business declines: cut costs. The first move was to change the schedule so that the passenger train would no longer tie up in Sisson overnight, but use the McCloud facilities instead. Engineer Caswell and conductor Miller moved their families to McCloud. The basic pattern of two round trips between McCloud and Sisson was continued. Timetables available show one and sometimes two scheduled trips east of McCloud during this era. The new schedule did bring one convenience and a low fare to match. McCloud children could ride the train to attend high school in Sisson and buy a 50 ride ticket for $12.50.

The spring of 1917 saw Tom Davis cranking up his jitney three times daily each way. In November the railroad shifted its schedule once again. This time the change was that service east of McCloud would not be by a separate train, but handled by the Sisson train through to Bartle and return.

The 1913 total of 28,311 riders was the all-time high, but with increasing activity east of McCloud and the post World War I surge of business the number of riders in 1920 again exceeded 25,000, and the passenger mile total was 607,070, highest ever because of longer rides. Even the traffic to the Mt. Shasta Power Corporation railroad in 1921 did not yield a total of 15,000 riders. Although business did pick up again after the 1921 slump, never again were 25,000 passengers carried and 500,000 passenger miles of service was provided in only one subsequent year, 1923.

The question of regular passenger operation over the PG&E (Mt. Shasta Power Co.) line operated by the McCloud River Railroad was seriously considered and negotiations between owner and operator were held. No regular service was ever established. Special passenger runs were made on a few occasions, however. In June of 1922 the McCloud baseball team chartered a Sunday special to Pit powerhouse No. 1. A press special for reporters to cover the PG&E power projects came in by rail, and the Masons had a trip to Burney using the railroad. Old-timers still recall the Masonic visit as pretty expensive. The extent of the expenses have not been detailed, but Masons are not noted for skimping on excursions.

The Davis jitney continued to siphon business away from the train, and on April 18, 1927, the railroad made its next countermove, by eliminating one of the two daily round trips between Mt. Shasta City and McCloud and substituting instead two automobile trips of its own to carry the mail and any passengers who might be enticed away from the Davis' bus. By this time that bus was being run, often both literally and managerially, by Mrs. Myrtle Davis, and was no longer launched from Kuck's Saloon. Ironically enough, when the Davis jitney started, the railroad had little choice but to watch it undermine train traffic. However, as soon as the railroad gave up the battle and put in its own highway substitute for the train it could no longer afford, Mrs. Davis promptly filed a complaint that her new competition was illegal, should be restrained and the officers guilty of the offense punished.

She had the law on her side and the McCloud management was aware that it had acted a bit prematurely in inaugurating highway service without the blessing of the regulatory authorities. The easiest way out of the dilemma was to buy out Mrs. Davis. Her price was $4,000, which appears modest enough under the circumstances, and by January 2, 1928, the State gave its formal permission and the railroad was legally in business by highway. Since that time, the railroad has operated both freight and passenger motor vehicle service directly and through several subsidiaries. This report will not include these corporate meanderings. At present the railroad no longer has any off-rail service, and there is no common-carrier passenger or express traffic provided by anyone.

The Davis family had not yet finished working on the railroad. Mrs. Davis started a line between Dunsmuir and Weed, through Mt. Shasta City, after withdrawing from McCloud, and apparently found time to figure out a plan to get more money from her previous experience. She brought suit for $35,000 damages against the railroad for its illegal competition to her.

Despite the high costs of dealing with Mrs. Davis, the company liked the comparative expense of running buses with those of steam trains well enough so that on October 31, 1929, it discontinued passenger train operation west of McCloud. Two more buses were added to

This bus was the McCloud River Railroad's substitute for train service. It is hard to believe anyone would prefer this monstrosity, even with its festive bunting for a local parade, to No. 12 and a comfortable railroad coach. That the bus was cheaper appears reasonably obvious. —T. E. GLOVER

the original fleet of one. More than 30 years of faithful service between the only communities of importance on the line and the rail link for McCloud people to the rest of the world meant so little that it was severed without even being mentioned in the local press. Evidently few cared, no tears were shed and there was little fanfare over the passing. Nobody even bothered to change the notices that appeared in the *Official Railway Guide,* which continued to claim a steam train operated when in fact it had long since ceased. Actually, the ending of service was a rather conditional thing. Because of the possibility of heavy snow a rail run might be substituted when the bus could not make it through, and the train evidently was pressed back into service a few times. Highway snow removal equipment became more effective and no more need for train substitution materialized, with the result that the last scheduled Mt. Shasta City-McCloud run by train is not even specifically identified. It probably came during the 1952 storms. Passenger service just fizzled out.

The bus was more satisfactory from a cost standpoint, but was hardly an attraction to additional traffic. It carried 2,353 passengers in 1929, and had deteriorated to fewer than 500 in five years. Depression had intervened, but far more travellers were able to afford an automobile than settled for bus tickets.

Passengers continued to ride east of McCloud, but this service also died out eventually and with vague records of its passing. The coach continued to bounce along behind log flats daily except Sunday, with advertized service actually extended beyond Bartle to Hambone. Before the end of the decade of the 1930's

McCloud River Railroad Company
McCloud & Mount Shasta
Daily Train and Bus Service
TIME TABLE
Effective May 6, 1928

Read Down				Read Up		
6 BUS	**4** TRAIN	**2** BUS		**1** BUS	**3** TRAIN	**5** BUS
P. M.	P. M.	A. M.		A. M.	P. M.	P. M.
5.20★	1.20	7.00★	Mount Shasta	6.35	12.45	4.50
6.10	2.15	7.50	McCloud	5.45	11.50	4.00
P. M.	P. M.	A. M.		A. M.	A. M.	P. M.

Busses Leave from Railroad Depots
Tickets Will Be Honored On Trains or Busses.
Train Service Will Be Substituted for Bus Service When Roads Are Impassable.
Checked Baggage Will Be Handled On Trains. Hand Baggage Will Be Allowed On Busses.
★Bus Will Wait One Hour If Southern Pacific Trains 12 or 13 Are Late.

A choice of a train or bus ride is offered by the timetable above issued May 6, 1928. —MCCLOUD RIVER RAILROAD (BELOW) Excursion train leaves Mount Shasta for McCloud. The Southern Pacific station may be seen in the background and parked alongside was the latest vintage McCloud River Railroad stage. —STAN KISTLER

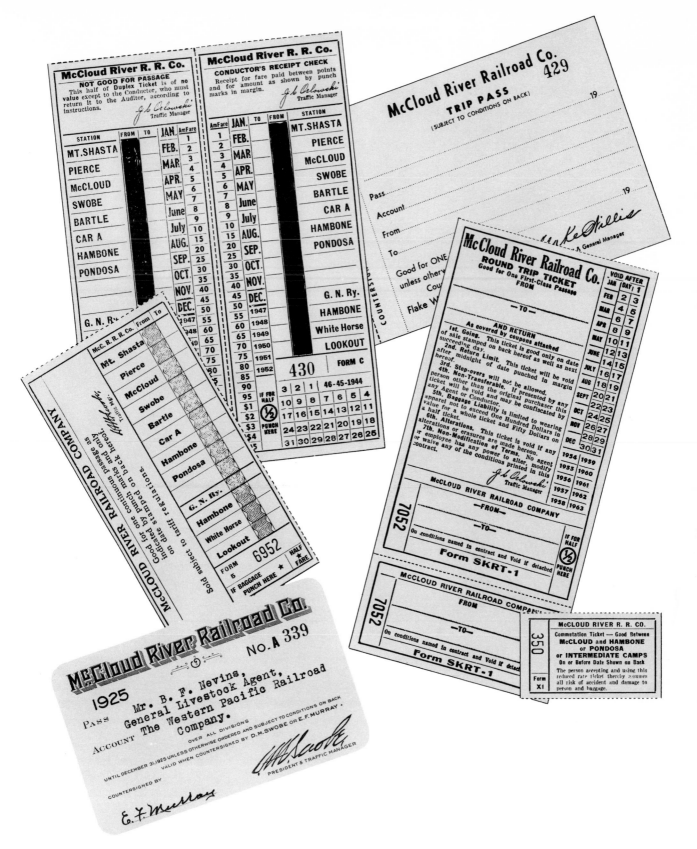

During a lifetime of passenger service, the McCloud River Railroad published all types of forms. The samples shown above are a perfect example of these issues. At the top a conductors receipt check, a trip pass issued to employees for a single ride, a regular round trip ticket, a commutation stub ticket to logging camps, an annual pass, and a one way ticket. —MCCLOUD RIVER RAILROAD

This homemade contraption called the *Vinegar Valley Express* hauled loggers between the base camp and the woods. Perhaps inspired by early vintage streamliners, it was neither speedy nor comfortable. The hulk still rests in the woods east of McCloud with a tree growing through its interior. —CHARLES M. HAINES COLLECTION

irregular service was the extent of passenger claims. The pattern was clear: woods employees could ride the train from McCloud out to the job, and fair numbers of them continued to do so, but this patronage gradually declined also. When the coaches wore out (the first was retired in 1936; the two remaining were reclassified in 1939) and their carrying capacity was no longer needed, passengers shared the ordinary cabooses with the crews. The same disease that brought down the Mt. Shasta City passenger train vanquished the east end passenger business as well. Loggers, too, preferred to drive their own cars.

There was no formal finish to east side service. According to the employee instructions still in effect: "Passengers will be carried in cabooses of freight trains east of McCloud, except to Pondosa and Burney." Few avail themselves of the service. In 1930, 1,738 revenue passengers rode; in 1933 the figure was still more than a thousand (1,195), double that for the bus. By 1940 traffic was down to 332 riders, who paid $228 for the privilege. A decade later the number was actually up to 625 (it had been substantially higher during the war years), but none are reported after 1955.

The lumber company also operated its own passenger trains independently of the railroad, in addition to purchasing employee and even commuter tickets for the passage of its employees over the railroad proper. The lumber company policy of modern permanent camps in contrast with the more portable or disposable temporary camp villages of earlier times dictated longer average distances to sides or working sites in the woods. Until good roads were provided work access was a rail function. There is no record of the lumber company operating passenger trains as such to the woods, but the regular woods log train often was timed to provide a dual function.

Because coordinating the schedule to haul both logs and loggers could be a nuisance to both passengers and logging operations, the fairly typical practice of using light rail-motor cars was used extensively: this use was a natural outgrowth of the development of a reliable gasoline powered small rail vehicle. The contraptions that evolved in wide variety were apt to resemble expanded and more sheltered section maintenance type cars.

With their customary flair for the unique, the McCloud mechanical geniuses came up with a logger coach for commuter service over lumber company rails that certainly had no precise counterpart. Working in the company shops, the builders started with a solid and ample bed that they may have filched from some existing truck or other vehicle, mounted it over suitable lightweight wheels and axles, and hooked up a standard Caterpillar tractor engine in the front end with direct drive. They covered the whole thing with a welded steel shell shaped in the best streamline tradition of the times, adding a row of what appear to be large paint can lids to the exterior for purely decorative effect.

Despite the sharp appearance when new and neatly painted, this vehicle came closer to the steerage passage of immigration legend than to bankers special rail commutation. Inside, seating was simply row on row of rather narrow planks, closely spaced, nailed to supports. The rig must have had a capacity close to 150. No divider separated riders from the works. Windows were small and few. When fumes from machinery and passengers blended after a hard day's work, the combination could have been remarkable, especially if certain rumors about national dietary habits were correct. Adding to the problem, the car, despite its modern appearance, couldn't get up enough speed to generate much of a breeze, even though generous clearances had been left in the floor around the engine that could provide for entry of fresh air.

Long disused, the relic of the streamliner, also known as the *Vinegar Valley Express*, still stands in the woods, virtually the sole remnant of the last permanent camp named Kinyon, about 15 miles east of McCloud. Its access rail is gone and the cold winter winds and hot summer sun have warped and twisted the steel body, but the engine is still in it, and it appears sufficiently durable to last a good many years yet if scrappers do not get it before rust makes its final claim.

In the depths of the depression, President Swobe made one effort to revive passenger service briefly in the form of ski specials. Highway and railroad are quite close together at the top of the climb between Mt. Shasta City and McCloud, and a ski slope known appropriately enough as Snowman's Hill was developed there.

On January 23 and 24, 1932, a meet of sufficient importance to draw visitors from far and wide was scheduled, and the railroad decided to participate by running special trains up from Mt. Shasta City and McCloud. The theme of not having to drive on the mountain, plus having a warm ski hut (the coach) to retire to between events, was advertised. The local newspaper wrote favorably of the opportunity to see superb winter scenery from the train as well, and characterized the train ride as a feature of the event. The one dollar round trip fare seemed reasonable enough, and hundreds of riders were hoped for. Some 1,500 people showed up at Snowman's Hill, but very few got there by rail. They were not to be given another opportunity.

Another breed of passenger did begin to show up and in increasing numbers after World War II. Railfans heard about the spectacular scenery and the trim little railroad with its well kept motive power and wanted to see it. Better still, to ride it, and a friendly management made riding possible. At first, a few extra cabooses were enough to accommodate groups, but a 1950 special required a full-fledged passenger train, using streamlined coaches operating through from the San Francisco area.

The influx of outsiders interested in seeing and riding the railroad reached a climax in 1955 with the opening of the Burney line. On July 3, three special trains ran to Burney, one originating at McCloud, one at Dunsmuir, and the third, sponsored by railroad enthusiasts, came from San Francisco.

Although driving a gold spike at Burney marked a high point in interest, decline thereafter in railfan patronage was severe for another reason. The Burney trip was the last use of a steam locomotive, and rail enthusiasts

The motor car also brought flexibility to the McCloud River Railroad. At first such vehicles had only railroad wheels, then combination steel wheels and rubber tires for better traction and comfort were used. In the view above, motor No. 100 was photographed grinding up from McCloud toward the switchback at Signal Butte. This station wagon type motor was a Ford *Model A* equipped with a large pair of rear drive wheels as shown at the right. At times a trailer was attached behind in order to handle the extra load. —BOTH CHARLES M. HAINES COLLECTION (LOWER-RIGHT) A later version of a rail-going station wagon was this 1941 vintage Ford. —T. E. GLOVER

Modern *Hy-railer* pick-up truck is capable of either highway or rail operation by raising or lowering a small set of flanged guide wheels, front and rear. The bulk of the vehicle weight is carried on ordinary highway tires. The 1968 photograph on the left was made on the turntable at Signal Butte, used only to turn these vehicles. —ROBERT M. HANFT

Few pieces of railroad equipment carried a McCloud River Lumber Co. identification, but railbus No. 50 was one of them. A four-wheeled caboose of the design shown here behind No. 50 is still in existence, off rail at Pondosa. It retains its wheels, which were mounted directly to the frame. No. 50 also shows evidence of homespun talent in the modification of a standard truck chassis. —CHARLES M. HAINES COLLECTION

Locomotive No. 25 smokes her way across Lake Britton bridge for the benefit of railroad photographers standing on the bank. This special train is the famous *McCloud River Rattler* of June 22, 1963. —KARL KOENIG

chased off in other directions to pursue remnants of the dying breed while they were still available.

As already pointed out, Prairie type No. 25 was quietly tucked away in the McCloud engine shed and little attention was paid to it as the years passed and bearings stiffened. For more than seven years it was idle, but observant railfans remembered. With steam railroading now extinct virtually everywhere, President Willis was asked to reactivate No. 25. It would be expensive, but excursionists were willing to meet the costs. In 1963 the old-timer was dragged out of retirement with a certain amount of complaint from long idle parts and readied for service once again. The passenger special, with more cars than one locomotive could handle, even though they were modern lightweight equipment, called for extra power, which was forthcoming from the nearby Yreka Western. The Yreka Western also had a steam locomotive, even though it did not have as much scenic trackage over which to run it. The Yreka Western No. 19 was certainly right at home lifting excursionists up the grade, for it had spent most of its working career on the McCloud River Railroad. About all that had changed since was the lettering; even the number was the same. It hadn't ever before moved so many people all at once, however.

In June, No. 25 starred again, this time as a solo performer. It made a round trip from McCloud to Burney with passengers, but without a passenger train. The consist included a tank car, a Great Northern box car, two logging flat cars, two additional flat cars rigged up with guard rails and benches, and a caboose. The idea was to simulate a freight train, even to the point of naming the excursion the *McCloud River Rattler*. Not as widely advertised as the earlier double-header, the freight provided photo opportunities for a steam run along the trackage that had been largely the domain of the diesel since it was built.

On this occasion the weather provided less than perfect cooperation. A rain and sleet storm met the unsheltered riders south of Bartle. There was no vestibule between caboose and open cars, and not enough room in the caboose for all the riders if they could get there anyway. Engineer Ray Piltz was working the No. 25 pretty hard trying to get somewhere fast when the rear end crew decided to do something before the passengers froze, drowned or both. Superintendent Sid Muma let a little air out of the train line, partially setting the brakes. Engineer Piltz put on more steam; more air was released, the engine labored mightily until awareness came. Everyone dashed for the box car when the train stopped, but the door was man high above the ground. Ray Piltz answered the call above and beyond duty by making himself into a human ladder, with cupped hands and sturdy shoulder for rungs, but fortunately only a few of the heaviest and least agile of the passengers had taken advantage of him when someone came forward from the caboose with a more suitably designed boarding device. Sheltered and under way again, many of the riders thus probably got their only hobo-eye view of this or any other railroad from the interior of an empty box car. A few minutes later the train stopped again, and camera buffs were able to photograph a snow scene with a freight train, even though it was late June. The ground was covered with several inches of glistening hail, a very realistic substitute for the more wintery stuff so common to the area. The balance of the trip was somewhat more conventional.

With people obviously attracted to the delights of steam railroading with the No. 25, not to mention the scenery of the Shasta wonderland area, President Willis decided to augment the two-flat passenger fleet with the purchase of some more weatherproof equipment. The Southern Pacific was parting with surplus elderly commuter coaches, two of which were purchased for a modest price and routed to McCloud. There they were painted a gay orange and fancily lettered in a style combination they certainly had never known in the sedate fashion of commutation. Now the McCloud River had a four-car passenger fleet, five if you included the spare caboose. A third commuter coach was purchased primarily to provide spare seats. It was not refurbished. The railroad was ready to lease a train to all comers who had the cash, preferably in advance.

In a way the railroad was thus back in the passenger business, but not on the old basis of running trains whether enough riders showed up or not, particularly the latter. A trip or two

Excursions with McCloud steam locomotive No. 25 are fun in the winter, too. In this scene, a special excursion of the Pacific Locomotive Assn. lives up to its designation as a "snow train" as it leaves McCloud for the woods at Pondosa. Orange coaches, green trees and white snow provide colorful contrast. (BELOW) Big flakes of falling snow add white spots to the photograph as the special makes a stop at Bartle for water. A small bucker-flanger plow has been added ahead of the locomotive to clear the track. — BOTH ROBERT M. HANFT

or several were being run every year, including some as local goodwill gestures, others for highly interested U. S. Plywood executives, and one or two for visitors belonging to the Young President's League, of which Willis was a member.

In 1964 Robert Classen decided to try a new sort of venture. He advertised the "Mt. Shasta Alpine Scenic Railroad" to the public, chartered the train to make three round trips a day between Mt. Shasta City and the summit, and waited for riders to show up on the dates advertised, particularly the Fourth of July weekend. Classen lacked the base that trip-charterers selling tickets in advance to people with known interest from the metropolitan centers had enjoyed. His effort was not a success.

Certain steam railroad passenger runs have been successfully revived at several locations around the nation, ranging from the heavily patronized line built new at Disneyland to the Durango-Silverton narrow gauge trip in Colorado that continues passenger service dating back to the 1880's, but which had slipped to one car twice a week before the tourists discovered it and spread the word far and wide.

The McCloud line offers scenery better than most of the presently successful passenger carrying railroads. It is farther than most from major metropolitan areas, but hardly as far as

Another variety of excursion followed the restoration of the 2-6-2 to serviceable condition in 1963. The McCloud River Railroad had no passenger cars of its own but ran trips on occasion for small groups without resorting to interline trains. First such passenger train was the *McCloud River Rattler*. The scene above shows the logging train excursion. Riders had a choice of the empty gondola or one of the cabooses. —CHARLES M. HAINES COLLECTION (BELOW) Brightly repainted former Southern Pacific commuter coaches today carry the riders. —ROBERT M. HANFT

Durango, Colorado, and is right on a heavily travelled tourist highway, Interstate 5, between California and the Pacific Northwest. Another young man dreamed of success where Robert Classen had failed.

Richard Lohse is the son of a Southern Pacific switchman so grew up with a railroad background. At an early age he became infected with the strange — but more widespread than recognized by those who do not catch it — virus of affection for steam locomotives. Young Lohse was just in time to witness the close of the steam era with full awareness of what it was like but subject to intense dissatisfaction and frustration over being closed out from further pursuit of his hobby.

He accumulated a college degree, a wife and a job as an electronics engineer at the Lawrence Radiation Laboratory, but determined to do something about his hobby gap. Perhaps to his own surprise he discovered others had a similar interest to the point of being willing to participate. He also heard about the McCloud River Railroad and went there to see one of the big excursions. Later he observed what Classen was doing. Lohse's desire was to get a locomotive that would be his own personal property and pay a railroad for storage privilege and for running it occasionally. With his kindred spirits available to share some of the expense, and President Willis ready to consider the McCloud River Railroad as the site of operations, Lohse decided to proceed. He found a locomotive available in the form of Santa Maria Valley No. 21, a 2-8-2 that appeared to be operable. The group purchased it and shipped it to McCloud, where they proceeded to learn some of the economic facts of life about railroading, in particular that railroads are exceedingly expensive to operate. The No. 21 was not ready to run again with a few minor touch-ups; it would cost a fortune to get it in shape to pass the ever vigilant safety inspectors. Even if they did fix it up, operations never would be something they really could afford.

There was another steam locomotive only a few feet away from their own in McCloud. It wasn't for sale at a price the group could consider, but it was available on lease; complete with cars and crew. Even lease terms were and are stiff for individuals, but the Lohse

group decided to share their kicks with the public. They were well aware of what happened to Classen, but decided to take the gamble, with a larger budget for advertising, and a more extensive schedule that they would adhere to.

Thus it was that the Shasta Huffen Puff came into existence. Lohse and 15 other stockholders are the Shasta-McCloud Steam Rail Tours, Inc. Their product, the Huffen Puff, was advertised for a few runs in late summer of 1967, then for every weekend in the summer of 1968. The tour group employed an advertising agency, which came up with the Shasta Huffen Puff name as one that would have public appeal.

Rail buffs were not particularly enamoured over the name *Shasta Huffen-Puff* for a steam run, but the title was suggested by an advertising agency as having widespread public appeal. Excursion operator Lohse attracted enough riders to run trains each year from 1967 through 1970 and his supporters hope for continued operation with the overhaul of No. 25. (BELOW) During the first summer of the *Shasta Huffen-Puff*, No. 25 was photographed as she worked steam between Mount Shasta and McCloud. — ROBERT M. HANFT

News and advertising coverage were obtained, including a color-illustrated feature in a Sacramento newspaper. Billboards were set up to attract tourists approaching Mt. Shasta City.

The Huffen Puff runs are two round trips across the mountain from McCloud to Mt. Shasta City each operating day. The railroad furnishes regular crews but Shasta-McCloud stockholders are along as a public relations crew and for their joy in steam railroading. They also staff the ticket window and the refreshment stand.

At the close of the 1968 season a look at the books tallied up more than 3,000 passengers carried, which meant they were a long way from running their train for their personal entertainment alone. At the same time the 3,000 fares failed to meet expenses by a fairly substantial amount. The shareholders decided to try another summer of scheduled operations and then to consider their position for the future once again.

Tiring of waiting until summer arrived they trouped back to McCloud for a winter weekend in January. Advertised as a snow special open to the public they were successful in attracting both riders and snow. No. 25 has been fitted with a special connection to provide steam heat to the coaches, and a ride between snow banks has its special appeal.

The real test came during the summer season, but results were not completely conclusive. Expenses were reduced with elimination of some of the less profitable schedules with ridership increased for each train that did run, so that losses for the season were reduced. The operators depended more on advertising from previous riders by word of mouth and less on commercial solicitation. They announced their intention to continue in 1971 and started out with another winter weekend in February, but faced an additional financial hazard in that the railroad will charge them a higher fee for the train operation. Expenses are up on the McCloud River Railroad as with all others. An increased charge to riders may be expected.

The motive power situation is not too encouraging, either. Although the No. 25 has not been worked day in and day out, certain repairs are scheduled for steam locomotives on a calendar basis, and the engine is required to undergo some of major nature this year. Originally slated for early in the year, sympathetic boiler inspectors have decreed that new flues would not have to be installed until after the close of the summer excursion season. For the company to do so it will have to be clearly convinced that use of the No. 25 will be demanded on a profitable basis for some time to come.

In the meantime from the public standpoint, after a lapse of almost 40 years it is once again possible to walk up to the ticket office and purchase passage on a regularly operated train between McCloud and Mount Shasta City. Furthermore, more people are doing that for each trip than ever was the case in the earlier days. Whether or not enough people will do so to make Shasta-McCloud a profit-earning corporation remains to be seen. At least a few somewhat similar ventures with no greater scenic attractions or finer railroading have.

From the railroad viewpoint, the Huffen Puff contributes something to net income as long as it runs under lease. Other groups are still accommodated on dates not reserved for the Huffen Puff. Maintenance of the locomotive becomes increasingly expensive with passage of time and obsolescence of skills and facilities, but revenues are higher too. A major failure of the No. 25's machinery could wipe out service even before the flue replacement date, but in the meantime it chugs away like a cross between an excited puppy and an oversize watch.

The Shasta-McCloud group may be the instrument to protect passenger service against engine failure, too. Being possessed of more than ordinary ingenuity to have gotten themselves in their present position in the first place, they may find a solution to making their No. 21 operable. They also have located and now own yet another locomotive that they would like to move to McCloud, but which now appears to require a prohibitively high cost for the move. It is by no means inconceivable that No. 25 could find itself with a working partner.

Passenger service, 1971, may be looking at a future on the McCloud River Railroad quite different from that faced by the pitiful remnants on our larger railroads.

This winter scene, in the grand manner of steam railroading, dramatizes the raw power of locomotive No. 25 as it pushes a plow toward Pierce, summit of the grade between Mc-Cloud and Mount Shasta. —DONALD DUKE

7

SNOW

NATURE'S abundance in the Mt. Shasta region includes not only rich timber but also a more than ample endowment of snow. The white capped Mt. Shasta standing like a giant overlord adds a measure of scenic beauty and inspiration difficult to equal, and snow at the lower levels adds a certain charm and change of pace to the landscape. Winter brings in tourists, fills up the motels and lodges with skiers bound for Shasta Ski Bowl, which has long since replaced Snowman's Hill along the McCloud River Railroad as the center for snow enthusiasts.

Snow is not a blessing to loggers or railroad men, it is a white menace. It comes each year, however not always in identical quantities or at the same time or place along the railroad. There is no such thing as a bare winter, and 20 inches would be interesting enough and no real hardship, but sometimes it is 20 feet! Dependably, the fall of snow makes it impossible for a locomotive to just brush it aside. The railroad has to either remove snow or shut down. In its earliest years the McCloud

River Railroad did shut down, but it is really more expensive to close up shop than to fight snow. Shippers have long since grown dependent on the railroad to move lumber when it was ready for the buyer, rather than to hold it for spring. Logs, too, were cut and moved year around in many of the rail-hauling years. Employees favor steady incomes; management makes nothing from idle machinery and must pay substantial investment and storage costs if goods are not sold as produced. At one time it was rumored that management was considering building snowsheds over the entire line to enable it to run all year. Even before the railroad became committed to full year service, the same economic pressures were causing it to push the natural season a bit by not waiting for the snow to melt enough for an unequipped locomotive to push through on its own. In the very first year, with no snow removal equipment, but unwilling to limit itself to the snow free season alone, the railroad asked the Southern Pacific for the loan of a snowplow which was granted.

In 1899 the railroad decided to open on March 1, and again brought in a SP plow to open the line the last week in February. The big road had a snowplow base at Dunsmuir, less than 20 miles away, which was convenient. The McCloud company found the problem had another dimension in this particular spring, however. On March 14, a Tuesday, the crystals began to accumulate again instead of melting off for summer. The Wednesday train got stalled short of the summit, where the depth was reported as two feet, and had to back (or did it run forward? Switchbacks are somewhat confusing) down to Upton and call for help again. This time the SP was having snow problems of its own in the same storm and naturally took care of them first. The McCloud railroad had to wait until Friday before big brother would lend a hand.

Six types of machinery are used for railroad snow removal. The McCloud River Railroad has used all six but has never owned the ultimate weapon to fight the massive accumulations.

The simplest tool is a hand shovel, powered by man. It works when all else fails. It is slow, and expensive when costs are calculated on the

Effective snow fighting on the McCloud River Railroad was accomplished with the wedge plow. The railway was unable to justify the expense of the massive rotary. In this scene, one oil burner is assisted by three wood burning engines as they push through Pierce. (BELOW) Manpower and shovels are the most versatile snow removal devices. A liberal supply of both pose on flat cars ready to move to the attack. —BOTH CHARLES M. HAINES COLLECTION

basis of cubic feet of snow removed per dollar. This method of hand powered removal is modified somewhat by substituting a pick for the shovel when necessary. A shovel gang can remove snow with little regard for an obstacle, such as a boulder or fallen tree that will stop a power device. The gang can also extricate a machine that has gotten itself stuck. Because the machines are not able to cope with every snow removal problem, manpower and shovels are still used.

The plow has moved forward until it stalled, the locomotives uncoupled and backed well away. Then the shovel gang moved in behind the plow to shovel out snow and ice that had fallen into the cut. The locomotives will recouple to the plow, yank it loose and then back far enough to get a run for the next charge into the drifted mass. (LEFT) McCloud country snow usually packs to a solid mass. A little help is needed to scale the white cliffs. (BELOW) Clearing out a junction. Where tracks diverge manpower is still necessary to provide a few touches more sophisticated mechanical devices find difficult to match. The broom is standard equipment at switch stands in country — not that eight foot drifts can be swept away, but even a few flakes between switch points and through rail from a light fall make bending a rail already stiff with cold almost impossible to move. —ALL CHARLES M. HAINES COLLECTION

Opening one of the logging lines in the Spring. Engine No. 9 wears a butterfly plow as, less obviously, does its partner No. 10. Both locomotives back against a bucker plow, which would hardly be needed if all the snow along the way was no deeper than this. (BELOW) Reason for the front end conference around this bucker plow appears to be a derailment. Massive dimension of the tall wooden wedge dwarfs the small locomotive pusher. —BOTH CHARLES M. HAINES COLLECTION

Another simple but efficient and widely used device is the so-callel "butterfly" or wedge-shaped gadget bolted to the front of a locomotive just above the rails. For modest depths this nose plow is quite ample. Used very extensively in snow country, butterfly plows are frequently attached to all power units for the winter season. They are often referred to as pilot plows because of their position on the locomotive. A larger version is sometimes called a headlight plow, presumably because it reaches so high up on a locomotive. The headlight plows have not found widespread popularity, but No. 7 was equipped with one.

The even higher wedge that has been more widely used is a separate unit designed to be pushed by a locomotive rather than to be a part of it. The great wedge or bucker plows, sometimes called Russell plows after the designer of one version, were the mainstay of McCloud River Railroad snow removal for many years and one still remains on the property, with another on display not far removed. The bucker plow has a gracefully shaped wedge reaching taller than a locomotive above the rail in the McCloud version, mounted on a sturdy chassis with a box covering the frame behind the wedge itself. Atop the body is a balcony of sorts with a few simple controls where the plow operator could ride. Control consisted mainly of signalling locomotive engineers pushing the plow and activating flap-like devices at the very bottom edge that provided varying clearances from the ground.

Bucker and pilot plows alike have a grave deficiency even apart from the fact that snow can simply get too deep for them. They do not clear all the snow out down to bare ground. That which they pass over can become compacted and turn to ice. If the plow has to reverse, when it backs up it actually gathers in more snow and helps compact it into ice. Ice will derail a heavy locomotive if there is enough of it in the wrong place. To fight this the flanger was devised. The flanger is basically an ice cutting blade located between the trucks of a sturdy car, again with controls to regulate the ice-gouging activity. The McCloud line used several of these machines, and put a wedge-shaped nose in the front of the car bodies, making them a combination flanger and small bucker plow. These medium-sized devices are the first line of defense against snow today. Huge shovel gangs of an earlier era would be prohibitively expensive. The buckers usually keep the line open at moderate cost.

The Jordan ditcher-spreader is a highly sophisticated combination of bucker plow and flanger, with a bag of additional useful tricks already described. This machine replaced the big bucker plows as the prime weapon against snow too deep for McCloud pilot and flanger plows.

The machine that moves snow when all other power devices fail is the rotary plow. It can actually tunnel into drifts substantially deeper than it is tall without simply pushing the snow ahead of it into a compact blob that stalls the plow train. It works by taking snow back through a rotating cutter blade that whirls it up, out and entirely away from the track through a path the plow has already opened above itself if the snow was that deep. Seldom could the rotary be stalled by snow alone. Its infrequent failures come primarily from debris mixed in with the snow. These plows may be equipped with their own flangers as well.

The last of the big wedge plows waits in McCloud during the summer of 1968 for a call apt to come only if other snow fighting tools fail. —ROBERT M. HANFT

Not particularly impressive but still useful, this little box is a flanger. Equipped with a small wedge on either side, it can cope with moderate accumulations of the white menace. —CHARLES M. HAINES COLLECTION

The Jordan spreader also awaits duty in McCloud during the summer of 1968. It could serve in a variety of maintenance-of-way functions in addition to being a prime mover of snow. —ROBERT M. HANFT

The McCloud line has never owned a rotary snowplow. It has leased one on occasion when its own tools could no longer cope with the problem.

Once the railroad was committed to running all year, a policy that grew inevitably out of its own success, snow fighting equipment was as necessary as locomotives or cars. Borrowing plows when the SP didn't need them was too expensive and time schedules too uncertain. The road soon had bucker plows on the equipment roster, supplemented by shovel gangs. The company turned to the Southern Pacific once again in early March of 1902 when the road became plugged too badly for home equipment. This time a rotary snowplow went over the hill to McCloud and back.

The McCloud River Railroad has a problem with snowplows peculiar to its own layout. If it is snowing hard enough while the removal is going on, the line may fill in deeply behind the work train soon enough so that supplementary removal — a pilot plow at least — is needed for passage. With switchbacks on the line a train has to back when it reaches one, either over the new segment or the way it came. Cabooses, the usual rear end of trains, are not well equipped to lead the way through snow that amounts to much. The solution to this problem was to build a snow plow turntable at Signal Butte switchback. Very much like an ordinary locomotive turntable, this one is smaller and lighter and never was intended for engines.

After clearing to the end of the line in a forward direction, the plow plowed the turntable lead, was turned around, and then faced forward again to make the assault in the new direction.

In recent years the unique turntable has fallen into disrepair and has been used only to turn flanged automobiles to keep from running them extensively in reverse gear. The turntable had to be shovelled out if the snow got too deep, which on occasion took 50 men eight hours or more. Rather than continue to maintain the turntable, plow trains now run forward from McCloud to Signal Butte, back down to McCloud, turn around, back up to Signal Butte, and then are ready to run forward from Signal Butte to Mt. Shasta City. If it is snowing hard enough, a bucker-flanger can be added to the rear of the train for back-up insurance. If this had been done more commonly on railroads in general, snow plow trains would have avoided entrapment and occasional tragedy.

Newspaper reports indicate that the winter of 1903-04 may have been the first for the railroad to attempt year around operation over the main line between McCloud and Upton. Winter train service east of McCloud was reduced because log camp winter activity did not follow until much later. All present trackage has been used regularly for many years.

The winter of 1912-13 was one of exceptionally heavy snow and with it came the usual problem of keeping the road open. On January

During the winter of 1912-1913 the snow was heavy and required the service of the Southern Pacific rotary in order to keep the road open.
—CHARLES M. HAINES COLLECTION

On January 14, 1913, the bucker plow derailed with the result that the McCloud River Railroad was closed tight. The Southern Pacific rotary was called to the rescue once again. Railroadmen ponder the problem of how to re-rail the bucker. —CHARLES M. HAINES COLLECTION

14 the bucker plow derailed with the result that the road was plugged tight until January 23. Twelve feet of snow covered the rail at the summit.

When a plow or any other piece of equipment derails in snow the first problem is access. The vehicle is ordinarily too close to the snowbank to even walk alongside it, let alone place rerailing equipment. Hand shovelers have to clear the snow away from the sides. When the snow is more than man deep the problem is far from trivial. To begin with, there isn't any place for the shoveler to toss his load if he starts work in a deep cut. Instead, a series of terraces are hand shovelled, starting on top well away from the derailment. As the terraces finally reach down to track level each shovelful is relayed from terrace to terrace to get it out of the way. This has to be done on both sides of the derailment in order that rerailing frogs can be placed to guide back

all wheels that are off the rail. In the meantime part of the snow has been disposed of in another fashion by scooping it into the tender to keep the boiler supplied with water to keep locomotives from freezing while waiting. Keeping them supplied with fuel may also get to be quite a problem if they are stalled long enough. Five engines were out with the plow on this occasion, each adding its power to force the wedge ahead.

163

The SP rotary made another trip to McCloud, rescuing the McCloud snow train in the process. While there it was used for something other than clearing the tracks. The roofs of the large buildings that served as depot and company offices — and a whole series of other useful functions ranging from store to town meeting hall at one time or another — were steeply pitched to keep snow from accumulating. This fall was not only deep but sticky enough not to slide off, and was heavy enough to cause concern about collapse of the roofs. Why not use the rotary to dispose of the roof snow? With a modest assist from shovel crews, the accumulation was urged down onto the adjacent house track. When the snow level on the track was roof high the rotary moved in with its usual full head of steam and with blade revolving at high speed, set to fling the nuisance way across the adjacent trackage. It did, clearing the street too, plastering the fronts of the houses facing the track with snow, which slowed down hardly at all at the window glass.

Black Butte is white as the 1913 Southern Pacific rescue train grinds upward from Sisson. (BELOW) The rescue train rounds Big Canyon fill. —BOTH CHARLES M. HAINES COLLECTION

The Southern Pacific rotary clears out the tracks adjacent to the depot. In addition to the fall of snow directly as a result of the storm, the rails were covered with most of the accumulation on the roof, which had been pushed downward. A slight miscalculation resulted in some of the snow being shot through the windows of nearby homes by the rotary. (RIGHT) The rotary moves alongside the depot and prepares to tackle the snow by the company store. — BOTH CHARLES M. HAINES COLLECTION

The PG&E extension was in snow country, inevitably. The original contract provided for plow and flanger leasing from the railroad operator to the power company owner, at a fee of $1.50 each per hour. In February of 1922 shovelers and the plow spent five days opening up the railroad between Bartle and Pit powerhouse No. 1, in order that construction supplies could be brought in. At the toughest part, on Dead Horse Summit, in three days little more than a mile was cleared. The new line had been in use for only six months. Four locomotives were used in the plow train, each costing PG&E three dollars per hour. With crew wages added to the bill, PG&E might have entertained some doubts as to the virtue of rail transportation in the Mc-Cloud country.

After more than a decade of winters that were relatively bearable, 1936-37 and 1937-38 both brought problems out of the ordinary. Trouble in the first winter came in the form of a massive accumulation on the hill west of Mc-Cloud that could not be handled with company equipment. Once again the Southern Pacific rotary came over to McCloud.

Keeping a wedge plow moving when snow is deep and heavy takes brute power. Five engines curve through the snow in this 1914 scene. (BELOW) Locomotive No. 4 appears to fit snugly in its white environment which nearly envelopes it. —BOTH CHARLES M. HAINES COLLECTION

The following winter was worse. On Saturday, February 12, the regular empty log train headed east from McCloud. It was snowing, but that was hardly unusual. With some delay the train reached Car A, and had to buck moderate drifts there, for which it had inadequate power even for the small bucker-flanger plow it had brought along. In backing up for another run engine No. 14 derailed, and then the real trouble began. The snow was too deep to get at the locomotive to rerail it. Car A had section people and shelter at least, even if the limited facilities were overcrowded and rations short. The snow kept piling up until it was 19 feet deep on the level at Car A, marked by cutting a notch on a telegraph pole at snow level. A rescue train with the big wedge plow left McCloud, but found the going rougher than expected, and more locomotives were added to team up all the available power on the railroad. Rescue slowly ground eastward.

Telegraph and telephone circuits were disrupted by the storm. Word was finally patched through to Pondosa that men were hungry at Car A. Logging foreman Charles Daveney improvised a homemade sled from fir poles and planking, loaded it with beef, eggs, flour and other foods, hooked it behind a logging cat and finally got from Pondosa to Car A with relief. Going was actually made easier because rain had come at the tail end of the storm and then froze into a tough crust atop the mass.

The dense fall and hard crust made going possible for the cleated machine and its tow, but only made it tougher for the bucker train. Bringing in a rotary plow was no solution, for clearances along the line east of McCloud were too narrow. Patient repetition of shoving forward with every ounce of thrust by combined effort from the locomotives until the plow was stalled, then backing out for another run — or shoveling loose if the plow was wedged in too tightly to reverse; over and over, with little rest for man and machine; frustration at dwindling supplies of fuel and water necessitating return for replenishment; sheer exhaustion of human bodies that lost track of time as day merged into night and then changed back again; this was the pattern of slowly opening the way to the stranded men and train. After the storm the sun came out and the world for these peo-

Until the plow passes after a storm, the countryside appears to be in the full possession of Mother Nature, as shown on the opposite page. The plume of smoke behind the wedge plow suggests that a railroad will soon reappear in this primitive landscape. (ABOVE) Wedge plow No. 1767 has met snow almost beyond its own height as it grinds eastward toward Car A where a train has been stalled and derailed in 1938. (RIGHT) Mid-day lunch is taken by the wedge crew atop the plow. No. 1767 was destined to be the last surviving wedge plow on the line. (LOWER-RIGHT) The wedge plow has been backed away from the drift that stalled it. Camera and crew survey the situation briefly, but the signal will soon be passed along for all the locomotives to charge forward with all their combined might once again. — ALL CHARLES M. HAINES COLLECTION

ple became dazzingly beautiful with the green of the forest breaking through the otherwise universal mantle of endless unspoiled white topped by the bright blue sky. Few had time to contemplate it and were much too tired of it all to appreciate it.

Eventually Car A was reached, with the disheartening discovery that car after car of the stranded train was off the rail, along with the locomotive. They all had to be rerailed because the line was blocked until they were cleared out of the way. The shovel gang started swinging.

Working in the snow cuts was quite restricted. If a man lost his footing there was only one direction in which to slide, which was not wise when wheels were turning. Brakeman Frank Green made the fatal mistake. Numbed by this tragedy the men could do little but lay the remains aside and keep working. Green was a young man, employed only for a short time, and popular with his fellows. He was one of a fortunate few to be hired in weakening days of the great depression and had impressed others with enthusiasm for his new job, one that had ended his personal hard times.

A sad and worn crew returned to McCloud dragging the No. 14 with the human victim of the storm. Their work still was not ended, for the town of Pondosa remained isolated and running dangerously low on food. Wires were all down or grounded out, but officials thought Pondosa people could be cheered if they knew help was on the way. Word got through in a novel way. A very popular news broadcast that originated in Los Angeles was asked to mention the isolation of Pondosa and add the word that the relief train should break through the next day, because the company was concentrating all resources on doing so. It was heard there on battery radios and the message spread through the little community.

Ironically enough, the Pondosa relief train found its work practically insignificant. Temperatures had risen (by contrast with 18 degrees below zero one night during the period of maroonment), the hard crust had melted and the whole mass was beginning to vanish almost as rapidly as it had fallen. A few days later trains might very well have gone through with only a pilot plow and none of the thousands

of man hours of earlier exertion and heartbreak.

The year following the big blockade saw the completion of two more bucker-flanger plows in company shops. They weighed 58,000 pounds apiece, much of which is ballast to help keep them on the rail while crunching ice, and cost $4,609. Some of these smaller plows were assigned to lumber company use on the log spurs that were kept open all winter. The company had accumulated a total of ten buckers by the time the Jordan plow was purchased in 1951.

Again, more than a decade elapsed with no really serious snow problems, but 1951-52 was another season of continuing storms. This time diesel locomotives and the Jordan plow were on the line and the problem was more in the nature of having to force the stuff day after day rather than endure long blockades. Snow could very well have hastened the dieselization program of the railroad, for a contrast of costs between diesel and steam locomotives in snow fighting was amply demonstrated, with steam reported most unfavorably.

The 1952 snow could have been a deciding factor for presidents as well as locomotives. President Myers decided to leave McCloud that spring. He had been around for many a snow campaign, and was in the thick of the rescue operation back in 1938, but a job offer had come along from a railroad where snow is virtually unheard of; one that doesn't own even a smidgen of snow removal equipment.

Myer's successor to the presidency, Flake Willis, had worked with snow before coming to McCloud. Because of his first name, Willis might have felt right at home in McCloud from the start. Less obvious is the fact that Willis was born in Snowflake, Arizona. Any play on names is hardly relevant, but with powerful diesel locomotives, the Jordan plow, and buckers in reserve the railroad again took snow in stride for years. Like the stiff grades, snow was and is a nuisance, but McCloud railroaders accept both as a way of life.

Capricious winter had not completely given up playing games around McCloud, however. Another chapter was written in 1969. The 1968-69 season snowfall again approached records. The railroad kept going, but crews got

It is March 2, 1969, and Southern Pacific rotary No. 208 is about to make its last steam-powered assault on McCloud snow. Shoved by McCloud River Railroad diesels it pauses briefly before getting under way from Mount Shasta. —TOM IRION

increasingly worried as banks got higher and higher, drifted in again with new storms, and made it more difficult each time to get rid of the new accumulation. One day management realized the line was blockaded again. On February 28, and again on March 1, men and machines worked long hours to get the Burney line open and finally did so, but the Pondosa branch was still closed and looked to be every bit as tough a job, or worse, than Burney had been. Once again the call went out to the Southern Pacific for help, and it was heeded.

Actually, the SP had been alerted to the possibility of need well before the call came, and had agreed to lease a rotary plow if the Mc-Cloud line could no longer get by with its own equipment. In late afternoon of Saturday March 1, the decision was made and Southern Pacific rotary No. 208 started out for McCloud.

This time the plow had to come all the way from Roseville rather than nearby Dunsmuir. It was brought in a special train movement and not without a certain amount of difficulty. The huge, heavy, awkward machine is not designed for speed even when towed, and this one hadn't moved for about three years. It weighs more than 100 tons, and is fed fuel and water from an extra-large (and heavy) tender salvaged from one of the company's last and largest steam locomotives. Journal bearings ran hot and worried its attendants for much of the run to Mt. Shasta City. Stops for inspection and cooling added to the time consumed.

Rotary No. 208 is the last Southern Pacific plow to have a steam-powered cutting blade. All the steam rotaries except this one have either been scrapped or had their boilers removed and electric drive machinery (interchangeable with that on diesel-electric locomotives) substituted. Presumably SP could best spare this little-used plow with less concern about what might befall it.

After almost a full day of limping journey from Roseville the machine arrived at Mt. Shasta City. The boiler had been fired up en route and everything was in readiness. To test it, the wheel was set spinning and a little snow thrown off yard trackage at Mt. Shasta City, giving rise to the distinct possibility that the occasion was the last use of a steam rotary on the SP. Shortly after 5:00 p.m. McCloud River power took over for the trip across the mountain. The line was open to McCloud, but the plow had work to do anyway. It was wider than the line cleared, and so had to enlarge a path for itself. Actually, the McCloud people had hoped the plow would have wider "wings" to make an even broader cut than it did; "wide-wing" rotaries have extension scoops for just this purpose. Night rolled around before the plow got under way, and McCloud crews were a bit jittery about how the behemoth would behave on steeper grades, sharper curves, and lighter rail than it usually experienced. It spun along without a flaw, however, arriving in McCloud after a four hour run.

The blockade was still ahead and the decision whether to plow on or wait for daylight had to be made. Plow attendants, including experts loaned by the SP, fortified themselves for the rigors ahead with a good meal before leaving civilization at McCloud, just in case. The word was "go" and go it was, for 11 more hours, this time into drifts up to 20 feet deep. This was the first occasion for a rotary plow

At rest in McCloud, Southern Pacific steam rotary No. 208 has just returned from a night spent successfully clearing the Pondosa line; the first and thus far only time a rotary has ventured east of McCloud. —KARL KOENIG

There is plenty of action and noise involved when a rotary snowplow, particularly one that is steam powered, gets into tough going. The scene was never more vividly portrayed or daringly captured than in this close up photograph of McCloud snow removal. —KARL KOENIG

run east of McCloud, but clearances had been improved. The track held up under the combined tonnage of the plow, tender, and three McCloud Baldwin diesel-electric locomotives (Nos. 29, 31, 32) pushing. Slow, steady progress, with no real crisis, and the road was open. Pondosa, now the home of a good sized independent sawmill, could have freight service once again. Widening the snow cut all the way to Burney was considered, but the load for the Lake Britton bridge would be more than management cared to impose on it.

On the return to McCloud, the rotary was tucked away inside the diesel shed and allowed to cool. On previous occasions the McCloud River Railroad was anxious to return a rotary plow to the SP as expeditiously as possible, but this time the SP was content to allow the machine to remain rent free. Thus, the railroad had a rotary snowplow available right on the property in the event that the storm continued. Southern Pacific was undecided whether to scrap No. 208 or rebuild it with an electric drive. Interested observers speculated as to whether or not McCloud management would buy it at scrap value and add it to the roster. The additional storms did not materialize, and with the threat ended No. 208 was towed back to Mt. Shasta City and placed on the rails of its owner.

Perhaps it is only a coincidence, but coping with the massive snow problem of 1969 was the last major McCloud River Railroad crisis faced by President Willis, just as the 1952 storms had been for his predecessor. Willis decided to return to his native Arizona, where he may find snow again, but almost surely in quantity less than that which visited the slopes of Shasta in March 1969.

Trainmaster Charles "Chino" Haines, who is also the roadmaster referred to earlier, in addition to being lineman, conductor and otherwise useful in one capacity or another during his long career with the railroad, claims that speed is the key to successful snow removal when a rotary plow is not available. If the bucker, or even pilot plow, gets out soon enough and runs fast enough it will throw snow from the rails clear outside the right of way. Momentum will break through short drifts. If the plow is run slowly it will build higher banks that impede the next removal and tend to fill up if any wind is blowing. A slow-moving plow may stall in drifts.

Haines practiced what he preached when given the opportunity. He directed snow removal from the hurricane deck of the bucker plow on many an occasion, though often not as early in the storm as he would have liked. Witnesses describe him as fearless under pressure, and it takes considerable courage to keep signalling for more speed from behind when the unknown is ahead. With tremendous power being applied from a battery of locomotives, if the plow ever stopped suddenly the locomotives would probably slam right through it before their engineers could even close their throttles.

Haines seemed to have a sixth sense for hidden dangers. One of the commoner hazards is the tree that falls down across the track early in the storm and is completely hidden when the plow comes along. Fast as he went, he always recognized a tell-tale change in contour of the snow ahead in time to signal the pushing locomotives to shut off and stop before they hit. The plow has emergency brake controls for the entire train, but if applied injudiciously every wheel in the train could be slid flat. By moving slowly at time of contact, the plow could raise the tree up out of the snow. Men with saws cut off the visible end wide enough to clear the train, then the engines pushed ahead a little more because the remainder would have dropped into the snow in front of the plow. It would rise again, and then a second cut would leave a loose log in front of the wedge. That section would soon work its way to the side when the plow resumed speed.

Haines comments that it was the height of his glory in railroading to go like a bat out of hell with a snowplow. Almost 20 years later the writer was told that the big mistake made in 1952 was spending too much money just *pushing* snow. Haines should have been turned loose to *throw* it, but others feared "that old bald-headed so and so would kill us and everybody else."

Whatever the answer, snow removal may continue to provide the question and the test.

8

McCLOUD POTPOURRI

ANY HISTORY is concerned with events over the passage of time. A railroad history rightly is heavily involved with hardware. A complete chronicle must also honor personalities, even though objectivity toward people is more difficult to achieve than is the record of things mechanical. Perhaps no tale under this heading will yield quite as vivid an impression as that just presented of a "bald-headed so and so" hanging to an open railing while five steam locomotives strain every rivet to shove him at break-neck speed along a railroad neither he nor anyone else on the train can see. Even so, imagination alone must fill in the crescendo of sound effects that come from full throttle and Johnson bar "down with the oil cans," and the sight of twin plumes of snow cascading far out from the speeding wedge splitting tranquility of the winter scene.

Each preceding chapter has followed a chronological pattern. The time sequencing will be less rigorous here, in part because following a time pattern would be awkward as well as meaningless.

Incidents on a railroad may well conjure up thoughts of wrecks. The McCloud River Railroad had wrecks, the first of which has already been described. The writer is anxious to put others in perspective. This railroad came into existence when mechanical and human failures on railroads were common and taken for granted. It is a line with special hazards to trap the careless to this day. As the record unfolds it becomes obvious that McCloud railroaders have gradually made it a safe railroad. There is no evidence that it ever was less safe than its contemporaries at any period, despite the operating difficulties. Railroaders have paid with their own and fellow workers' lives for mistakes. The survivors are not proud of the lapses from safe routine, but they can be proud they were so few and so long ago. Day after day trains leave their terminal, do the required work and return hundreds and even thousands of times on end without incident. Frank Green was not the first train employee to lose his life, but none has perished on the job since. Thirty-two years have ticked away in the meantime.

173

No locomotive was ever smashed so badly as to put it beyond repair. In the early years most of them spent a fair amount of time on the ground and occasionally suffered a few bruises in the process. In June of 1900, one engine headed into the timber and took on a two-foot-thick tree with substantial damage inflicted to both, but without harm to humans. A three sentence news item indicates this derailment was the first reported accident on the line involving a train. Locomotives were not identified, but No. 6 could have been on the line by then and showing its lack of affinity for the rail.

The first railroad fatality followed within a week. Spurs in McCloud were more often slanted than level and on this occasion a crew of Chinese laborers loading cars with wood decided to let gravity assist in moving a ten car string to a new spot. Somehow instead of stopping again after a few feet the cars got out of control and raced down the grade. Several men leaped off, but four stayed aboard. The ten cars jumped the track and piled up in a jumble of kindling from car and load alike. One man was killed, one seriously injured, and the other two shaken up. A jury met, investigated, and came up with a verdict typical of the times. Death was the result of an accident and the company was exonerated of any responsibility.

Two more train accidents in 1900 each resulted in a fatality, this time to trainmen. Both were runaways on the hill. Brakeman Donaghue had the unenviable distinction of being the first trainman to lose his life on the railroad. He was working a five car train west up the hill from McCloud which not only stalled but then rolled back down the way it came. At a

sharp curve the cars left the track, carrying Donaghue to his death. Surprisingly, the locomotive held to the rail and was stopped where the line levelled off in McCloud.

The other accident seems almost incredible, especially in the light of following hardly three months after the Donaghue runaway and to a man who had been with the railroad almost three years. Old timers still talk of it and shake their heads. Engineer Frank Moran was proceeding over the steepest part of the grade (which the news account refers to as seven percent!) when something went wrong with the locomotive. Moran stopped the train, clambered underneath the locomotive and began to tinker with the mechanism. When gravity prevailed he could not get out.

About a year later another brakeman lost his life. Faulting the company for this death would be somewhat difficult, for even steep grades could hardly be considered a contributing factor. The problem was and is that workers do not always get along well with each other, and railroaders are no exception. Conductors have been known to report misdeeds of engineers to management, and both pick on brakemen. In this case brakeman H. V. Newby believed he was being abused by conductor William Page. Tempers had been raw between them for at least a couple of weeks prior to Thursday, October 24. On that day after the train left Upton enroute to McCloud they

The result of an early runaway. Cars in the above scene are Southern Pacific wood racks indicating fuel supply service for the larger road. (RIGHT) This mess of spaghetti was structural steel designated for the Pacific Gas & Electric Pit River project. —
BOTH CHARLES M. HAINES COLLECTION

Detailed information is no longer available for either of the above mishaps. The flat car problem was a runaway in the early days when such incidents were relatively frequent. The box car difficulty was a derailment in the 1930's somewhere east of McCloud. —BOTH CHARLES M. HAINES COLLECTION

evidently quarreled bitterly, and Newby threatened to kill Page. On arrival at McCloud, Newby dashed to his room, picked up his revolver and told his roommate he was going to kill Page on sight. He returned to the train, climbed aboard to get at Page, who drew his own revolver, fired two shots and killed Newby almost immediately.

Coroner Fairchild came down from Yreka, and held a hearing, with the jury reporting justifiable homicide. Page went free. Upon receiving details and having some second thoughts District Attorney Lodge wired McCloud to rearrest Page, but the conductor had decided he had had enough of McCloud and departed town without leaving a forwarding address. Interestingly, a year later Page's wife, Nellie, then living in Ashland, Oregon, filed suit for divorce. Page's whereabouts was still unknown, but she claimed no great loss in that regard. He had threatened her life on several occasions, and once tried to carve her with a chisel. Fortunately he had missed her and drove it into the wall instead. Before he got the job at McCloud she had been forced to support him in idleness by taking in washing.

Railroads are an attractive nuisance to children, which generated a 1903 tragedy to one Italian family. While several children were playing on a flatcar another car being switched bumped into it and threw one of them beneath the wheels. Again indicative of minority status, the news report of the period let "Italian" stand in lieu of any name.

Two adult brakemen had a narrow escape by jumping in a somewhat similar circumstance a month or so later. This time they were working on a car that rammed another hard enough to be heard over much of the town.

Later in the same month, August 1903, the railroad managed still another form of negative accomplishment in its diversified list of mishaps. It staged an interline collision with the Southern Pacific. Damage was very slight; and only the spirit of the occasion in accomplishing something new merited the record. Trains of both railroads were switching in the yards at Upton and came together with a modest amount of splintering of an SP locomotive and a McCloud car.

Head-on collisions or "cornfield meets" have been rare in McCloud history. They are a worse than ordinary hazard for this line with its many blind curves. It is entirely single tracked and has never had automatic signals. To reduce the probability of men overlooking orders and trains colliding as a result, schedules have typically been arranged to avoid meets entirely. This wasn't always possible.

The first recorded "head on" (wreck) was staged in 1906 between a lumber train and the afternoon passenger run. The passenger consist was the usual coach plus some empty flat cars returning to McCloud. The loaded lumber train was running very slowly on the heavy pull. They met on a curve with little time for braking, but slow speed helped avoid casualties. Both engine crews jumped and must have found relatively soft landings. This might have been the incident that converted No. 1 to No. 12.

In recent years radio has been a great boon for all concerned to keep posted about what is on the tracks. Getting crews to accept and use radio took a little tact. One conductor grumbled that his hands had been quite adequate for signalling all the years he had been running trains, and he needed no new-fangled nuisance to burden him now. Rather than argue, the boss simply suggested that he throw a set in the caboose, just in case. Only a few trips later this same conductor had a helper engine to the summit at Pierce. After cutting off the helper the train started down to Mt. Shasta City, only to stall in snow that was a bit deeper than anticipated. The previous winter a man would have had to trudge for miles in the winter snow to get help. This conductor remembered his scorned gadget, dug it out, made a call, and it worked. The helper reversed, came back over the summit, coupled into the stalled train and broke it loose before it had a chance to really freeze in. Radio had gained another convert.

Lumber company lines also used radio in their last years, but for much of their existence had neither radio nor dispatching of any kind. When two crews used the same log line, an uncommon situation but one that did occasionally happen, they worked out their meet arrangements together. Ora Anders tells of one experience where he had a positive meet set up with the other crew that didn't come off as planned. He had to work much longer than he expected switching a loader to a new position. As he came down the hill toward his meet he saw a light through the woods and set the brakes in emergency, just in case. Sure enough, moments later the other locomotive, also with brakes set tight, came sliding around the curve. Fortunately they stopped in time. When the two crews put their hearts back in place and started breathing again they had a brief confab, with one crew doing the talking and the other mostly stammering. From then on, Anders insisted that his meet arrangements be in writing. Not that he could stop the other train by rolling the paper up into a wad and throwing it at the culprit, but at least it would establish who was at fault.

Apart from radio orders, written orders, telephone orders and mutual agreements, the Mc-Cloud River Railroad used another form widely discussed amongst railroaders but never condoned in actual practice — well, hardly ever. These are the so-called "smoke" orders, where one train comes onto track that belongs to an-

other. The crew of the train not entitled to occupancy looks for smoke of the other job. If smoke is seen the train waits where it is supposed to. If no smoke is in sight, rather than wait indefinitely the smoker proceeds, running the risk of collision and knowing the blame will be entirely on him as the violator of the right of way.

The lumber company had a line that joined the main track about two miles out of Pondosa. To get into camp, log crews had to proceed against the rights of a railroad company train or wait until it passed — if it hadn't already done so. Good practice required that a man walk well ahead of the train that held no rights to stop the one that did if it showed up. The actual practice was to smoke. The smoker stopped at the junction, where the crew listened carefully, inspected the sky ahead and proceeded, keeping a sharp lookout for the enemy. Once around the last curve, they could see clear track to the sanctuary of their own siding in Pondosa. The smoke orders never resulted in a collision. Probably the main line crew was thoroughly aware of the propensity

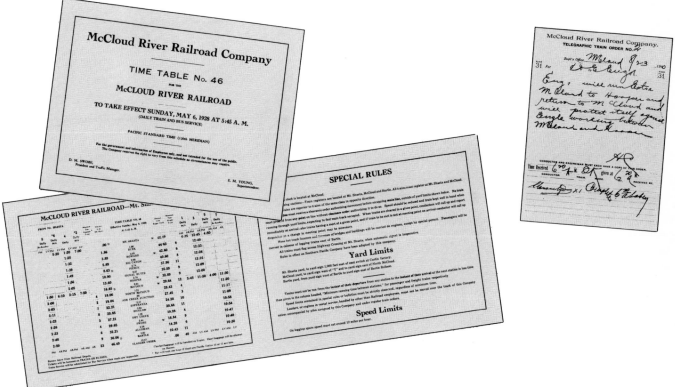

Employees timetable and train order form. —MCCLOUD RIVER RAILROAD

of the loggers to sneak on in, and made certain that there was plenty of smoke and racket if they wanted to head on out when the woods turn was due in.

The *Vinegar Valley Express* got into a head-on one day. Perhaps it didn't make enough smoke. It ran on regular train orders, which gave it clearance to Car A only, eastbound on this trip. It must have been making better time than customary, for it got to Car A and kept right on going. From there on it was on smoke orders against a steam train, but one crew had forgotten and the other was unaware. The startled crews applied emergency brakes when they saw each other rounding the inevitable curve, and had things pretty well under control when the noses kissed. Nothing even derailed, but when the No. 63 tried to back off, it was found to be tightly coupled to the locomotive. Not a formal coupling, just that the tin was bent that way. The steam locomotive had to drag its front end festoon into Hambone where tools were available to put them asunder.

When railroad and highway share the same space, vehicles of the two varieties will inevit-

Three locomotives on the head-end move a string of cars across the mountain between McCloud and Mount Shasta. Appearance of riders on top the cars along with the photographer suggests a fine day. (BELOW) Locomotive No. 14 heads a mixed train toward the logging frontier. The second car behind the locomotive appears to be a load of fresh ties, suggesting a logging spur extension into the woods.
—BOTH CHARLES M. HAINES COLLECTION

ably contest for simultaneous occupancy of that space. The McCloud River Railroad has grade crossings; it follows that it has a record of collisions there. None was fatal until 1967 when two Dunsmuir men were killed at the Pilgrim Creek road crossing east of McCloud. The men, one of whom was a former McCloud railroad employee, were driving so fast along the dirt road that when the driver saw the approaching locomotive he was unable to stop the car or turn away.

This collision ended a dozen years of freedom from fatalities on the railroad. The last previous casualty was Peter Alkoff who was new to McCloud and had just gone to work for the railroad. He was one of several maintenance men riding a speeder on the Burney extension then being built. A flat car had been left standing on the main line and the driver of the motor did not see the flatcar in time to stop. Rain and darkness hampered vision. Eight other men were injured.

Conductor Haines reports a grade crossing accident with a happier outcome. He was bringing the passenger train into Mt. Shasta City one day when an automobile crashed right into the side of the coach. The train, which was running very slowly, stopped immediately and the crew discovered the auto was wedged underneath the steps but was not seriously damaged, nor was the driver. The driver pleaded with the trainmen *not* to send for help or medical aid. A little prying, pounding and bending got the vehicle loose, after which the driver apologized profusely for the inconvenience he had caused. The rather considerably battered remains of the automobile still functioned after a fashion and the train was not harmed.

A night or two later, four jugs of the locally produced mountain dew were mysteriously deposited on the Haines doorstep. Perhaps the town bootlegger had his mind more on a precious cargo and interruption from the rear than the presence of the train in front when he had plowed into it.

Haines didn't explain what he did with the potent stuff once he had it. The railroad has the usual Rule G injunction against the use of intoxicants, and this writer has never seen Haines accept a drop, even in retirement. Per-

haps railroaders used it in barter with those who could imbibe.

Actually, the company did hire men who had been discharged from other railroads, some of them for violations of Rule G elsewhere. Good railroaders were often scarce but badly needed, and officials hoped that past slips might not be repeated. Another chance did not mean free license, and men were let go if they did not measure up to the demanding job.

Rule G was only one of those fractured by an early-day engineer who got tired of doubling the hill with a six car train. The usual procedure then was to make up the train with three cars ahead of the locomotive and three behind. When the train stalled, the rear three loads would be cut off and the head three pushed to the summit. The crew would then return for the remainder. Attempting to take all six one day, Jack Borman decided to screw the safety valve down a little bit, which he did. The crew set handbrakes on the first and last cars in order to let the engine get a slack advantage. With 225 pounds of steam in a 185 pound boiler, Jack yanked the throttle open, the handbrakes were spun off, and everyone expected to see the locomotive go straight up in the air. It might have been interesting to see the crew's reaction if someone had fired a shotgun at that moment!

Jim Robinson tells of an engineer who started violating Rule G regularly after losing his wife. Jim was firing for this man, and was offered a cup of coffee. He turned it down, but the engineer insisted, and he finally shared the contents of the engineer's thermos. "Gee, whiz, it liked to knock my head off," is his recall. Knowing what would happen, Robinson avoided firing for this engineer again. Sure enough, when the man was discharged, his fireman was included. Robinson stayed on for virtually a half century, less some time out for military service.

Perhaps as close as Robinson came to getting fired was right after he was hired. He went to work stoking lump oil into one of the tree burners switching in the yard. The weather was hot, but the boiler was cold. A stranger stepped into the cab as Jim was bailing wood into the hungry maw at a furious pace in anticipation of an uphill pull. An ensuing conver-

179

sation went something like this:

Stranger: "Hey, Kid, you want to ring that bell when you come down to a crossing."

Kid: "If you want that bell rung, you ring it yourself because I'm plenty busy."

Stranger: "You're a pretty smart kid. I don't think you'll be here long."

Shortly afterwards the stranger got off.

Kid: "Who is that guy?"

Engineer: "He's the trainmaster."

Kid: "Has he got anything to do with me?"

"Sure has!"

Years later engineer Robinson gave the trainmaster, then superintendent, his last ride over the hill in the passenger train. The earlier indiscretion had long since been forgiven.

Recent labor strikes have not been highly significant in McCloud. Railroad and mill have been unionized for years, and when union policy called for a work stoppage, one ensued. They were always part of a larger strategy and without great bitterness because other men and other managements were in the same dilemma. In late May of 1909 a strike with considerably more import than modern day stoppages adds a more colorful page or two to the record.

At that time the lumber company employed hundreds (one account states 700) of Italians. That there was any formal organization of Italians as a work group is highly doubtful, but that they were regarded as a distinct entity both by themselves and non-Italians is more likely. In any event, a spokesman presented a demand for more money to management. The request, reportedly for 25 cents per day, was refused. Within a few days the workmen backed up their demand with threats, not only calling on all their countrymen to join the instigators, but promising to bar others from working, if need be. A specific threat was that no trains other than those carrying United States mail would be allowed to run. The resulting strike was reported as a riot, which was an exaggeration, and "one of the biggest and most dangerous that ever occurred in this part of the country," which was quite possibly true.

Local management called for Siskiyou County Sheriff Charles B. Howard, and also informed President Queal, who was in Chicago. Both headed for McCloud, but travel

That McCloud was not all showplace housing is evident in this 1909 photograph as tense men gather in the Italian section of town to discuss the strike. — MILLER PHOTO FROM CHARLES M. HAINES COLLECTION

Strangers in town in June 1909 were warned to leave or suffer the consequences. The company referred to these new arrivals as guards, but Italians regarded them as strikebreakers. Discretion overwhelmed valor and the advice to depart was heeded. (BELOW) When troops arrived much of the town turned out to witness events, but were more curious than hostile or aggressive. Shoving flat cars ahead of the Southern Pacific locomotive, the special militia train arrives in McCloud on June 3, 1909. —BOTH MILLER PHOTOS FROM CHARLES M. HAINES COLLECTION

from Chicago took several days in 1909. Howard deputized some 60 men to "aid in protection of the property," and stationed himself in the box factory in an attempt to keep that unit running. The strikers surrounded the building, informed the sheriff that any person who attempted to work would be killed, and demanded that he leave. This happened on May 31, and the sheriff promptly telegraphed Governor J. N. Gillette, asking that a company of militia be sent.

Gillette replied that he needed additional evidence of necessity, but passed the buck to Adjutant General J. B. Lauck, requesting him to "use your own judgment" as to whether or not militia should be used. Lauck communicated with the sheriff, who advised that the strikers had just taken over the company powder house. Lauck had a subordinate, too, assistant Adjutant General Colonel A. W. Bradbury, who was ordered to proceed to McCloud immediately in person and report. Bradbury arrived the next day, found that the strikers had not actually gotten into the powder house, but was told they had seized the Bartle mail train and a log train. The sheriff and company officials again appealed for troops. Bradbury saw little evidence of actual violence and little desire on the part of the sheriff to face it if it did occur. In late afternoon he advised his

boss to alert four guard companies for use if the need did arise.

The next day Bradbury asked that a few railroad cars be loaded so that he could see what would happen. Horrified officials refused, greatly to the relief of the sheriff. Through an interpreter, Bradbury asked to confer with strike leaders. They refused to meet with him, but notified him that they would demonstrate later in the day, and close down the electric plant. They did demonstrate, and did force the power plant engineer to draw his fires. Both lights and fire pumps were then disabled by lack of steam to generate electricity. Bradbury believed more drastic action would follow, and the sheriff had shown no evidence of coping with the problems of the day. The wire for troops was sent.

Three infantry companies, a cavalry troop and a hospital corps detachment had been alerted. Adjutant General Lauck assumed personal command and at 8:20 p.m. June 2 boarded a special train at Sacramento with the troops, save for one company that joined the special en route at Chico. Colonel Bradbury met the train at Sisson the next morning and held a strategy meeting with his chief, following which the special train switched onto McCloud River Railroad tracks locomotive and all, and proceeded up the hill. To protect the train

The guardsmen promptly set up an encampment near the lumber sheds and engaged in military formations and exercises of the sort for which they were trained. Doubtlessly the McCloud townspeople were impressed with the antics of the visitors as they gathered by the railroad station. —MILLER PHOTOS FROM CHARLES M. HAINES COLLECTION

three flat cars were placed ahead of the engine. Perhaps Bradbury felt the train would be mined, now that he was away from McCloud and only the sheriff and 60 deputies stood between the rioters and the dynamite in the powder house. Ten sharpshooters were placed out on the flat cars. One wonders if they knew why empty cars run ahead of locomotives in military zones, and how naked they felt if they did know! Every open coach window also had an armed man, as did the vestibule platforms.

President Queal arrived in Sisson just in time to join the soldiers. He stated that the company could not and would not meet the strike demands and that he "was prepared to fight to the bitter end." Unfortunately the record does not tell whether or not he then jumped astride the front coupler of the first flat car and rode fearlessly to the battle, leading the troops.

The train was not molested by the strikers, but it proceeded with great caution, taking three hours to get across the mountain. The slow progress resulted largely from too much train, too much grade, and too stiff and heavy a locomotive. One of the flat cars was set out and then the struggle was a bit easier. Perhaps the ten guardsmen felt a closer kinship when spread over only two cars instead of three. The menage arrived at McCloud at 12:15 p.m.

Men, women, children, and even a photographer were out to meet the train when it pulled up to the station, but no battle lines were apparent. The troops detrained and made camp, the men setting up tents and the general moving into the Queal mansion. Guard units were established to protect the powder house, water lines, and the mill. One casualty was reported, details of which do not appear in contemporary reports, but do by word of mouth from old timers.

It appears that one of the first military orders was that all pedestrians would keep to the sidewalks. Hardly had the edict been issued when one older Italian, with some broken comprehension of English, came walking along his customary path beside the track and encountered a guard, who ordered him to the authorized route. "Me no go," was the reply. The order and the reply were repeated and the worker angrily brushed past the guard. The soldier applied persuasion with his bayonet to an obvious target from the rear. "Me go," howled the anguished civilian. No further "battles" ensued.

A complication to the whole problem arrived with a telegram from the governor on June 3, that the Consul General of Italy had been alerted to the situation and requested that any Italians *not* engaged in rioting had better be protected. Lauck replied that "Any Italians not engaged in riotous action will have our best protection," but not everyone was fully convinced that best would be good enough. Consul General Rocco and an editor of *La Voce del Populo*, an Italian language newspaper, took off from San Francisco for McCloud. The governor advised Lauck that "you will kindly meet him (Rocco)."

Lauck arranged a conference between company officials and Italian leaders on the morning of June 4. Spokesman Frank Levati promised that no further violence would occur and Lauck promised Levati that the guard would prevent unlawful acts of the company. Later a cordon of troops surrounded the Italian section of town and thus reinforced the sheriff moved in and arrested the three strike leaders. Rocco arrived, discovered his countrymen were exceedingly bitter, but advised them it would be wise to leave McCloud and seek employment elsewhere.

The railroad enjoyed a spurt of passenger business with Italians leaving on June 9, and the guard on June 10. On June 12 another special train ran. The employees' (presumably non-Italian) dance originally scheduled for May 29 but postponed because of the strike was held then, with revelers from Sisson joining in the fun.

Five years after the troops departed, another "invasion" came to McCloud. This one was not human, but in the form of countless hordes of caterpillars. The wiggly crawlers ate every leaf in the whole countryside and continued to search for more, swarming up the railroad grade and over the rail in such numbers that they stopped passage of trains. Despite liberal applications of sand, locomotive wheels just spun futilely in the greasy mess of crushed worms. Creosol was spread to kill them, myriads more advanced over the dead bodies. Men with brooms, themselves sliding in the mess, tried to sweep them off the rails, but crushed as many on the rail as were swept off, and more got back on before the locomotive could pass. If a train did get going, its brakes were completely ineffective on the downslopes. Shutting the railroad down until the caterpillars decided to move on and metamorphose seemed ridiculous, but management was at wits end. Again local ingenuity saved the day. Master mechanic John Kennedy had an idea and mounted two pipes ahead of the cowcatcher on engine No. 11, aimed downward to end in two nozzles just clear of the track, one to each rail. The rear of the pipe was hooked up to the boiler, live steam cracked through improvised jets, and the worms were blown clear. The train ran. Steamed bodies were banked alongside the track for miles.

A section on flood problems might logically have been appended to the snow chapter, for

A work crew hunts for the railroad underneath solid overflow from Mud Creek in 1924. One wooden trestle became the bottom of a cut and three miles of track required digging out as a result of this situation.
—BOTH CHARLES M. HAINES COLLECTION

snow makes water when it melts. Actually drainage in the porous lava soil of the region is good and floods have been a comparatively minor difficulty for this company. The most important flood trouble came only indirectly from snow, at a time when the weather was dry, sunny and hot. Furthermore, water was not the principal ingredient of the flood. Clues to the flood potential were observed as early as 1875 when a civil engineer noticed vast sand deposits on the surface of the land for several miles east of McCloud. In 1924 the railroad and the town discovered how the sand deposits had come about. Konwakiton glacier high up on the mountain rests on a bed of volcanic ash and lava estimated to be 1,500 feet thick. Summer melt from the glacier is the source of Mud Creek, so named because the melt water carries volcanic ash with it. Mud Creek has a canyon on the upper slopes, but banks broaden out when it reaches more level country east of McCloud. The railroad crossed the active channel with a minor timber bridge hardly worthy of being called a trestle.

Mud Creek flow always increased in midsummer as a function of glacier melt. In 1924 the increase in water volume came early and by August 12 was the highest ever observed and over the banks. With more water flowing and cutting into the volcanic ash in the upper reaches the viscous flowing mud got heavier and heavier. By August 14 the railroad was blocked with dirt and debris carried down and deposited on the right of way. On August 16, the McCloud city water supply was cut off when the pipe line serving it from the source was washed out. On August 18, the problem was temporarily solved by a change of weather up on the mountain, when it turned cold and snow actually fell at higher elevations, slowing down the melt. The railroad dug itself out and raised the level of its grade some 30 inches across the mud flow area. The problem then was what to do about future flows of this sort. The goop that came down was estimated to be more than 80 percent solids, with massive boulders weighing a ton or more included with smaller particles down to fine silt-like ash in great quantity. The overflow strip was more than a mile wide in places. Men who had climbed up on the mountain reported extensive collapse of the channel banks and an

Two Mikado type locomotives in this scene, Nos. 26 and 19, were a common arrangement for the run east from McCloud until the end of steam. —W. C. WHITTAKER (BELOW) Locomotive No. 27 urges flats toward a loading area. The tanker and lone box car contain supplies for an outpost. —GUY L. DUNSCOMB

The doubleheader with locomotives No. 24 and No. 18 is more than just a superb portrait of McCloud steam power in action. When engines on this line were used in multiple they were usually coupled directly to one another— or at opposite ends of the train. Also, 2-6-2's such as No. 24 shown here on the point did not ordinarily work the mainline freight trains with box cars. —JOHN KRAUSE

185

Flood waters were too much for a box culvert and took out a chunk of fill. Men with hand tools and cold feet prepare the stream bed for a replacement culvert. (BELOW) A ballast train of homemade gondolas (flat cars with sideboards) loaded with cinders will provide new fill once the culvert is placed. — BOTH CHARLES M. HAINES COLLECTION

Nature's caprice evens things out. In this scene flood waters removed part of the railroad; here men and tractor are called upon to cope with a slide that has been added to the right-of-way. —CHARLES M. HAINES COLLECTION

ominous grinding roar from the tumbling mixture quite unlike any ordinary water stream. What if there was no cold spell next time?

For some time there was no shortage of suggestions about what someone other than the suggester ought to do about preventing recurrences. Most agreed that the government should take steps of some sort. The eventual outcome was, of course, a study. The railroad management wasn't too confident that its raised grade would be protection enough, and a study might be fine but wouldn't keep trains runnning either. The following summer many individuals and certain issues of the public press tingled with eager anticipation of disaster, but nothing much happened. By early summer of 1926 the railroad decided to take action on its own, and built a wing dam up the hill designed to divert flow from the Mud Creek channel to that of Elk Creek, believed to be better capable of handling the runoff. The project was timely indeed, for the 1926 flow proved to be as much or more than that of two years earlier. Railroad traffic continued without interruption this time, but not without additional anxiety and effort. At some peril a crew kept the diversion to Elk Creek functioning during the flood time, and others worked frantically at the railroad grade putting in additional culverts and boxing the mud flow. Again the grade was raised. Cost of these efforts was listed as $3,000.40, but where the 40 cents was spent remains a mystery.

Again a great hue and cry was raised over the problem. The Sacramento River was discolored for miles with pumice silt and Redding was afraid of what might happen to its water supply. The beauty of the McCloud River was also of prime concern. A couple of more enterprising McCloud residents who had seen the flow collapse great chunks of land into the upper channel decided to see if the new surface presented anything interesting by way of minerals. They actually panned a little gold, and found cinnibar, but after assay decided their future was somewhat more secure in the lumber business. The furor over water pollution died down, too.

The mud flow crisis presented another little problem to the railroad, with regard to its relationship with the lumber company while independent. Although the original 1924 flow was largely stopped by the weather change, the lumber company had sent men up the mountain to work on diversion. The town and the mill were not, it proved, in direct danger, so the railroad was the principal beneficiary of lumber company efforts. When the pipe line was severed, lumber company forces repaired it, but the railroad again was aided substantially. During the period that water was cut off from the normal source the railroad brought in tank cars of water for public use. The regular city lines were hooked up to the mill pond for fire protection. Directors had to thresh out who owed whom how much.

Wetter water than that of the mud flows occasionally topped the rails and added a bit of extra excitement for the train crews. Usually the engineers felt their way cautiously along the flooded right of way and kept going. On one occasion east of McCloud the crew found the whole railroad afloat, which was something else.

With light rail and loose (if not negligible) ballast the track across a water-covered meadow simply floated away from the ground with the lift of previously well-dried ties. After a pow-wow with the crew to discuss the floating bridge across the newly formed pond, conductor Haines started walking across. All appeared reasonably sound and the locomotive sloshed along behind, depressing rails back beneath the surface until the train passed, when they bobbed back up again.

When the flood subsided later, so did the railroad, little the worse for having broken loose from its roadbed.

A few more details of the exhibit at the Panama-Pacific International Exposition of 1915 are appropriate to this story. Three Northern California lumber firms, the McCloud River Lumber Company, the Red River Lumber Company, and the Weed Lumber Company, pooled resources to sponsor an exhibition building and accompanying displays. Appropriately enough the structure was called the White and Sugar Pine Building. California materials were used to the maximum extent, starting with concrete foundations from local cement mills, framing of white and red fir, sidewalls, flooring, windows and doors of sugar and white pine. The interior was finished with white pine veneers trimmed with sugar pine. The exhibitors reached beyond their own forests for the shingles, which

were redwood. A fireplace and its flues were constructed from lava rock brought from the base of Mt. Shasta.

The McCloud River Railroad furnished the logging train that accompanied the building display. It consisted of locomotive No. 18, caboose No. 15, a box car, and two flat cars loaded with flawless specimens from the forest. All equipment was scrubbed, painted and polished to a condition hardly typical of its working environment. To keep the display of logs from checking and discoloring in the sun, their sawed ends were carefully fitted with protective covers until arrival at the exhibit site.

Apart from the hope that lumber users might consider their product favorably, the spirit prompting the sponsors of the fair exhibit was that visitors from all over the world might get some notion both of what the industry and the beautiful forest itself was like. Few of them would have the opportunity to actually visit such a forest and see it for themselves. At that time the timber tracts were still so endless that the mill operators probably didn't regard themselves as the mortal enemy of the beauty they wished to display.

When you visit McCloud a drinking fountain bubbles merrily away alongside the post office just where it can be of benefit to a maximum number of pedestrians. Few of them pay attention to the neat bronze plaque dedicating the cool (naturally refrigerated) stream to the

Destined for the Panama-Pacific International Exposition of 1915, select logs and a spic-and-span caboose are admired by local residents prior to the departure of the cars from McCloud. Ends of the logs are covered to prevent sun checking before display. —CHARLES M. HAINES COLLECTION

The date is July 1950, and No. 18 has the eastbound freight under way. It will add No. 26 for extra power across the sags before it finally reaches town, for it is still within the confines of the McCloud yards. — ROBERT M. HANFT (BELOW) Locomotive No. 17 was photographed working one end of the hill freight. Snow on Mt. Shasta is typical of the late summer. — CHARLES M. HAINES COLLECTION

McCloud engine No. 17 lifts lumber across the mountain toward the Southern Pacific interchange and the market place. The train is resisting progress as it finds the grade leaving McCloud yards. (BELOW) The locomotives of the same train have shut off and No. 17's safety valve pops off with the lack of demand for steam as the train drifts toward Mount Shasta. — BOTH CHARLES M. HAINES COLLECTION

memory of B. W. Lakin. Bert Lakin was the general manager of the lumber company in 1936 and on October 1 lost his life in a forest fire. Remarkably enough, his is the only recorded fire fatality to an employee of either railroad or lumber company, despite the ever present hazard and occasional outbreak.

The 1936 fire was right on the west edge of McCloud. Lakin and fire fighters walked up the railroad track to inspect damage and control activities. He separated from the rest of his party, according to a survivor, and plunged through a brushy area alone. When he did not return to McCloud a search party went out the next day, and the same man who had last seen him the day before found the blackened corpse. Prudence had saved the companion, but one does not tell the boss where he should go — at least not to his face!

Lakin had been a popular leader and a monument to his memory was erected at the scene of his death in addition to the fountain. The woods momument consisted of a marker plaque perhaps two by three feet in dimension embedded into the face of a natural boulder some eight feet high alongside the track.

The very first fire in the railroad era has already been narrated. Its combat set a standard of getting whatever manpower was needed for control to the fire area. If this meant closing the mill to ship all hands to the front it was done. A combination of precaution, capable combat when preventative measures failed and, perhaps, good fortune, has yielded a record of less fire difficulty than might be expected. Damage certainly, but never such as to end or bankrupt the company.

A 1905 blaze at the end of the railroad near Bartle raised a threat not only to McCloud timber but also to the Bridgeford-Cunningham mill at Algomah. The Algomah employees were all at the fire lines, but were having little success until the McCloud mill closed down and some 500 of its men joined forces at the front. Special trains were also loaded at McCloud with whatever available containers could be found and filled with water, and rushed to the fire lines. The Algomah mill was saved, but extent of the damage to timber was not reported. Apparently 1905 was a dry year, and hot summer weather brought pitch to the surface of the bark, which burned readily and tended to damage standing trees more than might otherwise have been the case.

Not only did the railroad have fire problems with the standing timber, but also with some that had already been harvested. In the same year a fire started in one of the big piles of locomotive fuel at Upton. The owners were concerned about the prospect of this wood, intended to be burned but under different conditions, going up in smoke prematurely. Townspeople were interested in the entertainment aspect and more in what it might do to the surrounding community if it really got going. Hasty and valiant effort forestalled the threat, with agreement that it had been a close call. A locomotive was accused of arson, perhaps for lack of any other certified culprit.

The town of Sisson learned the next year that forest fires are not respecters of forest boundaries, for a substantial part of the town was burned out. The railroad was not directly affected, but Scott and Van Arsdale lost several buildings. The local lumber salesyard and office of the McCloud company was among those destroyed.

On at least two other fire runs the train did not get through according to reports. One of them was carrying William Randolph Hearst to Sisson. A blaze in the brush on the outskirts of town stopped progress, but the decision was made to walk around. Hearst was a pretty good outdoorsman, but his companion, Marion Davies, was not as athletically inclined and found stumbling along the ties breathing hot smoke and eyeing nearby flames rather distressing.

One of the more extensive fires struck in the White Horse country in the late 1930's. To aid the fighters from White Horse camp, a train with support was dispatched from McCloud with "Chino" Haines in charge. As it approached the fire front, Haines stopped the train in an open area and put out a flagman with strict orders to hold any following traffic. The relief train then plunged ahead into the fire zone. After a few more miles the crew found continuing further into the inferno was no longer possible, and Haines instructed the engineer to back the train to safety as rapidly as he could. Haines took a position on the rear platform, which was then the front of the train,

Back in the days when steam was king of the rails on the McCloud River Railroad, a triple header snaked a tonnage train through a junction east of McCloud just six months before Pearl Harbor was bombed.— W. C. WHITTAKER

with his hand on the emergency brake control.

Visibility was only sporadic, with the usual series of curves, complicated by waves of smoke that made it impossible even to keep eyes open and breathe for moments at a time. As the train roared around one curve and into a brief tangent, the smoke lifted enough to see a speeder covered with men charging ahead into the same straightaway. Haines "wiped the clock" with every ounce of braking power at his disposal. The engineer at the other end of the train immediately shut off his power. The speeder driver locked his wheels too. The combined efforts were in the nick of time.

Everyone then resumed the backward movement out of the fire zone to the clearing where the flagman was stationed. A conference followed. It seems that the speeder was manned by a government forest service crew en route to fight the fire. The flagman had stopped it, but the forest supervisor informed him that the federal government was not subject to flagman's orders.

Haines' comments to the supervisor are not, unfortunately, recorded for posterity. Veteran railroaders seldom suffer from a deficiency of vocabulary in circumstances such as this, how-

ever. It might well be the case that if the nearby woods had not already been on fire the discussion would have kindled a blaze. Apparently Haines would not have minded grinding up speeder and supervisor under the train, but didn't relish the thought of including the innocent and endangering the train.

The record of fire incidents is one largely of days long gone, yet the potential for disaster from this hazard remains very real. Airplanes and chemicals have been added to the arsenal of defense, but a large enough fire in the timber resource to change the whole outlook for McCloud is not impossible. If fire destroyed the McCloud mill, the need for the railroad could vanish overnight. The vigil against the monster continues and the truce with flames is not a completely easy one.

A happier and differently exciting occasion was the opening of the White Horse line as a new main link to the outside world. This connection with the Great Northern Railway included hopes for better service than was provided with a single outlet, which implied expanded markets. Coming as it did in time of severe depression, the opening may have been more deeply symbolic of prosperity ahead than was actually warranted. In any event, the circumstances appear to have added up to an occasion.

The Great Northern reached Lookout Junction from the north and continued on to meet the Western Pacific a few miles south at Nubieber. The McCloud River Railroad and the Great Northern would not wait for the actual completion, but decided to run out a special from McCloud in advance. With no great market pressures for immediate delivery, shipment was postponed until a total of 57 cars of finished lumber had accumulated, which was then sent out as one solid trainload from McCloud.

Although the McCloud companies tended to be somewhat shy, this was one occasion when

The McCloud depot was new and the occasion was festive when the Shevlin Pine Special pulled into the stub end of the depot track to pose for photographs. The chill gales of depression were blowing and haste in getting this first train out over the Great Northern connection was hardly imperative. The complete special was 57 loads, only a part of the show here. (BELOW) Reason for the goat mascot is not entirely clear, but identification with the Great Northern's trademark is likely. —BOTH CHARLES M. HAINES COLLECTION

the publicity was turned on. Each of the loaded cars had a placard tacked to its side to announce the contents to all it passed en route. Instead of heading east directly from the McCloud yards, the locomotives brought the train, or enough of it to fill a picture, at least, south into the stub-end track past the depot. Here a banner proclaiming this to be the Shevlin Pine Special was held in front of locomotive No. 19, which had been duly spruced up. Photographers, professional and amateur, recorded the scene, with the attractive new depot in the foreground and the mighty sentinel in full display to the rear. People, including the local band, turned out in numbers to observe and take part.

Once the special had been duly serenaded, recorded, and ceremoniously wished-well, engines No. 19 and No. 14 backed around the curve, tied everything together and went to work. Although almost all of the Lookout line had been in use for some time, this was the first tonnage train eastward. Retired locomotive engineer James Robinson, who was a fireman on the special, says there were some anxious moments. Superintendent Kennedy was along and became concerned as the heavy loads started down a grade east of White Horse, asking the engineer if it wasn't time for brakes. Robinson was silently agreeing with the super that it was, but the engineer was more nonchalant. When the application was finally made, Robinson remembers a surge sufficiently vio-

lent through the train to uncouple the lead locomotive and set all brakes in emergency. Before everything got stopped, a gap opened up between the locomotives and then closed again with a noisy jolt.

The somewhat shaken crewmen inspected the damage, but it was mostly to their own nerves. They recoupled the broken fitting and went on into Lookout Junction without further incident, probably quite relieved to turn their charge over to the Great Northern crews.

In the scene below, McCloud River Railroad locomotives No. 19 and 14 roll the Shevlin Pine Special out of McCloud, as the first tonnage trip eastbound moves toward Lookout Junction and the connection with the Great Northern. (ABOVE) The Great Northern took over the banner and the train of 57 cars moving them north on its main line and east to St. Paul. —BOTH CHARLES M. HAINES COLLECTION

Not only did this train officially open the Mc-Cloud line to the east, but also the Great Northern's California extension. The Shevlin Pine Special was handled intact as the first revenue train into Klamath Falls from the south, and continued northward to Spokane where it was routed eastward over the GN main line, still unbroken, to the east end of the GN at St. Paul, where it was finally split up to send the lumber cars to their several separate eastern destinations.

After almost 40 years old timers' memories of the sequence of events at the opening of the new line are understandably somewhat hazy. That the special ran, with fanfare, from Mc-Cloud as described above, is well remembered. The date was September 15, 1931. Most do not agree that two special trains were involved, but the record strongly indicates that there were two in fact, with the second following in November.

Rival Red River Lumber Company at Westwood decided to run a special train that would eclipse McCloud efforts. It used the same idea, but ran its special in conjunction with the completion of the entire high line or Northern California extension. The first McCloud train ran when the new line was opened from the north to Lookout Junction, but while a gap still existed to the south. Completion ceremonies did not come until November 10, as mentioned earlier. Completion of the new line offered its shippers including the McCloud River Lumber Company a choice of three quite divergent routes: north to the Pacific Northwest, then east to Minneapolis, St. Paul, Chicago and the East; south via Keddie to San Francisco and Los Angeles; east via Keddie to Denver, Chicago and the East. The McCloud River Railroad had another 50 cars ready for movement to Keddie and beyond on November 10. Red River had 171 cars and a bigger battery of press releases. Its three-locomotive special stole the show.

Despite the more clever publicity from Westwood, the McCloud train was probably the first through Nubieber, just as one had been from Lookout Junction north. Instead of coming as one unit from McCloud with the tub-thumping repeated all over again, evidently a few cars at a time were taken east, some parked

194

The Shelvin Pine Special of September 15, 1931, was repeated again in early November of the same year with a different cast of characters. This time the box cars carried the Western Pacific herald and the McCloud locomotives handled the action to Lookout Junction. In these two scenes the Shelvin Pine Special stands in the McCloud yards. —BOTH CHARLES M. HAINES COLLECTION

The Shelvin Pine Special with McCloud locomotives Nos. 19 and 14 whistles off and moves out of Mc-Cloud. —CHARLES M. HAINES COLLECTION

along the way temporarily, then finally all were assembled at Lookout Junction. They were combined there with a like 50 cars that had come down from Bend, Oregon, to make a 100 car train through Nubieber to Keddie, where it was broken up for movement to separate markets as the Western Pacific saw fit. Red River put this whole show into eclipse with an extra 71 cars.

The Lookout line, and to some extent the entire inland gateway route, is D. M. (Milt) Swobe's personal monument. As mentioned earlier, his was the driving force to convince the larger roads to build. He also is the one who swung the deal for GN ownership of the Hambone-Lookout segment at a time when capital was needed in McCloud, with operation to improve revenue at the same time. Less well known is the fact that his efforts resulted in GN's inheriting a small memorial to prostitution.

Some years before GN took over, a log spur branched off the main about four miles east of Hambone, with a camp at the end of the spur. In good McCloud tradition a fine dining facility was operated, supported by a cook with established culinary talent. First-rate camp cooks were valuable assets that tended to be treated with considerable care. This one approached the local camp manager one day with the story that his niece in Washington State had just been orphaned. He asked that she be allowed to stay in camp until she recovered a bit from her loss.

Camps were beginning to include families of married loggers in contrast with the almost exclusively bachelor living of earlier days. Permission was granted for this slighty different version of family life, and in due time the grieving orphan arrived and was solicitously installed in a camp unit adjacent to her uncle's quarters.

Before many weeks had elapsed, a logger rode to McCloud from the camp in question and was treated at the company medical facilities there for a disease by no means unheard of in logging camps or unfamiliar to company doctors. The man proved to be just the first of what rapidly bid to be a source of important new commutation revenue for the railroad. Lumber company spoil-sports made a reverse-direction run that dried up the activity. Discreet inquiries had been made, and a supervisor and a new employee boarded an eastward train. On arrival at camp, the supervisor introduced the cook to his successor, who presumably had no orphan nieces, and suggested that if the ex-cook and niece were on the train for its return journey, it would spare them a long walk.

From this apparent sensitivity to decentralization of and competition to Red Cloud enterprise (actually chronology of events is such that Red Cloud could have vanished before the above incident took place), one wonders who really owned Red Cloud.

The camp got a name after this. The name was passed along to the spur track. Today the camp has vanished without a trace, and all that is left of the spur is a switch and a few lengths of rail, now part of the Great Northern. The name remains. Chippy Spur.

Judged by today's standards, the early McCloud companies would appear far from liberal toward their employees, with disclaimer of blame in accidents a case in point. Actually, the companies were strongly paternalistic, which resulted in better conditions than typical for the times. Under paternalism the company judged its own liberality, and management was intent on minimizing overall costs. It wanted to get and hold first class workmen, but didn't exactly pamper them either. The presence of Chinese as mill workers, and their earlier use in construction demonstrates an unwillingness

Against a backdrop of pine trees, McCloud locomotives No. 26 and No. 14 move the daily eastbound freight toward Bartle with the final destination of Lookout Junction and the Great Northern-Western Pacific connection. —W. C. WHITTAKER

The rhythm of crossheads and reciprocating siderods announce the departure of Nos. 15 and 26 as they leave the mill behind but still in sight. The shuffle of emtpy log flats into the woods, and logs back to the mill did not end until U.S. Plywood entered the McCloud scene. (BELOW) McCloud No. 14 smoking up a storm with a short train of logs and one of cut lumber from the Scott mill. —BOTH CHARLES M. HAINES COLLECTION

to appease local white labor by doing whatever was necessary to employ only their kind.

Employment meant more than just hiring people who rode the train over to McCloud looking for a job. The companies actively solicited and recruited in areas where labor was cheap. The Chinese track gangs were probably invited in the first place. In 1899 a special train was run from Upton to McCloud just for mill workers coming in from Michigan. The Chinese eventually disappeared, but Italians came in large number, and at least one group of Greeks was recruited. The railroad found men of Mexican descent particularly skilled for track work. Around the time of World War I, Negroes augmented the hard pressed labor force. Yet there is no record that local Indians ever were hired.

Management looked to leaders in the minority groups for liaison, since direct understanding and communication was difficult, often including a language barrier in addition to cultural differences. Roadmaster Haines provided an outstanding exception, since he had lived and worked in Mexico for several years.

Management was deceived on one occasion. The lumber company found what it regarded as a Negro leader in the deep South who agreed to forward workers to McCloud for a fee. This agent reported he had 15 men ready to load and requested that McCloud send the fare, which it did. The company is still waiting for the workers to show up — and looking for the con man.

No passenger ever lost his life nor is there a record of a serious injury to a fare paying rider as the result of a McCloud River Railroad mishap. Sometimes a statement intended to convey a message of no fatalities will be worded "never lost a passenger." This wouldn't be quite literally correct for the McCloud line which did, in a way, lose a passenger. It is somewhat difficult to imagine the McCloud passenger terminal being so busy that people would become confused about what train to board, but on July 20, 1905, William H. Garrett, a 70 year old pioneer of Siskiyou County, did get on the wrong train. He had been ill for several days at McCloud, but felt well enough this Thursday to go home to Little Shasta, some distance north of Upton. Once aboard the train in the wrong direction bound for the logging frontier his illness was apparently aggravated by the jolt and jar and his pain became intense. When he and the crew discovered the mistake the trainmen suggested that they make him comfortable by the wayside, pick him up again on the homeward trip, and then set him straight for Upton. About 10 miles east of McCloud the train stopped and the trainmen fashioned a crude couch in the shade, leaving Garrett there with drinking water and the promise to stop inbound. He thanked the crew for their thoughtfulness and the train proceeded. About three hours later they did return and stopped. The old man was stretched out on the couch, but had evidently died quietly and certainly alone.

Myron Burkhalter, superintendent of the railroad, died June 6, 1907, of a heart attack. The manner of his passing might not be significant to this record, but the location of his death is of interest. The company had opened up a coal property in Kosk Creek canyon not far from one of the logging spurs serving the Harris Mountain area, south of Bartle. The coal was dragged out by wagon, then loaded onto railroad cars for shipment to test the market. Burkhalter had come in to inspect the coal mining operation and to check feasibility of extending rail service directly to a tipple. The attack came while he was in the mine. That his death had anything to do with the failure to further exploit the coal deposits is doubtful. In any event, the mine did make the railroad an originating coal hauler of record, but many more cars of this fuel arrived inbound over the years than the scant two or three loaded out from this local mine.

Light and worn rail, little or no ballast, modest engineering standards for grades and curves, and minimum maintenance combined to keep railroading on the log spurs more like old times right up to abandonment. Conductor George Tolosano, who worked the last log runs out of Burney, claims that the most important difference between early day log train operation and that of the last was that steam locomotive crews rapidly became expert at rerailing loaded log cars, diesel crews at rerailing the locomotive. He says he learned more about what is underneath a diesel locomotive on the log job than he did about its superstructure, with as many as five derailments in a single day.

Experienced crews learn to appraise how long it should take to rerail. When the locomotive parted company with the rail, the first thing to do was test to see if it would move a little on the ground. If it would, it probably could be rerailed under its own power. If the wheels just spun, a "cat" was usually sought to give a boost.

Locomotive No. 16 with a short train pulls into the yard from the stub-end station track at McCloud. —W. C. WHITTAKER

The steam railroaders customarily had their locomotives remain on the rails, but cars often strayed far from the track. Because costs of calling out a wrecking crew ran around $500, trainmen were expected to get their cars or pieces thereof back on the iron if at all possible. The "at all possible" came close to meaning anywhere within reach of a cable.

Ruel Methvin recalls one occasion at Clark Creek with a double-header where both locomotives derailed. By the time one of them was worked back on the rail, the other had settled so far in soft dirt that the crews were afraid it would tip over. A block and tackle was rigged up to the loaded cars. With tightly set hand brakes, the cars served as an anchor or "dead man" for the cable. Judiciously applied power from the available engine slowly righted the tilted twin and got it back into position for placing the rerailing frogs.

A typically critical work area was right at the jammer or log loader. The loader was usually at the end of track, and on a sharp upgrade for incoming empties. They had to be pushed hard because of the grade, but if shoved too hard and too far, they would go off the end of track and pile up. If the man riding the far end wasn't alert in getting them stopped in time, he had better be able to jump promptly or get tangled up in the ensuing mess. That this work was often done at night and with snow on the ground didn't help. When shoving empties in total darkness, the trainmen substituted sound for sight. If the first car struck a downed tree, rock or livestock, the brakeman applied emergency braking from a following car, then jumped off, and after everything got stopped, tried to find out what happened. If he had acted fast enough, the pileup wouldn't be too bad.

To add to the hazards at the jammers, they had a cable alongside the track to move cars through for loading in the absence of the locomotive. Getting slapped against the cable often meant internal injuries that were not particularly apparent at the time.

Even when crews made their exchange of empties for loads at the jammers without mishap, they were never sure they would not have a mess to clean up regardless. Sometimes the cars got away from the loading crews, ran free

In the early years of the McCloud River Lumber Company the boom loader was the simpliest means of loading the logs onto rail flats. —CHARLES M. HAINES COLLECTION

The McGiffert Log Loader was a popular type of steam jammer found in the McCloud woods between 1915 to the end of railroad logging. It pulled empty cars from the rear, loaded them and winched the loaded cars down the track. —CHARLES M. HAINES COLLECTION

The first successful power loaders were placed on the market in 1885 and since that time many forms have been brought out, which differs in the manner of locomotion, character of booms, and other details. The main feature of a steam power loader are a hoisting engine and drums and an upright boiler. These are mounted on railroad trucks with some appliance for transporting itself, and also carrying a rigid or swinging loading boom. (ABOVE) The Lidgerwood Skidder and Loader was the ultimate development in steam woods technology. This car-mounted monster was able to load logs with a heel boom, skid logs on ground leads, haul logs through the air by means of the portable spar and jockey cars into loading positions—sometimes all at once. (LEFT) A double-ended homemade device which lifted logs bodily with cables and placed them on log flats. In case of heavy logs, one end was lifted at a time. — BOTH CHARLES M. HAINES COLLECTION

Heading for the reaches of Lookout Junction, this manifest with Nos. 18 and 26 pause at Bartle for some of that magic elixir that makes steam. —JOHN KRAUSE

Until 1970 McCloud had narrow gauge trains, too! An early user of gasoline powered dinkies, the diminutive pike was used to shift lumber in the mill area. More extensively used in earlier years, the slim gauge remained but largely out of sight from curious visitors. —TED WURM

Locomotive No. 19 was right at home moving logs in a new career. Displaced by diesels on the McCloud River Railroad Co., this locomotive moved north to Yreka, where it is shown switching logs, a hardly remarkable chore for this engine. Logs are an import on this railroad; although forest products are a mainstay on the Yreka Western, none grow alongside the track as they do so profusely in the McCloud country. When diesels again displaced No. 19 at Yreka it was retained, restored to service in 1970 and shipped on again, to Cottage Grove, Oregon, to haul excursionists in 1971. —ROBERT M. HANFT

and piled up somewhere down the grade, usually at a derail strategically located for maximum inconvenience.

Methvin told the writer of his taking a tumble from a load of logs to the ground while switching and losing his footing. He found soft dirt and after some doubts decided he had not been injured. He was lucky. Perhaps the greatest killer on the railroad in its early years was falls from trains, occasioned by changes in speed, shifts in the log load, by slipping while straining against the hand brake, and at least once by act of local juveniles in placing a barricade on the track right in McCloud. The subsequent derailment threw a brakeman to the ground and his death.

The lumber company was an early user of small four-wheel Plymouth gasoline locomotives. These machines were the mainstay of tracklaying and removal, a constant practice with rail logging. They were occasionally used out on the main line to move a few cars, despite the fact that they made no smoke for smoke orders. Skylarking youthful operators would run them as fast as they could turn a wheel between Pondosa and Car A. On the level that speed wouldn't amount to much, but downgrades were something else. If a cow had wandered onto the track in one of the sags, it is a good question whether cow or Plymouth would have made the best hamburger. The gas buggies didn't have a semblance of a train brake. Apparently luck held and none ever came to serious grief.

A bottle of whisky was a common wager. This, too, seems a bit strange in the light of Rule G, but new crewmen often paid this price as initiation to the woods engine service. A favorite quart bet was with men who had worked elsewhere, especially on larger railroads, and who had confidence in their own ability.

The bet: the new man was to stand at the nose of the locomotive, which would then be started up. He was to board it at the rear foot board. There were no gimmicks (such as a missing grabiron). The locomotives used were the 20-series 2-6-2's which had small drive wheels and plenty of snap; more than the victim could usually visualize. If he "bit" the rail would be carefully sanded to insure traction, positions taken, especially by the eager gallery, and the engineer would adjust valve and throttle control. The throttle was opened wide with the brakes set and the engine then put into motion by releasing the brakes.

If the victim just stood flat-footed and tried to swing on as the rear end came by he was in real danger of having his arm bones yanked right out of their sockets. If he started running too soon, the engine swiftly gained more speed than he was by running. The best thing for him to do was just watch the rear end go by and pay up more or less cheerfully. What usually happened was that he tried, but had to turn loose and went sprawling head first into the lava dirt. That way he still had to pay, took just as big a razzing, and had to soak his sprains and bruises, mend his torn clothing and pick cinders out of his hide besides.

Railroading at McCloud has its lighter moments, as well as its everyday accomplishments under difficulties accepted by talented men as routine. Failures to complete the usual work tour are rare indeed and have become part of this story because they are the exceptions rather than the ordinary.

The rugged, winding right-of-way of the Burney line offers some of the most spectacular diesel operations in America. Brand-new diesel No. 36 was photographed on the return to McCloud from Burney. —DON HANSEN

9

WHAT THE FUTURE
MAY HOLD

IN THE PREVIOUS eight chapters, variances from the ordinary were heavily emphasized. Ways in which this line distinguished itself from its neighbors were pointed out, along with relating its own particular trials and triumphs. Detailed reports of income and expenses for every year of the corporate existence were available, but this book was not intended to be a report of the annual financial standing. By contrast with the earlier emphasis on the exceptional, in this final chapter the writer uses a very ordinary crystal ball to proclaim that the future of this railroad is subject to virtually the same whims and economic forces that will decide the future of other short line railroads of the nation. Because these forces are not widely understood, they are discussed here in some detail.

One obvious fact that makes putting this story together a particular pleasure is that it is not a summary of the total life of the railroad as is the case with so many histories of abandoned lines. The McCloud River Railroad is very much a going concern. May this pleasant state of affairs long continue.

There are bases for both optimism and pessimism about the future. One of the insidious things about crises is that any one can finish off a railroad forever. Once removed, railroads seldom return, even though the Burney line provides one of the rare examples to the contrary.

On the other hand, windfalls of good fortune, such as the PG&E pipe hauling, need have no effect whatever on longevity of the carrier beyond their own duration. To use an analogy, even if your hula-hoop factory made you rich, there is no point in keeping hoops in production once the fad passes.

Selling out to U. S. Plywood-Champion Papers Inc. is typical of the times. It has one sure effect on the railroad in the foreseeable future. The railroad used to be part of Mother McCloud's brood, even after it was formally divested. The paternalism thread was a strong force to continue the established tradition. There will be no such consideration with the present ownership, where control is remote. The dollar figures will themselves make the decisions for the future of the railroad. The example is already at hand. Before coming to

205

McCloud, U. S. Plywood had convinced itself that rail logging was the high cost method. Within days of the takeover, log trains rolled no more.

Two omens are favorable, but their limitations will also be pointed out. USP would not have spent a million dollars for the railroad if it had not anticipated a return for its money. It would not have spent almost that much again in 1969 for locomotives if it did not anticipate a return on that investment also.

There is no quarrel with the logic. If, however, through change of circumstances that will be described later in this chapter, or for any other reason, anticipated or not, the ability of the investment to earn a return is destroyed, U. S. Plywood-Champion Papers Inc. will not hesitate to liquidate it.

The locomotive investment is not as completely committed as it may appear to be. Perhaps a better way of expressing the thought intended here is to point out that the company would lose comparatively little of the money it has tied up in the new engines if it decided to get rid of them. They are a standard design, for which a high resale price can be anticipated as long as they are currently in demand. If they are around long enough to become obsolete, they can be expected to have earned their keep. Hopefully, this will prove to be the case.

The timber resource available not only to the McCloud mill but to the other shippers on the line is another conventional concern. Whether or not there is enough timber growth in the area to support mills and railroad indefinitely on a sustained yield basis is not within the purview of this writer to appraise meaningfully. The company still owns some virgin forest. Second growth is coming along in others. The demand for lumber is such that the company has long since departed from its early policy of selling little except virtually flawless clear sugar pine. On the other hand, some of the timber holdings of the old McCloud Company were sold by the new management. More could be sold if selling would appear to maximize financial return. As already pointed out, a devastating fire could change the picture in short order. Certainly those who wish the railroad well will hope that failure of the resource is not close at hand, even while being aware that exhaustion of the natural resource has, in fact, been the main cause of demise for many a little railroad.

The very financial sophistication of U. S. Plywood-Champion Papers Inc. could actually lead to restoration of a lost traffic, namely logs to the mill. Strange as it may seem, the freight tariff or price charged by the railroad has absolutely no bearing on this possibility. What it would cost the railroad to handle the logs does,

but requires a costing approach long ignored by too many railroad managements.

The reason rates are irrelevant is because U. S. Plywood-Champion Papers Inc. owns the railroad outright. If rates on company-owned traffic are "high" the owner benefits from railroad profits rather than shipper earnings. If rates are "low," shipper profits go up accordingly because of transportation charges being small. In the final analysis of overall earnings of the principal corporation, what subsidiary company charges the parent for moving the parent's property is devoid of any meaning whatever.

Traditional railroad accounting is rigidly prescribed by rules of the Interstate Commerce Commission. All a railroad management has to do to determine cost for any traffic is to put revenue and expense figures into various slots on ICC reports, turn a calculating crank, and costs will emerge. The figures have significance in some circumstances, yet are almost as meaningless as rates on company traffic in others. To get more specific with the case of potential log traffic, a hypothetical example will be used.

Suppose that the company were to restore log rail hauls from Burney, with the same tonnage of logs each day as the total of other traffic now moving in the regular train. The log movement would then be costed out with a share of maintenance, taxes and the president's salary about the same as that charged to the

Baldwin diesels Nos. 33 and 32, the two 1,200 h.p. RS-12's, bring the Burney train around one of the many curves near Obie (junction with the Pondosa branch) en route to McCloud late in their career. They were destined to continue as a pair hauling lumber on the California Western where the emphasis is on redwood rather than pine. —KARL KOENIG

other traffic. It is traditional for each segment of traffic to bear its fair share of overhead costs. ICC and conventional accounting practices demand that this be done. Allocating costs in this fashion does not make economic sense, however.

What does make sense is the avoidable cost approach. In essence, avoidable costs include costs incurred if logs move, but which are not present if no logs move. The taxes paid on the right of way ought to be the same whether a single log is hauled, no logs, or a million logs. If the regular daily train that runs from Burney to McCloud adds a few cars of logs the avoidable costs are going to be negligible. In other words, it costs a railroad almost nothing to add a car to a train that will run anyway. Even a second train over an existing track comes far from doubling total costs. The belief of the traditional manager that putting a tenth car on a nine-car train means that it will incur one tenth of the cost of running the train is simply fallacious.

Log hauling would add some expense, of course. Costs of loading them, plus investment, repairs and depreciation of cars used in this service are avoidable by not hauling logs. Unloading goes on regardless of how logs get there. If it costs more to unload rail than trucked logs, the extra amount is an avoidable cost; if it costs less, there is an avoidable savings.

Even though calculating avoidable costs is simpler than finding total costs, both are subject to arbitrary judgments that are far from being precise. Again, an example: say that a lift designed to slide under truck logs and transfer them to a rail car costs $30,000. You believe it will last three years and that you will load one million feet of logs per year. Your calculated annual cost of the log loader itself is $10,000 per year or $10 per thousand feet of logs. You could, however, use a perfectly legal accelerated depreciation figure of $20 per thousand in the first year. It is also possible that the machine could last for six years and actually load six million feet and you could then say that its cost was $5 per thousand. $5, $10, $20 are all proper figures; there is no agreement that one is more correct than another. Advance planning tends to be conservative in estimating costs. Conservative typically means overestimating unknown costs to minimize unpleasant surprises. If costs of any new approach are overestimated, the present method, with known costs, is automatically favored. The figure that the cost estimator selects and incorporates in his report to the decision maker might well determine whether or not logs move by rail or truck. Yet the real cost per log cannot be determined until the machine has finished its service to the company.

Once a truck is loaded and rolling, costs added per extra mile of operation are high compared with those of a rail car loaded and rolling. Logs moved a substantial distance to the mill from rail-served territory still offer a very real potential for rail traffic.

Rail enthusiasts tend to be over-optimistic about passenger traffic helping rather than hindering a railroad. McCloud management has a rather fortunate position with passengers in that it cannot really be hindered if it doesn't so choose. It has no passenger losses to contend with and does get a modest contribution to income from them. For this driblet of income, management probably devotes a disproportionate share of its own time and attention, but enjoys it. Perhaps even the upper echelon dignitaries get a kick out of their passenger train when they come to McCloud, although it is not fashionable to admit that such sentiment could interfere with fiscal reality.

Looking beyond McCloud, at least one railroad branch line makes a modest contribution to company net from passenger traffic alone today. The hard-headed new management of another California short line has decided to invest money in passenger equipment because it anticipates a return, even though freight is still the mainstay of that company. The odds appear small for McCloud passenger traffic to become important enough to save the railroad; neither is it completely impossible that a Mt. Shasta City-McCloud rail ride may someday become a self-supporting tourist attraction. In the meantime avoidable costing has relevance to passenger service, too.

Turning to the areas that pose a threat to the railroad, one is its labor cost. Men want good incomes and pleasant working conditions, and progressive managements want them to have both. With few exceptions, railroads have had to face rapidly rising wage scales, but comparatively stable freight rates and traffic volume. Because wages take about half of every dollar of all railroad revenue, to keep the industry alive management has to find ways of doing with less labor. When men see their fellows laid off and services eliminated, resentment and concern for their own future may follow, along with counterattacks at management in a number of ways, all of which aggravate the basic problem. In talking with McCloud employees the writer detected sentiment ranging from highly supportive of company policies to bitterly resentful.

Resentment can develop refusal to cooperate in any new situations except for a price. When the price gets too high the railroad itself is in trouble. The McCloud River Railroad has a wage cost somewhat higher than the national average in proportion to revenue. It has found the labor price for certain services it would like to offer its customers too high to afford

them.

Holding labor costs down is sometimes accomplished by reducing and postponing maintenance. Maintenance deferred too long can result in higher total costs than maintenance performed when due. You can save money for a while by not adding oil to your automobile as it runs low. If you continue this policy until the engine runs out of oil, expensive trouble is not far removed. McCloud probably has skimped on its maintenance of the locomotives in recent years. With replacement in the offing, this didn't matter much. The highly sophisticated second generation machines it has now might be more demanding.

This report is neither an anti-labor nor anti-management statement, but rather an acknowledgment that different viewpoints exist, that friction does follow, and that seeds of corporate disaster are planted in this kind of soil. Level heads, which are in fact available in McCloud, are needed to preserve good incomes for both men and the enterprise.

One solution proposed to the dilemma of costs too high for an independent railroad to continue is for a larger railroad to take over. In order to interest a big railroad it has to see

Diesel locomotive No. 33 pairs here with No. 28 as they growl toward Burney in 1964. No. 28, pioneer of the McCloud diesels, was damaged sufficiently shortly afterwards to be withdrawn from service and never repaired. —DON HANSEN

profit opportunities. In the case of the McCloud line, profit could come in one of two fashions, or perhaps both. First, the big road could operate the McCloud properties as a branch more cheaply than the present independent company can function. Second, the new owner can develop traffic not presently available.

The question of whether or not enough operating economies could be attained to make operation by a large railroad profitable when it is not under independent management is a complex one. Crew costs per train mile would be higher, for McCloud trains can be run now with less than a full crew. Separate managerial and accounting staffs, on the other hand, would not be required. As a guess, cost savings

Three Baldwin road diesels with a string of loaded log cars are ready to take off from Berry on the Burney line for the run back to McCloud. The caboose that came in from McCloud is still attached to the empty log cars. —DON SIMS

At the left, a loaded log train going back to McCloud. The flats are stacked high with various sized logs, lurching from side to side with every curve. (ABOVE) A log flat back at McCloud ready for dumping into the millpond. —BOTH DON SIMS

McCloud No. 32 and No. 33 pose for a combined portrait at Lookout Junction and defy the viewer to find a difference between them. —DONALD DUKE (BELOW) A little bit of line work appears in prospect as Nos. 33 and 28 near Lake Britton in 1964 with gondola cars of ballast and flats with a bulldozer and earth moving equipment. —DON HANSEN

would not be enough to make purchase attractive to SP or GN.*

Either of the big roads would probably be very happy to get the McCloud line for its own because it would then get the traffic that the other now enjoys. Neither is going to let the other do so. There is no question of one outbidding the other for a purchase, because the ICC would not approve the purchase by one without protection of the interests of the other.

If the line were to be abandoned, little of the large road rail traffic would be lost. Lumber would simply be trucked to the nearest station and loaded there. If this were done, Southern Pacific would gain a very substantial advantage over Great Northern because of its proximity to McCloud. The SP could be expected to show little interest in taking over the McCloud lines to protect its traffic position, but the GN might well decide to purchase the short line if abandonment threatens. If GN

*The Great Northern was merged into the new Burlington Northern system March 3, 1970. The Western Pacific still holds rights into Hambone and could be involved as well.

McCloud River Railroad No. 29 hums outside the shop and services building. After 20 years at McCloud, this locomotive now hauls copper for the Magma Arizona Railroad. —KARL KOENIG

does so, SP will seek to protect SP traffic. It could request that historic proportions be imposed on GN to split business with it. Joint SP-GN ownership of the McCloud line is somewhat more logical and traditional as well.

The fact that this line is an important feeder to two trunk railroads rather than just one, and that they are not at an equal advantage in the event of discontinuance, gives all the present McCloud trackage a strong chance for longevity that wasn't even dreamed of when Milt Swobe masterminded the GN connection.

The survival of independent railroads in their present form largely depends on divisions or splitting up the revenue received for moving each shipment. For an example, take a car of lumber moving from McCloud to San Antonio, Texas. The figures used are all approximations.

The freight bill is $1,000. For moving that car 18 miles, McCloud River gets $100; for moving it 1,800 miles, SP gets $900. Through truck service to San Antonio is not competitive at this price, which averages out to 50 cents per mile. McCloud River gets more than $5 per mile for its share, please notice.*

The lumber could probably be trucked over to Mt. Shasta City and loaded there at a cost of $50. Why doesn't the lumber company do this and save $50? Because the freight rate from Mt. Shasta City to San Antonio is $1,000, exactly the same as it is from McCloud. Notice that this means SP has two different revenues for identical cars of lumber moving from Mt. Shasta City to San Antonio. If SP picks the car up from the McCloud interchange, it gets $900; if from a mill spur across town, it gets $1,000. Few who know about this arrangement are overly happy. The McCloud shipper figures he should be able to save $50 by trucking to Mt. Shasta City. The Mt. Shasta City mill owner resents having to pay an extra $100 for exactly the same transportation provided to the McCloud car. SP would prefer to keep more of the $1,000. Perhaps best off in this example is the short line, but its position is precarious, too.

*It should be noted that the share paid to the McCloud River Railroad is not based primarily on mileage, but more substantially on services provided as the originating carrier. It gets no more for cars moved via Lookout or from Burney.

Alert short line railroad managements have asked that they be allowed to substitute cheaper truck service for the rail haul and still keep their divisions. The ICC has usually refused to allow them to do so. If it ever changes its mind, this action could finish most short railroads and branch lines as well, especially with the spread of piggyback freight, where reloading for the highway haul is not necessary. An exception to the ordinarily hard and fast rule was made not too far from McCloud.

In that case, the Feather River Railway was allowed to substitute trucks for trains and still keep its corporate identity as a railroad because a new dam flooded out the tracks. If trucking makes economic sense, that should be as good a reason for it as a dam. If the government preferred to sacrifice dollars simply to protect railroad integrity, it could have relocated the line. The ICC is thus on record in allowing a railroad to be abandoned in fact, yet to continue providing its service by truck and to receive its divisions when the cost of keeping rail service going is very high, but not if that cost is only moderate. The distinction is arbitrary.

The $1,000 figure for the car moving from the West Coast to San Antonio is dangerously near vulnerability from truck competition. If

Three Baldwin built diesels head the consist across Lake Britton bridge. Low water level is consistent with the August 1964 date. —DON HANSEN (BELOW) McCloud No. 31, least powerful of all the diesels, receives attention at the McCloud shops in order to keep her 800 horses pulling. —DON SIMS

Wind whipped snow from the rugged crest of Mt. Shasta was blowing up a storm while 26 miles southeast at Bartle, the eternal silence of the countryside is shattered by the sounds of two separate diesel horns. Diesel No. 37 working west off the Burney line grinds her train into town and stops at a switch. Soon No. 36 running light eastbound pulls into a siding for a run-by. —DON HANSEN

a trucker could count on finding a return load regularly, a $950 highway rate might become feasible. If this happens, the ICC can be in a highly unpleasant dilemma. It has told all the parties that they will live with the division schedule as it exists. If a $950 rate by non-rail competition is logical, the ICC may not be able to stop it since it cannot regulate all trucking and has not traditionally prevented motor carriers from undercutting rail rates in any event. Other things being equal, shippers will substitute $950 trucks for $1,000 cars. If SP sees its business threatened, it may request a $940, $925 or even $900 rate for its vulnerable traffic, but no longer be willing to yield a $100 division to the McCloud line. Even though SP might want to keep the McCloud segment of business on an avoidable cost basis, the Supreme Court ruled in 1968 that it cannot.

If the situation comes to pass where trucks can compete with present rates, SP will have to reduce its rate to hold business on which it does not share divisions. It cannot reduce the rate on the traffic it receives in interchange because to do so would incur a loss. If the ICC attempts to maintain the status quo, all business will shift to trucks. The short line will be dead regardless of whether the ICC kills it by taking away the favorable division or by the truck undercutting its traffic.

In point of fact, the McCloud River Railroad and indeed most railroads already have lost most of their once quite varied traffic to trucks. In the past, virtually all goods came to McCloud by rail, few do today. Logs fit the same mold. The railroad has survived because revenues from forest products shipments alone are enough for it to do so. It makes its last stand with them.

Talent of the ICC and the courts is largely trained in legal and accounting concepts. Economic pressures have only reluctantly been comprehended and no broad policy developed to shift from the theory of monopoly control to recognition that transportation is, in fact, subject to intense competition. Plenty of precedent is to be found for predicting that the very existence of the McCloud River Railroad is in danger from exactly the pressures posed. Unhappily, no regulatory solutions are in the offing because our regulatory agencies do not

The McCloud mill pond was used until 1970, but today the lumber company has returned to dry storage. In the view above, logs in storage with towering Mt. Shasta standing guard. (BELOW) A close-up view of prime McCloud timber waiting its turn at the saws. —BOTH DONALD DUKE

Majestic Mt. Shasta looks down on the new order of things as Nos. 37 and 36 team 4,000 General Motors horsepower to move McCloud pine across the mountain. The diminutive wood burners have come and gone, geared locomotives and the twins tried and failed, oil burning steam engines served their time faithfully, as did the diesels built by the once great name among locomotive erectors. One may ask what the future has in store for this same scene? —HENRY BRUECKMAN (BELOW) The new locomotives of the McCloud River Railroad arrive on home rails at Lookout Junction, delivered there by the Great Northern. (LEFT) An early revenue run for one of the new General Motors units, as it heads for McCloud after crossing Lake Britton on the Burney line in June 1969. —BOTH DON HANSEN

even admit the problem exists until it hits a company specifically. It is often too late to do anything about it then.

The railroad has tried to take advantage of another regulatory quirk. This is the so-called "milling in transit" privilege. In general, the farther a freight shipment goes, the less it costs per mile to move it, and rates reflect the lower costs. Accordingly, it is ordinarily less expensive to ship one car 200 miles than two cars 100 miles each. From this it follows that processing plants locate either at the major market or at the source of raw materials rather than somewhere in between. The transit privilege is a tariff device used to encourage processing plants to violate this particular economic force and, in fact, locate between their market and their source of supply. It does so by calling, for rate making purposes only, the two separate movements, from raw material source to processing plant, and from processing plant to market, one single through shipment. In effect, a 200 mile rate then applies rather than two 100 mile rates (or whatever distances actually are involved).

Even though the McCloud line is not part of a through route to anywhere, the company has tried to sell the notion of using its rail under the transit privilege. Veneer blocks could start from Seattle, come to Mt. Shasta City, take a side trip to Burney, be processed into veneer panels, come back to Mt. Shasta City and go on to Los Angeles, all billed as one through shipment from Seattle to Los Angeles. The McCloud River Railroad would benefit from a combination of divisions and the transit privilege.

A modest amount of this kind of traffic has developed. A hoped-for expansion of paper warehousing at McCloud under this principle has not materialized. To the extent that this rate advantage can be used, McCloud management should pursue it. The long range problem is that this traffic is particularly vulnerable to competition for exactly the same reasons that traffic protected by an artificially high division is.

If rates on transit privilege traffic are cut to meet competitive rates on through traffic, a monetary loss to the carrier will result. If rail rates on the through traffic that doesn't use the transit privilege are not cut to meet those of competition, the traffic will be lost. If the through rates are less than the transit privilege rates, the transit privilege will not be exercised. Inexorably, the McCloud line would lose this traffic.

Bridge traffic is another hope for the company, but a slender one. A bridge carrier is one intermediate to a separate originating carrier and a destination carrier. At the time of World War II, a study was made of the feasibility of using the McCloud River Railroad as a bridge route if one of the major lines was blockaded for any reason. For example, if a landslide bottled up the SP near Dunsmuir, at least some of its northern traffic could be carried to and from San Francisco by a combination of the McCloud River, Great Northern, and Western Pacific around the closed line. The necessity never in fact arose.

For traffic moving between certain points along the SP in Northern California and Southern Oregon and the GN-WP to the east, such as Reno, Nevada, to Ashland, Oregon, the shortest route is via the McCloud River line. No traffic goes this way, however, again because of a rate convention. A shipper in Reno can request that it does, but he will be charged short-haul rates by the separate companies rather than one through long-haul rate. The reason is that SP serves both Ashland and Reno and doesn't want to share the business with anyone, for which it can hardly be blamed. It will set up a through rate over its own route, although longer. If it gets only an Ashland-Mt. Shasta City haul, it wants the full Ashland-Mt. Shasta City price for it. Without a satisfactory arrangement for through rates and suitable divisions of them, the bridge route possibility is dormant. A few cars have moved, but under the high "sum of the local" rates. Prospects for change in the future do not appear particularly bright.

In summary, this interesting little railroad is by no means facing certain extinction in the near future, neither is it vested with any substantial security. In the meantime, a visit, and, hopefully, a ride in the passenger train will reward the effort well.

APPENDIX

STEAM LOCOMOTIVES

No.	Type	Builder and Construction Number		Date Built	Dimensions Dr. - Cyls. - Wt.	Tractive Force	Boiler Pressure	Remarks
1	2-6-0	Baldwin	11627	1891	50 - 16x24 - 78,000	14,600	140	From California Ry No. 2; Became No. 12
2	Heisler 3T	Stearns		1897	40 - 18x15 - 120,000	24,000	170	Disposition uncertain
3	Heisler 2T	Stearns	1003	1896	40 - 16x14 - 90,000	17,500	160	From Blakely RR; to Weed Lumber Co.; Nevada County Narrow Gauge RR; Willamette Valley Lbr. Co.; scrapped 1930
4	2-6-2	Baldwin	16239	1898	44 - 16x24 - 96,000	19,000	160	Scrapped 1936
5	0-6-0T	Baldwin	17684	1900	40 - 11½&19x30- 75,000	17,750	200	Sold to Weed Lumber Co. (1919); Lystul-Lawson Logging Co. No. 5; Scrapped
6	0-6-6-0T	Baldwin	17684-5	1900	40 - 11½&19x30- 161,400	35,500	200	Engines Nos. 5-6 were built as a single double ender numbered 6. They were separated and used as two engines.
6	0-6-0T	Baldwin	17685	1900	40 - 11½&19x30- 75,000	17,750	200	Sold to Atkinson Construction Co. No. 6; A.D. Schader No. 6; Permanente Metals Co. No. 2515; scrapped
7	4-6-0	Baldwin	7935	1886	57 - 17½x24 - 92,000	17,400	150	See Note A
8	2-6-2	Baldwin	18595	1901	44 - 16x24 - 107,000	19,000	160	Sold to Amador Central RR No. 7 (1939); preserved on display at Ione, California
9	2-6-2	Baldwin	18596	1901	44 - 16x24 - 107,000	19,000	160	Sold to Yreka Western RR No. 9 (1939); to Amador Central No. 9 (1944); to Nezperce & Idaho RR No. 9; to Mid-Continent Ry Museum No. 9 (still lettered Yreka Western) for operating exhibit.
10	2-6-2	Baldwin	18674	1901	44 - 16x24 - 107,000	21,330	180	Sold to Yreka RR No. 10 (1925); scrapped 1944
11	2-6-2	Baldwin	23875	1904	44 - 13&22x24 - 147,000	21,240	200	Sold to W. S. Zimmerman (1926); scrapped 1939
12	2-6-0	Baldwin	11627	1891	50 - 16x24 - 78,000	14,600	140	Former No. 1; scrapped 1932
13	Vacant							
14	2-8-2	Baldwin	30850	1907	48 - 20x28 - 179,000	35,700	180	Scrapped
15	2-8-2	Baldwin	30851	1907	48 - 20x28 - 179,000	35,700	180	Scrapped
16	Shay	Lima	2401	1911	36 - 14½x15 - 180,000	40,450	200	Sold to Fruit Growers Supply Co. No. 4 (1924); scrapped
16	2-8-2	Baldwin	39394	1913	48 - 20x28 - 176,000	35,500	170	From Silver Falls Timber Co. No. 101 (1939); scrapped
17	Shay	Lima	2402	1911	36 - 14½x15 - 180,000	40,450	200	Sold to Fruit Growers Supply Co. No. 5 (1924); scrapped
17	2-8-2	Baldwin	42912	1916	48 - 20x28 - 179,700	35,700	180	From Pacific Portland Cement Co. No. 102 (1942); scrapped
18	2-8-2	Baldwin	41709	1914	48 - 20x28 - 178,400	35,700	180	Sold to Yreka Western RR No. 18 (1956); preserved
19	2-8-2	Baldwin	42000	1915	48 - 20x28 - 178,400	35,700	180	From Caddo & Choctaw RR No. 4; Choctaw River Lumber Co. No. 4; United Mining & Smelting Co. No. 2069 (1924); sold to Yreka Western RR No. 19 (1953); preserved
20	2-6-2	Baldwin	57617	1924	46 - 17x24 - 132,000	23,700	185	Scrapped
21	2-6-2	Baldwin	57618	1924	46 - 17x24 - 132,000	23,700	185	Scrapped
22	2-6-2	Alco-Schenectady	66316	1925	46 - 17x24 - 130,000	23,700	185	Scrapped
23	2-6-2	Alco-Schenectady	66317	1925	46 - 17x24 - 130,000	23,700	185	Scrapped
24	2-6-2	Alco-Schenectady	66434	1925	46 - 17x24 - 144,000	23,700	185	Scrapped
25	2-6-2	Alco-Schenectady	66435	1925	46 - 17x24 - 144,000	23,700	185	In Service
26	2-8-2	Alco-Brooks	55492	1915	48 - 20x28 - 195,000	35,700	180	From Copper River & Northwestern Ry No. 72 (1938); scrapped
27	2-8-2	Alco-Brooks	57291	1915	48 - 20x28 - 195,000	35,700	180	From Copper River & Northwestern Ry No. 73 (1938); scrapped

Note A — Built as Atlantic & Pacific No. 52. Sold to Weed Lumber Co. prior to 1897, later sold to McCloud River Railroad about 1900. Sold by McCloud about 1915 to F. Rolandi a contractor on the Hetch Hetchy water project from 1916-1917 where engine was used from Hetch Hetchy Junction to the foot of Priest Grade to eliminate the slower time of geared engines. Rolandi moved engine about 1918 to the Yosemite Valley area. Disposition unknown.

DIESEL LOCOMOTIVES

No.	Type	Class	Builder and Construction Number	Date Built	Eng. Weight Wheels - Nominal - HP	Remarks
28	C-C	DRS-6-6-15	Baldwin 73653	9-1948	42 - 292,000* - 1,500	Scrapped 1970
29	C-C	DRS-6-6-15	Baldwin 74812	7-1950	42 - 292,000* - 1,500	Sold to Magma Arizona RR No. 10 (11-22-69) delivered (1-6-70)
30	B-B	S-12	Baldwin-Lima-Hamilton 75912	10-1953	40 - 233,000 - 1,200	Sold to Rayonier, Inc. No. 202 (7-15-1963)
31	B-B	S-8	Baldwin-Lima-Hamilton 75913	10-1953	40 - 202,000** - 800	Sold to Magma Arizona RR No. 9 (7-10-69)
32	B-B	RS-12	Baldwin-Lima-Hamilton 76024	4-1955	42 - 240,600 - 1,200	Sold to Chrome Crankshaft Co. (6-5-1969); to California Western RR No. 55 (9-10-1970)
33	B-B	RS-12	Baldwin-Lima-Hamilton 76105	4-1955	42 - 240,600 - 1,200	Sold to Chrome Crankshaft Co. (6-5-1969); to California Western RR No. 56 (9-10-1970)
34	C-C	AS-616	Baldwin-Lima-Hamilton 75449	3-1952	42 - 325,000 - 1,600	From Southern Pacific No. 5253 (7-15-1963); to Oregon & Northwestern RR No. 4 (8-29-1969)
35	C-C	DRR-6-6-15	Baldwin 74261	5-1949	42 - 325,000 - 1,500	From Southern Pacific No. 5207; bought by Chrome Crankshaft Co. (9-10-1963); sold to McCloud 3-25-1964; became US Steel (Geneva, Utah) No. 39 (9-2-1969)
36	C-C	SD-38	General Motors 34880	4-1969	40 - 356,000 - 2,000	In service
37	C-C	SD-38	General Motors 34881	4-1969	40 - 356,000 - 2,000	In service
38	C-C	SD-38	General Motors 34882	4-1969	40 - 356,000 - 2,000	In service
5204	C-C	DRR-6-6-15	Baldwin 74258	5-1949	42 - 325,000 - 1,500	Note A

* — Built at this reduced weight at the request of the railroad to permit operations on 50 lb. rail laid at that time in McCloud Yard and McCloud River Lumber Company mill.

** — Built as standard S-12 a duplicate of No. 30 for updating later by McCloud if desired by adding turbo-charger and changing camshaft and adding ballast.

Note A — Former Southern Pacific No. 5204 purchased from Chrome Crankshaft March 25, 1964. When delivered at McCloud the No. 36 was placed in its train indicators and without repainting ran it around the yard in limited assignments. McCloud intended to maintain this engine and former SP No. 5207 by cannabilizing No. 28. By this time McCloud was phasing down their log hauls and decided not to overhaul No. 5204 but to use it for parts. Officially No. 5204 was not a regular road engine as first No. 36, but just used in yard service and can't be considered as part of the official McCloud River Railroad diesel roster. Sold to Chrome Crankshaft in 1969.

BIBLIOGRAPHY

BOOKS

Jones, J. Leroy, *Saddlebags in the Siskiyou*, Yreka, News Journal Print Shop, 1953.

McGowan, Joseph A., *History of the Sacramento Valley*, New York, Lewis Historical Publishing Co., 1961.

Poor, Henry V., *Manual of the Railroads of the United States*. Volumes 23-64, New York, H. V. and H. W. Poor, 1890-1930.

Wagner, Jack R., *Short Line Junction*, Fresno, Academy Library Guild, 1956.

PERIODICALS

"All-door Box Cars Available for Lease." *Railway Locomotives and Cars*, New York (August 1965).

Apperson, Orville O., "Excerpts from the Sisson Story." *The Pioneer*, Volume II, No. 2 (Fall 1952).

Berry, Swift, "Lumbering in the Sugar and Yellow Pine Regions of California." *Bulletin*, Washington: United States Department of Agriculture, No. 440 (1917).

"Compound Duplex Locomotive for the McCloud River R.R." *Engineering News*, New York, Volume XLII, No. 26, (June 28, 1900).

"Duplex Compound Locomotive for the McCloud River Railroad." *The Railroad Gazette*, New York, Volume 32 (June 1, 1900).

"Geared Locomotive for the McCloud River Railroad." *Scientific American Supplement* No. 1294, New York, (October 20, 1906).

"Great Northern Rails Reach California." *The Timberman*, San Francisco, Volume 33, No. 1 (November 1931).

Hillyard, Kay, "A Dramatic Pageant of McCloud 1830-1940." McCloud, 1940.

Hudson, James J., "The McCloud River Affair of 1909." *California Historical Society Quarterly*, San Francisco, Volume 35 (1962).

Koenig, Karl R., "S.P. Rotary on McCloud." *Pacific News*, Burlingame, No. 90 (April 1969).

Masson, Marcelle, "Alexander Roderick McLeod." *The Pioneer*, Volume 1, No. 3 (1949).

"McCloud River Railroad." *The Western Railroader*, San Mateo, Volume 11, No. 9 (July 1948).

"McCloud's Baldwins." *Pacific News*, Burlingame, No. 100 (February 1970).

Official Guide of the Railways, New York, (1898-1971).

"Pit River Railroad." *The Western Railroader*, San Mateo, Volume 10, No. 1 (November-December 1946).

Railroad Gazette, New York, Volumes 29-43, (1897-1907).

Railway Age, New York, Volumes 67-170 (1919-1971).

Schrader, George R., "Sawmills of Southwestern Siskiyou." *Yearbook*. Yreka: Siskiyou County Historical Society (1948).

Sims, Donald, "Logging Line, 1959 Model." *Trains*, Milwaukee, Volume 19, No. 4 (February 1959).

The Timberman, San Francisco, (1901-1969).

Wetzel, Gerald, "McCloud River Railroad." *The Siskiyou Pioneer*, Volume III, No. 7 (1964).

————, "Mud Creek in Action." *Ibid.*

"White and Sugar Pine Building at Fair." *The Timberman*, Volume 16, No. 7 (May 1915).

NEWSPAPERS

Bush, C. C., "McLeod River." *Independent*, Redding, California (September 12, 1878).

Glover, Malcolm, "Free Enterprise Revives Company Town." *Examiner and Chronicle*, San Francisco, California (October 13, 1968).

Johnson, James, "Old-Style Train Trip." *Bee*, Sacramento, California (August 6, 1967).

Lawson, John, "Winter Lingers in McCloud." *Record-Searchlight*, Redding, California (March 5, 1969).

"Railroad Buffs Get all Steamed Up Over Trip." *Record-Searchlight*, Redding, California (February 3, 1969).

"Whistling Its Swansong." *Bee*, Sacramento, California (October 12, 1970).

Courier, Shasta, California (1895-1898).

Headlight, Sisson, California (1905-1922).

Herald, Mount Shasta, California (1922-1968).

Mirror, Sisson, California (1896-1905).

COMPANY RECORDS

Annual reports of the company to the Interstate Commerce Commission (1898-1967); Annual reports of the company to the California Public Utilities Commission; Correspondence of the McCloud River Railroad; Minutes of the Meetings of the Board of Directors of the McCloud River Railroad (1906-1967).

INDEX

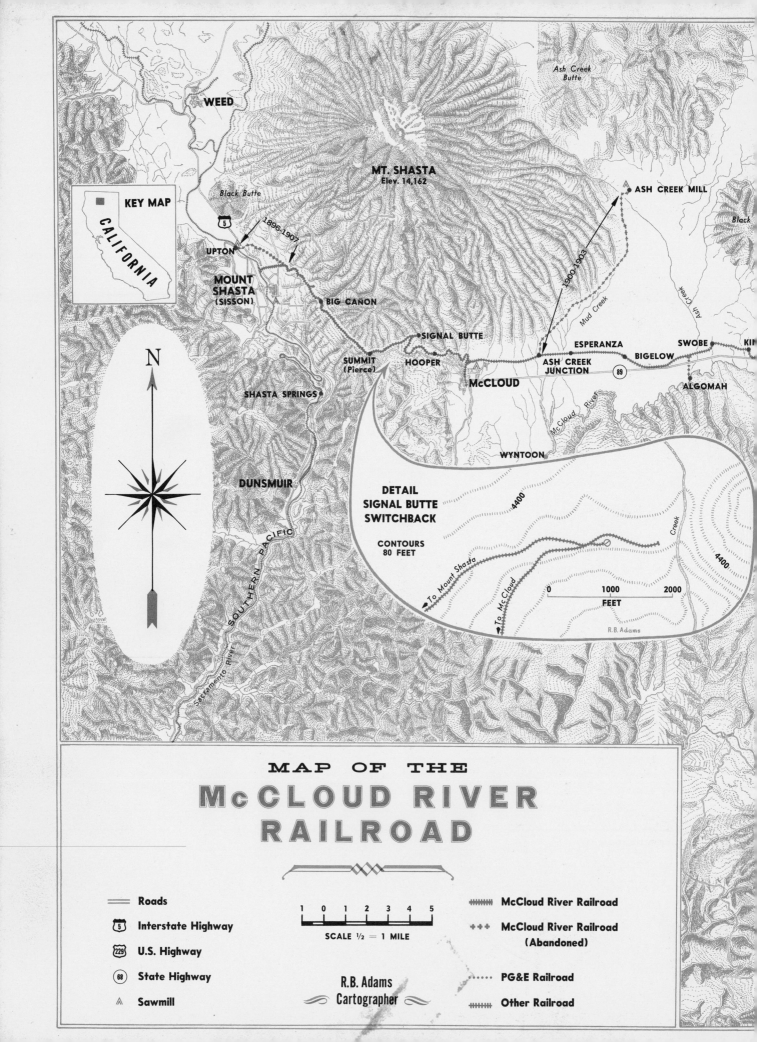

KEY MAP
CALIFORNIA

WEED

Ash Creek Butte

MT. SHASTA
Elev. 14,162

Black Butte

ASH CREEK MILL

Black

1896-1907

UPTON

1900-1903

MOUNT SHASTA (SISSON)

BIG CAÑON

Mud Creek

SIGNAL BUTTE

ESPERANZA

SWOBE

KIN

SUMMIT (Pierce)

HOOPER

ASH CREEK JUNCTION

BIGELOW

89

SHASTA SPRINGS

McCLOUD

ALGOMAH

McCloud River

WYNTOON

DUNSMUIR

DETAIL
SIGNAL BUTTE
SWITCHBACK

CONTOURS
80 FEET

4400

Creek

4400

To Mount Shasta

To McCloud

0   1000   2000
FEET

R.B. Adams

Sacramento River

SOUTHERN PACIFIC

MAP OF THE
McCLOUD RIVER
RAILROAD

R.B. Adams
Cartographer

Roads

🛡5 Interstate Highway

🛡229 U.S. Highway

68 State Highway

⛰ Sawmill

1 0 1 2 3 4 5
SCALE ½ = 1 MILE

McCloud River Railroad

+++ McCloud River Railroad (Abandoned)

PG&E Railroad

Other Railroad